# THE IMPORTANCE OF
# BEING EARNEST

broadview editions
series editor: L.W. Conolly

Oscar Wilde, 1882. Photograph by Napoleon Sarony.

# THE IMPORTANCE OF BEING EARNEST
## A Trivial Comedy for Serious People

Oscar Wilde

*edited by Samuel Lyndon Gladden*

broadview editions

**Library and Archives Canada Cataloguing in Publication**

Wilde, Oscar, 1854-1900
    The importance of being earnest : a trivial comedy for serious people / Oscar Wilde ; edited by Samuel Lyndon Gladden.

(Broadview editions)
Includes bibliographical references.
ISBN 978-1-55111-694-5

    I. Gladden, Samuel Lyndon, 1967-   II. Title.   III. Series: Broadview editions

PR5818 I4 2009    822'.8    C2009-905936-3

**Broadview Editions**
The Broadview Editions series represents the ever-changing canon of literature in English by bringing together texts long regarded as classics with valuable lesser-known works.

Advisory editor for this volume: Denis Johnston

Broadview Press is an independent, international publishing house, incorporated in 1985. Broadview believes in shared ownership, both with its employees and with the general public; since the year 2000 Broadview shares have traded publicly on the Toronto Venture Exchange under the symbol BDP.

We welcome comments and suggestions regarding any aspect of our publications— please feel free to contact us at the addresses below or at broadview@broadviewpress.com.

*North America*
Post Office Box 1243, Peterborough, Ontario, Canada K9J 7H5
2215 Kenmore Avenue, Buffalo, NY, USA 14207
Tel: (705) 743-8990; Fax: (705) 743-8353
email: customerservice@broadviewpress.com

*UK, Europe, Central Asia, Middle East, Africa, India, and Southeast Asia*
Eurospan Group, 3 Henrietta St., London WC2E 8LU, United Kingdom
Tel: 44 (0) 1767 604972; Fax: 44 (0) 1767 601640
email: eurospan@turpin-distribution.com

*Australia and New Zealand*
NewSouth Books
c/o TL Distribution, 15-23 Helles Ave., Moorebank, NSW, 2170
Tel: (02) 8778 9999; Fax: (02) 8778 9944
email: orders@tldistribution.com.au

www.broadviewpress.com

This book is printed on paper containing 100% post-consumer fibre.

Typesetting and assembly: True to Type Inc., Claremont, Canada.

PRINTED IN CANADA

# Contents

# Acknowledgements

Perhaps better than anyone, Oscar Wilde appreciated the social component of writing, and surely the published versions of his Comedies of Society provide the best evidence of the ways in which the perfection of Wilde's work derived to no small degree from the influences imposed on him by audiences, performers, producers, and his culture at large. In the time I've spent editing this volume, I've drawn on the energies, talents, and support of many people, each of whom I applaud.

At Broadview Press, Julia Gaunce and Leonard Conolly shepherded this project from its beginning, and I am grateful to them for their encouragement, their insights, and their quick responses to my questions. Marjorie Mather helped secure final permissions from the Wilde estate, Judith Earnshaw steered the final revision through to page proofs, and Denis Johnston offered countless suggestions at the copy-editing stage that made for a tighter, more effective book. Many of my colleagues, former professors, and students provided input on the book's proposals and on the Introduction, and I have benefited enormously from their wisdom. These include Thomas Connors, Nicholas Frankel, Melanie Hawthorne, Mary Ann O'Farrell, James Rosenheim, Philip T. Smith II, and Richard Utz; also, Brett Billman, Sarah Cowger, Heather Gruber, Gary Gute, Greg Holt, Julie Husband, Susan Santha Kerns, Dianna J. LeFevre, Kim MacLin, Nathaniel Nieman, Jesse Swan, and Nathan R. Wieting. Caity Grace and Amanda Valentine assisted in proofreading the typescript at a key stage, and in the end, Kyle Wilson, T. Matteson Toenjes, and Zachary Umsted labored over the copy-edits and page proofs. My priest, Father Ron Osborne, who wears a chasuble and wields a wit Wilde would envy, helped me work through some relatively obscure theological points that pepper the play, as did his successor, Father Mitchell Smith, whose enthusiasm in responding to my queries might have shocked those like *Earnest*'s Lady Bracknell, who would no doubt find in such youthful excess clear cause for alarm! Charlotte Mitchell of University College London illuminated specific cultural references, and Patrice S. Fox of the Harry Ransom Humanities Research Center at the University of Texas helped me locate a number of documents, including Wilde's corrections to Leonard Smithers's proofs for his 1899 edition of *The Importance of Being Earnest* and several copies of Smithers's first edition of the play. Colin Harris at the

Bodleian Modern Manuscripts Collection provided access to a host of documents that proved central to my thinking about Wilde, his play, and his culture, and Dorothy Fos of the Sterling C. Evans Library at Texas A&M University furnished references for a few sources unavailable to me at my own university. Virginia Bartow, Curator of the George Arents Collection at the New York Public Library, advised me in selecting texts as the basis for this book, and Marilyn Bisch, the President of the Oscar Wilde Society of America, put me in touch with Merlin Holland, Wilde's grandson, who offered support for my project at a crucial moment in its evolution and who, in his capacity as executor of the Wilde literary estate, kindly permitted me to draw on a vast number of documents written by his grandfather.

I remain grateful, as well, to the other individuals and entities who furnished permission for the use of many of the materials in the Appendices:

A.1 From *Oscar Wilde* by Richard Ellmann, copyright © 1987 by The Estate of Richard Ellmann. Used by permission of Alfred A. Knopf, a division of Random House, Inc.

A.2 From *Oscar Wilde: Trial and Punishment 1895-1897*. Reproduced with permission from The Raymond Mander and Joe Mitchenson Theatre Collection.

B.4 Reprinted by permission of *The Sunday Times*, London. ©NI Syndication, London.

B.5 Reprinted by permission of The Society of Authors on behalf of the Bernard Shaw Estate.

C.2 Reproduced by permission of the Wilde Literary Estate.

F.1 Reproduced with permission from Pryor Publications of Kent, <www.pryor-publications.co.uk>.

G.4-7 Reproduced by permission of Harcourt Inc. Copyright © 1936 by Harcourt, Inc. and renewed 1964 by Katharine Lewis and Harold P. Smith.

H.1-12 Copyright extracts reprinted by permission of the estate of Oscar Wilde. Copyright © the estate of Oscar Wilde 1956, 1962, & 2000.

I.1-3 Reproduced by permission of the Wilde Literary Estate and the George Arents Collection, The New York Public Library, Astor, Lenox and Tilden Foundations.

More locally, at the University of Northern Iowa, my Provost, James F. Lubker, my Dean, Reinhold K. Bubser, and my Department Head, Jeffrey S. Copeland, provided intellectual support for this project as well as the financial support that allowed me to draw on the enormous talents of a group of undergraduate and graduate students whose careful work and patient editing have saved me much time, energy, and worry. Among these, my thanks go first and foremost to Nathan R. Wieting, the editorial assistant who worked with me for over a year and a half on this project, and then to all the others who played similarly important roles in its completion: Alissa Stickler Burger, Aneta Dygon, Lucas Greene, Aaron James McNally, Holly Overturf, and Matthew Ross. The undergraduate students in the Spring 2005 and Fall 2008 sections of my Critical Writing about Literature course, which was called "Wilde, Utterly," class-tested this book and offered meaningful insights about what amused them, what helped them, what mystified them, and so on. Like my editorial assistants, these students embody the best and brightest of our campus population, and I feel truly fortunate to have had the opportunity to work with them so closely on a project so near and dear to me.

Finally, I thank my close circle of friends who had a hand in all of this, especially Ian Mewaka Rockwell, who proved invaluable in assisting with research in the final stages of this project, as well as Molly Cormaney, Trudy Eden, Janet Hurley, Z Hammer, John Swope, and Jeffrey "That book isn't going to write itself!" Taylor. I remain deeply grateful to my parents, L.K. and Helen Gladden, who encouraged me to be the earnest dandy I am today. Last, but certainly not least, I thank Magnolia for all she does, now as ever, and I dedicate this book to my good friend Kevin Gaffney, truly a Jack to my Algy.

# Introduction

"Indeed, [Wilde] made dying Victorianism laugh at itself, and it may be said to have died of the laughter."
—Richard Le Gallienne, *The Romantic '90s*

By the time Oscar Wilde attended the final dress rehearsal for *The Importance of Being Earnest* at London's St. James's Theatre on 13 February 1895, he had ascended the heights of popularity to become one of the most celebrated playwrights of his day. None of that, however, seemed to guarantee the play's success: Wilde wrote to his dear friend Ada Leverson that "The rehearsals were dreary. The uncultured had caught colds" (Holland and Hart-Davis, eds., *Complete Letters* 631). Wilde's remark crystallizes characteristics found throughout many of his works: the link between artifice and life, the shift in focus from issues of aesthetics to issues of reality, and the move from a psychological response to a physiological one all pepper Wilde's works, especially *The Picture of Dorian Gray*, "Phrases and Philosophies for the Use of the Young," and "A Few Maxims for the Instruction of the Over-Educated."[1] Sometimes through wit, sometimes through direct criticism, and sometimes through ideological and rhetorical subversion, these works collectively confront pressing issues that beset Victorians as their century of certainty sped to an anxious close.

Wilde's was an age in which customs and manners were coming increasingly under scrutiny as an older, traditional, resolutely rigid way of life threatened to be subverted—or at the very least made to look ridiculous—by a younger, progressive, seemingly superficial perspective. In *The Importance of Being Earnest*, such a social tension finds form in two sets of figures: the embodiments of traditional morality, including Lady Bracknell, Miss Prism, and Canon Chasuble; and the pairs of young lovers, Jack and Gwendolen and Algernon and Cecily.[2] Gwendolen and Cecily predicate their love for their suitors on the false assumption that each is named "Ernest," as both men claim, although neither is—at least not for most of the play. In so doing, Gwen-

---

1   See Appendix H for selections from these works.
2   See Appendix F for examples of traditional Victorian attitudes about behavior, dress, courtship, and other matters relevant to the aspects of social life Wilde explores throughout *The Importance of Being Earnest*.

dolen and Cecily offer Wilde's audience the spectacle of something new, not so much the so-called New Woman they disparage in an earlier draft of the play, who insisted on equal rights in legal, political, educational, and social spheres, but new sorts of women nonetheless, women unafraid to admit that their love depends entirely on a superficial quality, one so much so that, for Gwendolen, its effect figures entirely at the surface: the name "Ernest," she explains, "produces vibrations" (*E* 84).[1] Gwendolen's love for Jack would disappear in an instant, she cheerfully admits, if she discovered that he had any name other than the one she so admires. Similarly, Cecily falls in love with Algernon, but she makes clear her disinclination to love a man with a name like "Algy," despite her suitor's fervent efforts to convince her that "Half of the chaps who get into the Bankruptcy Court" share his real name, which she has yet to discover (*E* 114).

If Wilde's play sounds complicated, that is because it *is*, and delightfully so, for its complications lend the play its comic effect and operate on seemingly endless levels of interpretive possibility. It is not merely a farce, for there is more here than the familiar devices of mistaken identity, the double life, and the constant threat of being unmasked, and not merely a Comedy of Society, as were his three other successful plays of the 1890s. *The Importance of Being Earnest* draws on all of these aspects to articulate what may be Wilde's most complete, most accessible statement about his views on life and society, sincerity and superficiality, and power and pleasure, as well as his witty criticisms of these signal aspects of late-Victorian existence.[2]

## Wilde's Well-Made Plays

Wilde composed three early dramas, two of which, *Vera; or, The Nihilists* and *The Duchess of Padua*, were only moderately successful, and the other of which, *Salomé*, was never staged during his lifetime. Yet *The Importance of Being Earnest* proved the fourth—and final—work in a triumphant series frequently referred to as Wilde's "Comedies of Society," following *Lady Windermere's Fan*

---

1  Throughout this volume, cross-references to the play will be indicated with the letter "*E*" preceding the page and/or note numbers.
2  Jeremy Lalonde argues that Wilde's plays incite "the systematic deconstruction of ... ideological state apparatuses" and that "the mechanical laughter of the audience effectively sanctions this deconstruction and simultaneously camouflages its operation" (665).

(first staged in 1892), *A Woman of No Importance* (1893), and *An Ideal Husband* (1895). Although these plays were sometimes compared to the stage pieces of the French dramatist Victorien Sardou (1831-1908), from whom Wilde pointedly distanced his own work, the Comedies of Society contribute more significantly to a subgenre deeply indebted to the so-called well-made play, or *pièce bien faite*, a form generally attributed to the French playwright Eugène Scribe (1791-1861). Constructed around aspects of plot that create a sense of anticipation as the audience waits for secrets to be revealed, the well-made play was particularly suited to Victorian melodrama, and it shaped contemporary farce, as well. Popular throughout the nineteenth century, the well-made play drew from complexities that, under Wilde's pen, celebrated mistaken identities, not-so-well-kept secrets, amusing double-talk, and, of course, sparklingly witty repartee. Although Wilde resented what he regarded as the reduction of his work to the well-made play—a reduction that took legible form in a drawing in *Punch* magazine in 1892 that featured Wilde leaning on a stack of the most famous of such works—the dramatic model of the well-made play nonetheless helps us understand the structural elements that make for much of the success of Wilde's Comedies of Society.

Structurally, the well-made play includes several key features: a plot that centers on secrets that members of the audience know, making for their delight in watching characters who are ignorant of those secrets; an increasing rise in action and suspense activated by comic entrances and exits as well as by the exchanges of secret knowledge, usually through diaries and letters; rapid rises and falls in the hero's fortunes, largely due to his interactions with a key adversary; sudden shifts from high to low points in the play, usually precipitated by the revelation of secrets the audience already knows; a significant misunderstanding to which the main characters remain blind, again to the amusement of a knowing audience; a logical explanation for the play's misunderstandings, coincident with the drama's *dénouement*; and the modeling-in-miniature of the overall structure and action of the play within individual acts.

In Wilde's day, the well-made play was regularly associated with several playwrights, two of whom, Arthur Wing Pinero (1855-1934) and Henry Arthur Jones (1851-1929), Wilde mentions in his correspondence at the very time he is composing *Earnest* (see Wilde's letter to George Alexander, October 1894, in Appendix H9). In Wilde's day and our own, many cite Pinero as chief among the playwrights who addressed contemporary social problems; likewise, Jones is regularly noted, especially for his interest in the drama as a vehicle for social criticism or what came to be known as "the drama of ideas." While both playwrights claimed many successes, among the most important of these were Jones's *The Silver King* (1882) and Pinero's *The Second Mrs. Tanqueray*, which was produced in 1893 by George Alexander, the very man who would stage Wilde's *Earnest* two years later. *The Silver King* and *The Second Mrs. Tanqueray* both draw on features of the well-made play not only to entertain audiences but, more to the point, to illuminate some of the most vexing social issues that beset the late-Victorian age.

Pinero's *The Second Mrs. Tanqueray* addresses the controversy of the woman with a scandalous past, here in the form of the title character, who enters into a marriage while concealing her history of adultery. When Mrs. Tanqueray's daughter becomes betrothed to her mother's one-time seducer, Mrs. Tanqueray is forced to admit her past and is left to hope desperately that her husband—and the Society he represents—can forgive her and accept her. Tragically, albeit predictably, Society cannot, and *The Second Mrs. Tanqueray* concludes with the title character's suicide. Pinero's closing of the play offers a serious and solemn comment on the dim prospects Society makes available to known transgressors, a comment Wilde will challenge, to some degree, usually through wit and humor: his plays conclude more often than not with the recuperation of the transgressor, such as in the last-minute revelation that the feckless Lord Arthur Goring, a typical dandy—stylish, witty, averse to work, and in so many ways the antithesis of traditional masculinity—is in fact the ideal husband of the play of the same name.[1]

Of Jones's many stage successes, the work most relevant to the issues Wilde explores in *Earnest* is *The Silver King*, which tells the story of Wilfred Denver, a worthy young husband and father ruined by gambling and drink, who is tricked into believing he has shot and killed a man. Denver flees to America in a desperate effort to conceal his guilt and, thus, to save his family's reputation. Stateside, Denver makes a fortune in silver mining,

---

1   Throughout late-Victorian culture, the dandy provoked ire by embodying what Richard Dellamora characterizes as "a loss of balance between the dual imperatives of leisure and work incumbent upon Victorian gentlemen. The dandy is too relaxed, too visible, consumes to excess while producing little or nothing," thereby "[reflecting] negatively on gentlemanliness itself" (199).

becoming so wealthy that he resolves to return to England to share his wealth with the family he abandoned, who now live in poverty. Having prepared to confess all, even if it means further alienation from those he loves, at the last minute Denver discovers he is not guilty of murder after all, and the exposure of the real murderer exonerates him completely. Like Pinero's *The Second Mrs. Tanqueray*, Jones's *The Silver King* is a serious drama, commenting (albeit to a lesser degree than *Mrs. Tanqueray*) on issues of identity and reputation as well as on the perceived "worth" of a key character. In addition to *The Silver King*, Jones wrote some of the most popular plays of the late-Victorian age; in an odd twist, it was his drama *The Triumph of the Philistines* (1895) that would replace *Earnest* when its run ended abruptly amidst Wilde's legal scandals and the playwright's ensuing ruin.[1]

Wilde's Comedies of Society remain indebted to the work of his predecessors, particularly in terms of their use of the well-made play to explore questions about identity and truth, about representation and reputation. In addition, Wilde's works drew from his culture's unprecedented debates about presence and power, especially for women, debates Henrik Ibsen explored in *A Doll's House*, which was first performed in London in 1889. Wilde's Comedies of Society return to these vexing questions, transforming them to some degree through Wilde's comic tone, so that through them Wilde lampoons the assumed seriousness of such subjects as well as the entrenched positions in which Victorians believed—or at least pretended to believe. Wilde's was an era of unprecedented change, and just as Ibsen's works explored these social and cultural shifts with powerful force, Wilde's located in such debates the comic element, ultimately showing, as had Ibsen, that Victorians occupied a rapidly, radically changing world.

Kerry Powell observes that "[Wilde's] plays depended for life upon dozens of now obscure but once well-known forerunners in the late Victorian theatre," but he adds that, for Wilde, "to be dominated was intolerable" (*Oscar Wilde and the Theatre of the 1890s* 13). Thus, we find in Wilde's Comedies of Society elements of the well-made play—mistaken identities, plot devices that reveal carefully concealed secrets, and so on—and we find, too,

---

1   In Wilde's day, the term "Philistine" circulated as an epithet for narrow-minded, usually middle-class individuals, many of whom would have been averse to the lifestyles, the manners of speech and dress, the relationships, and the interests of many of Wilde's characters, not to mention to the general topics Wilde's work explores.

the protracted investigations of identity, voice, and power that underwrote Ibsen's masterpieces. Wilde's combination of these aspects made him, perhaps, the master of them all—the dominator of the stage, whose works combined the serious and the ridiculous, the tragic and the comic, in ways that both amused audiences and asked them to question their own positions in the leading debates of the day. *Lady Windermere's Fan*, for example, considers personal relationships as one among many sites of the struggle for power, as Lady Windermere, believing her husband has committed an indiscretion, prepares to elope with a lover of her own, only in the end to be saved by the very woman she believed was her rival for her husband's affections. *A Woman of No Importance* weighs the relative worth of men and women and raises the shocking possibility that women are perhaps not only better than men but, in fact, more important; further, the play considers the tension between public and private lives, between reputation and responsibility. Finally, *An Ideal Husband* examines the double aspects of gender, locating sharply distinct embodiments of masculinity in two men, Robert Chiltern and Lord Goring, and of femininity in two women, Gertrude Chiltern and Mrs. Cheveley; in the end, *Husband* shows how the good woman rescues the man whose secrets might have been exposed and how the dandy—Lord Goring—is ultimately transformed into the good man, the "ideal husband."

## Composition, Performance, and Publication History

Wilde composed *The Importance of Being Earnest* while vacationing with his family and, later, with his lover Lord Alfred Douglas at Worthing, a city that lends its name to one of the lead characters in Wilde's play.[1] Originally composed as a four-act piece, Wilde's work was promised to George Alexander, the manager of the St. James's Theatre, who secured it with what Americans today might call "earnest money" of £150. When Alexander refused the play, however, *Earnest* was offered to Charles

---

1   See the Chronology (below, 53) for a listing and description of significant developments in Wilde's personal relationships and professional achievements. For more extensive study, readers should consult the standard biography, *Oscar Wilde* by Richard Ellmann; the psychoanalytically based biography *Oscar Wilde: A Certain Genius* by Barbara Belford; and the close examination of Wilde's social and sexual relationships in *The Secret Life of Oscar Wilde: An Intimate Biography* by Neil McKenna. Full citations for all footnoted works are provided in the Bibliography.

Wyndham for production at the Criterion Theatre. Caught off-guard by the withering failure of the St. James's production of Henry James's *Guy Domville*, Alexander asked for the return of the production rights to *Earnest* with the promise and proviso that Wyndham would have the first right of refusal for Wilde's next play—an eventuality that was never to materialize. Alexander asked Wilde to cut the text of his play from four acts to three, and Wilde did so, albeit somewhat reluctantly, omitting sections of lines here and there and, most importantly, deleting an entire scene that featured a character named Gribsby, an attorney who goes to the country from London to arrest Ernest for unpaid debts at the Savoy Hotel, the very place where Wilde himself kept expensive rooms and entertained lavishly.[1]

The Importance of Being Earnest opened on Valentine's Day, 1895, to generally positive reviews and a near-rapturous response from Wilde's audience, all while the playwright was still enjoying the success of *An Ideal Husband*, which had debuted just five weeks earlier; in short, by the time of *Earnest*'s première, Wilde was surely the toast of the theatre world.[2] Such pleasures proved short-lived, however, when Wilde became enmeshed in the series of court cases that would culminate in his conviction for acts of gross indecency and his incarceration for two years of hard labor in Reading Gaol. Alexander hoped to continue *Earnest*'s successful run, but given the scandals attached to Wilde's name, the play closed on 8 May, leaving Alexander with a loss of £300 (Hyde, ed., *The Annotated Oscar Wilde* 326n).[3] That the production succeeding *Earnest* was entitled *The Triumph of the Philistines* proved an odd coincidence, surely much appreciated by Londoners: "philistine," an epithet popularized by Matthew Arnold in his influential study *Culture and Anarchy* (1869), aptly characterized the very people who would certainly have felt a sense of triumph as Wilde was taken away from the glamorous life he had enjoyed to be locked up in prison for two years. Philistinism was not confined to England alone, however: across the ocean, an American staging of *Earnest*, produced by Charles Frohman at New York's Empire Theatre, closed only one week after its première on 22 April 1895, it too a victim of the circumstances surrounding Wilde's scandal and fall.

---

1  See Appendix I for selections from the original four-act version that were excised when Wilde reduced the play to three acts.
2  See Appendix B for a selection of reviews of *The Importance of Being Earnest*.
3  For a comparison of the St. James's playbills before and after the scandal broke, see Appendix A.

Wilde's play languished, unpublished, during his incarceration at Reading Gaol, and it was not until 1899, the year before his death, that the play was finally made available to readers by Leonard Smithers and Company of London. The sole publisher of Wilde's works after his release from prison in 1897, Smithers was notorious for publishing materials that walked the dangerous, provocative line between art and pornography (Guy and Small 183); that Wilde would turn to Smithers not only suggests the depths to which Wilde's star had fallen but also reminds us of the potentially subversive nature of his works, of their purportedly provocative, dangerous effects.[1] Smithers's edition of *The Importance of Being Earnest* drew from the opening night script for the three-act version of the play as performed at the St. James's Theatre; this Broadview edition of *Earnest* is taken from the Smithers edition, which since its publication in 1899 has generally been regarded as the authoritative version of *Earnest*.[2]

*The Importance of Being Earnest* would not be produced again on the English-speaking stage until 1902, when Alexander revived Wilde's most famous work, as he did subsequently in 1911 and 1913 (Hyde, ed., *The Annotated Oscar Wilde* 326n). Alexander's profit from the 1902 revival alone brought him over £20,000, a sure sign of Wilde's resurgence after his fall from grace less than a decade before (Bristow, "Introduction" 22). In the century since, *The Importance of Being Earnest* has become recognized as a modern classic, performed each and every year by countless theatre groups, adapted to the screen in the middle of the twentieth century and at the beginning of the twenty-first, and variously appreciated and lampooned in plays, musicals, and even a novel based on Wilde's work.[3]

---

1 Smithers also published *An Ideal Husband* and *The Ballad of Reading Gaol*, a prison-era work in which Wilde advocates compassion for criminals by arguing that while all people are criminals, only some are made to suffer for it.

2 For a more detailed history of the composition, editing, and publication of *The Importance of Being Earnest*, see the Note on the Text (below, 61).

3 Film versions include an adaptation of the three-act *The Importance of Being Earnest* with Dame Edith Evans as Lady Bracknell (1952) and an adaptation of the four-act with Dame Judi Dench in the same role (2002). Musical versions include John Biggs's *Ernest Worthing: A Musical Play in Three Acts* (1997), John Sean O'Mahoney's *The Musical Importance of Being Earnest* (1988), and Lee Pockriss and Anne Croswell's *Ernest in Love* (1960). Charles Osborne's *The Importance of Being Earnest* (1999) adapts Wilde's play to novel form.

The adaptation of Wilde's play into other forms extends the intellectual and artistic history of the play itself, for *Earnest*, like many of Wilde's works, was not a wholly original production, a fact well known in Wilde's day. Wilde was routinely accused of outright plagiarism, most notably by his sometimes friendly, sometimes acrimonious rival, the American painter James McNeill Whistler. On one occasion, when Wilde admitted that he wished he had said something clever that the men heard together, Whistler replied, "You will, Oscar, you will." More pointedly, in a letter to the editor of *Truth*, Whistler accused Wilde of a complete lack of integrity, saying that "Oscar has the courage of the opinions—of others!", and in a letter to the members of the Royal Academy, which was published in *The World*, Whistler complained that "[Oscar] dines at our tables and picks from our platters the plums for the pudding he peddles in the provinces" (Holland and Hart-Davis, *Complete Letters* 419; Whistler qtd. in Ellmann, *Oscar Wilde* 273).

Certainly, Wilde borrowed freely from the works of others as he concocted the plots and sometimes even the dialogue for his works, as the excerpts from three of Gilbert and Sullivan's operas in Appendix D suggest. Many critics argue that Wilde's plot for *Earnest* draws heavily on F.C. Philips and Charles Brookfield's *Godpapa*, which contains a character named "Bunbury" and which had played at the Comedy Theatre four years before *Earnest*. The most convincing of these is Powell, who also points to W. Lestocq and E.M. Robson's *The Foundling*, which opened at Terry's Theatre about six months before *Earnest*'s première. *The Foundling*, Powell observes, "contains the dramatic basis of Wilde's play—the story of a twenty-five-year-old foundling in search of the parents he 'lost'" ("Algernon's Other Brothers" 138-39). Powell's chapter provides a fascinating catalogue of works that may have inspired specific aspects of Wilde's play, including *Mr. Boodle's Predicament, Crime and Christening, Jane, The Schoolmistress, The Late Lamented, Two Johnnies, Charley's Aunt, The Lost Child, Man Proposes, Your Wife*, and *Tom, Dick, and Harry*.

Plagiarism aside, Powell argues that although a number of contemporary works contribute aspects of plot or turns of phrase that find an echo in *Earnest*, Wilde's so-called plagiarism operates in the service of a much greater artistic achievement: "What distinguished Wilde's play ... was an undercurrent of seriousness which was mostly absent among other farces of the day" (139), for "*The Importance of Being Earnest* is characterized, above all, by an intellectual coherence and thematic solidity which are notably absent in its precursors" (148). Josephine Guy and Ian Small agree, arguing that "the derivative aspects of a play such as *Earnest* do not diminish our sense of its distinctiveness or of Wilde's comic genius" (264). While Wilde may well have been a serial appropriator of the works of his contemporaries, his takes on existing ideas far outpaced—and certainly outlasted—all of them.

In addition to these contemporary sources, Wilde's comedy of courtship remains heavily indebted to one of the best-known tragedies of heterosexual love, William Shakespeare's *Romeo and Juliet*, particularly given its negotiations of loyalty to family and beloved, its misunderstandings, and its secret sites of meeting. In fact, *Earnest* might be thought of as a perverse—from the Latin *perversus*, or "backwards"—version of Shakespeare's play: in *Romeo and Juliet*, the lovers negotiate their romance despite the resistance of their families, only in the end to plan to rendezvous at a secret location to celebrate their clandestine marriage; but where in Shakespeare's tragedy the lovers meet in a tomb and die, primarily because Romeo misinterprets Juliet's pharmacologically induced state as death, in Wilde's comedy the lovers meet at a country house, the center of well-heeled domestic life, and, having found out the truth of who they all really are— having interpreted themselves correctly—they celebrate their engagements, all under the watchful and ultimately consenting eye of the play's key embodiment of parental responsibility, Lady Bracknell. In Shakespeare's tragedy, Juliet's nurse and Friar Laurence enable the lovers' secret romance to continue; in the four-act version of Wilde's comedy, Lady Bracknell purchases knowledge of her daughter's amorous whereabouts from a maid,[1] and Cecily's governess Miss Prism proves finally responsible, albeit indirectly, for bringing everyone together and for delivering to Jack Worthing the truth of his identity, thus guaranteeing the success of his courtship of Gwendolen. In Shakespeare, the lovers die because their families cannot accept who they are; in Wilde, the lovers thrive only after their identities have been revealed, only after their families have, quite literally, found them out.

---

1  This significant detail is one of many that appear in Wilde's original four-act play but were cut for the three-act version.

## *Earnest's* Cultural Contexts

*The Importance of Being Earnest* emerged from a culture on the verge of collapse: the Victorian Age, which stretched from 1837, when Her Royal Highness Princess Victoria of Kent ascended to the throne, until the death of the monarch in 1901, six years after Earnest's première. During that era, Britons enjoyed an unprecedented period of expansion of territory, influence, and power. "The sun never sets on the British Empire," as the saying went,[1] and indeed this was the case, for Queen Victoria reigned over more than half the globe, her power centered squarely in London. With the development of railroads and steamships, Britons could travel at speeds and go distances that, just a generation before, would have been unimaginable—not to mention quite literally impossible. Telegraph services bested the Royal Mail for speed of communication: that Wilde, for example, could send his thoughts within an hour to someone on the other side of the world must have seemed, to Victorians, a marvel and a convenience not unlike e-mail and text messaging have become today.

Two technological developments typify the late-Victorian experience as it is rendered in *Earnest*. The popularization of the photograph and the ability of the untrained individual to produce it—to make "Kodaks," as such pictures were generally known— provided means of accurate representation to all who could afford the price of the equipment, a boon to collectors of images and anathema to those who feared losing control of representations of themselves. More technically, and literally more deeply, the x-ray exposed Victorians' bodies to themselves and to others in ways never before seen, and the mysteries of x-rays, which required special readers to interpret them, rendered the photographed body as a text-to-be-read, a mystery to be solved. Together, the photograph and the x-ray produced a double-image of a subject: the photograph recorded a surface image of the person more or less as he presented himself or herself to the world, and the x-ray revealed an in-depth image of that person, now wholly unable to escape the supposed representational truth the x-ray exposed. Outside and inside, the fiction of identity and the exposure of its truth, the superficial self and its other—all of

---

1   The popular version of a phrase coined by John Wilson for his "Noctes Ambrosianæ" (1822-35) in *Blackwood's Magazine*. Wilson, who wrote the column under the pseudonym Christopher North, referred to "[King George IV's] dominions, on which the sun never sets."

these resonate throughout the twin technologies of the photograph and the x-ray, and together these developments threatened wholly to expose the individual, to "see" and to show a person, inside and out.

*The Importance of Being Earnest* examines exactly these two perspectives, these two views of, and on, the individual: the surface, or superficial, and the depth, or what is imagined to be true. Throughout his work, Wilde voiced a resistance to such a double-vision, warning readers of the Preface to *The Picture of Dorian Gray* that "All art is at once surface and symbol. Those who go beneath the surface do so at their peril. Those who read the symbol do so at their peril" (3) and observing in "Phrases and Philosophies for the Use of the Young" that "The first duty in life is to be as superficial as possible," for "[o]nly the shallow know themselves" (1244). Throughout Wilde's play, these representational sites—superficiality and symbol, surface and depth—take specific and meaningful forms: Wilde's young characters' ideas about love and behavior exemplify the most superficial of perspectives, those attitudes likely to fall apart upon closer examination, a sort of "touch it and the bloom is gone" fragility, to borrow from the language of the play (*E* 86). On the other hand, the play's representations of traditional morality see *through*, or at least they pretend to see through, the "age of surfaces" in which the characters live (*E* 133), to peer x-ray-like beneath the superficial self all the way to its very depths, to recognize the truth beneath the "shallow mask of manners" that comprises one's surface—quite literally one's superficial—image (*E* 119). Perhaps it is no surprise that at the play's end, it is Lady Bracknell who sees through Jack Worthing's surface identity to tell him who he *really* is, but it is Wilde's genius to show us that, unbeknownst to him, Jack *really is* the person he has been pretending to be all along. Thus, Wilde's play closes by asking who has the right to claim truth, the right to occupy the position of transparency: the progressive liar (Jack) or the traditional moralist (Lady Bracknell).

Wilde's decision to assign to Lady Bracknell the privilege of revealing the truth of Jack's identity may seem to suggest that Victorian culture empowers the moralist at the expense of the liar, but Jack's lie-turned-truth and the reward he receives for it—being allowed to marry Gwendolen—show that in this battle of wills and ways, Jack, the progressive liar, emerges the ultimate victor. That he triumphs by lying, all the while claiming to "have realised for the first time in my life the vital Importance of Being Earnest" (*E* 114), further shifts the victory in Jack's favor, for not only has his lie become truth, effectively overtaking the claim on "truth" held by traditional moralists, but Jack has turned his culture's totem of truth—earnestness—into its very opposite, just as in its closing moments the play suggests the reversal of tradition into progressiveness and thereby looks forward to the post-Victorian age looming over the horizon. In these ways, *The Importance of Being Earnest* structurally and ideologically bears out Richard Le Gallienne's claim in the epigraph to this Introduction: audiences for Wilde's play laughed even in the face of the death of their very culture.

Wilde's play was staged against a larger cultural backdrop that featured a host of divisions similar to the Jack/Lady Bracknell, progressive/traditional dichotomy. Such animosities pit the safe world-as-it-had-been (or at least as it had been nostalgically constructed by traditional Victorians) against the world of the uncertain-that-is-to-come, a backdrop as frightening to traditionalists as it was promising to progressives. Wilde's age was not unique in this *fin-de-siècle* psychology: scholars of history, anthropology, psychology, and literature have found similar rifts at the end of almost every century of recorded history, and one has only to think back a bit to recall the very real fears of the so-called Y2K bug, which seemed poised to throw the whole of the electronic age into complete collapse. In Wilde's day, London audiences labored under not dissimilar threats to their personal safety, their cultural security, and their perpetuation into the next century, as long-held standards of belief, behavior, and social relationships were coming increasingly under attack. Seemingly countless religious movements gained momentum as the century drew to a close, including radically different versions of Christianity and other forms of monotheism as well as agnosticism and atheism, the latter of which took its cue, in part, from Charles Darwin's theories about evolution as articulated in *On the Origin of Species by Means of Natural Selection* (1859) and *The Descent of Man, and Selection in Relation to Sex* (1871). Increasing numbers of Britons resisted their culture's restrictions on the expression of the self and its needs and desires by developing new modes of behavior and new models of identity, collectively embodied in the problematic figures of the dandy and the New Woman.[1] The explosion

---

1   Lalonde notes that "the effeminacy" of Wilde's dandies "signifies in a
    host of ways," making the dandy "as much a performance of class as it is
    potentially a performance of sexuality" (660). See Appendix G for cari-
    catures and critiques of the dandy as embodied by Wilde.

of a middle class threatened the long-held privilege of the wealthy as more and more Victorians appropriated the powers and pleasures traditionally associated exclusively with society's most privileged. In short, the whole of British culture seemed ripe for revolution, and the reminder of the French Revolution just a century before surely encouraged Britons to think twice about questioning the status quo, not to mention toppling it—an anxiety Lady Bracknell intones early in the play when she aligns the French Revolution with excess, disrespectability, cultural chaos, and utter social collapse.

Less than ten years before the première of *Earnest*, the many and complicated fears that beset Wilde's audiences took a very real and present form: Jack the Ripper, that notorious serial killer who virtually held the city of London hostage during his reign of terror in 1888. A sort of come-to-life version of Dr. Jekyll and Mr. Hyde, one of late-Victorian literature's most fearsome double-selves, Jack the Ripper embodied the most terrifying form of what Wilde's play treats as purely comic: the respectable gentleman engaging in not-so-respectable pursuits under the cover of darkness and beyond society's all-seeing eye—in short, the double-life.

The most notable among *Earnest*'s characters who enjoy double-lives are surely the play's male leads, Jack and Algernon. Yet it is neither of these but a character from Wilde's original, four-act version of the play, the attorney Gribsby, who offers the most precise embodiment of the Ripper-like double-life, of the Jekyll-and-Hyde, two-competing-realities-in-one that Wilde's play explores and extols. Gribsby proved a casualty of the cuts Wilde was asked to make to the four-act version of the play, and for the most part, that character has been forever lost to literary history.[1] Appearing briefly in act 2 of the four-act text, Gribsby presents a calling card from the firm "Parker and Gribsby, Solicitors" (Wilde, ed. Dickson 1: 74), but he confides to Jack that, in fact, Gribsby and Parker are one person, not two. Under the guise of "Gribsby" he bears stern tidings, while as "Parker" he engages in more pleasurable business:

JACK. You are Gribsby, aren't you? What is Parker like?
GRIBSBY. I am both, sir. Gribsby when I am on unpleasant business, Parker on occasions of a less serious kind. (Wilde, ed. Dickson 1: 81)

---

1   See Appendix I1 for the so-called Gribsby scene, which does not appear in the three-act version of *Earnest*.

In this two-in-one character, Wilde poses the embodiment of extremes—prudery and pleasure, responsibility (that is, *earnestness*) and its other—all of which masquerade under the sign of respectability and find form in Gribsby, a socially sanctioned figure charged with carrying out the nation's legal business. Like Jack/Ernest and Algernon/Bunbury, Gribsby/Parker emerges as a progressive figure, a liar who assumes the mantle of morality and tradition as he goes about the pursuit of diverse pleasures, sometimes claiming one identity and sometimes retreating to the other. Gribsby thus functions as a synecdoche—that is, he stands as a miniature—for the sutured self Wilde's play explores, a self constantly split between "the duties expected of one" (*E* 87) and the pleasures one privately seeks: a Bunburyist, pure and simple.[1] Although this key character disappears from the canonical, three-act version of *Earnest*, Gribsby figures prominently throughout the material in Appendix I1, for an understanding of Gribsby's tricky embodiment of duplicity will surely help readers of the present edition appreciate more deeply the wild divergence of the other-selves embodied by many of the play's characters.

## Wilde's Rise and Fall

It is a mistake always and only to read Wilde's works autobiographically and even more so to limit one's autobiographical readings of Wilde to a retrospective vision that finds in them the seeds of the playwright's undoing, so that "Wilde's 'fate' as a tragic figure gets read back into his life ... as [a] totalizing, life-defining myth" (Kaye 210).[2] Nonetheless, readers attuned to

1 Christopher Craft reads the Parker/Gribsby double-character even more pointedly as "a structure in which transgression and law, homosexual delight and its arrest, are produced and reproduced as interlocked versions and inversions of each other" (33).

2 Such a retrospective reading is sometimes applied to all late-Victorian representations of men in general and dandies in particular, an overly specific view against which James Eli Adams inveighs: "... the force of Wilde's spectacular and wrenching downfall, with all the forms of emblematic closure that have been attached to it, has tended to distort our understanding of Victorian masculinities, by suggesting a misleadingly narrow, rigorous, and persistent association of dissident masculinities with transgressive sexuality" (230). Alan Sinfield argues that while "it might be nice to think of Algernon and Jack as a gay couple, ... most of their dialogue is bickering about property and women; or Bunburying as cruising for rough trade, but it is an upper-class young heiress that we see Algernon visiting, and they want to marry" (vi).   (Continued)

Wilde's private life cannot help but find echoes of it throughout *The Importance of Being Earnest*. By the time of the play's prem... ière, Wilde had become famous and infamous throughout Europe and America, not only for his much-celebrated personality but also for his dramas, his novel *The Picture of Dorian Gray*, his essays on criticism, philosophy, and the arts, and, to a lesser degree, his poetry and children's stories. In the early days of his career, when his literary output was known only to a small readership, Wilde nonetheless became something of a character in British culture when he was repeatedly parodied throughout the pages of *Punch; or, The London Charivari* as the embodiment of the emerging Aesthetic movement, which was usually represented under an "Art for Art's Sake" banner. As an Aesthete, Wilde modeled an apparently superficial appreciation for beauty in all its forms—in literature and the arts, in clothing and interior design, and in the physicality of the bodies of women and men.

Wilde's fame became sufficiently widespread for a British theatre impresario, Richard D'Oyly Carte, to hire him to accompany the 1882 American tour of the Gilbert and Sullivan opera *Patience; or, Bunthorne's Bride* (excerpted in Appendix D1) in order to introduce Americans to the Aestheticism *Patience* lampoons. Wilde's lectures functioned, in effect, as mini-theatre, his costumes and backdrops suggesting that this Aesthete/dandy was, at every moment, playing a role—and an excessively dressed and decorated one, at that.[1] *Patience* delightfully parodied prevailing modes of masculinity, offering for its viewers three representatives of Victorian manliness. The Dragoons (military soldiers) and their officers embody a muscularity and a commitment to action traditionally associated with masculinity. Reginald Bunthorne, a composite character drawing on aspects of Wilde, Whistler, and the controversial poet Algernon Charles Swinburne, represents the so-called Fleshly Poet associated with the Pre-Raphaelite Brotherhood, dedicated to the exploration of forms and styles from an earlier period that were saturated with color, suffused with lust, and devoted to the worship of beauty. Finally, Archibald Grosvenor represents a mode of masculinity in transition, the "Idyllic Poet" who apes Bunthorne's feminine poses and flamboyant costumes in an attempt to woo women, just as

Lalonde agrees, adding that "both Algernon and Jack ... display heterosexual desire. If anything, there is the suggestion that Algernon might be promiscuously heterosexual in spite of his effeminacy" (660).

1 On Wilde's costumes and stage sets for his American tour, see Mary Warner Blanchard, *Oscar Wilde's America: Counterculture in the Gilded Age*, 18.

Bunthorne, despite his (pretended) disinterest, does without fail (Gilbert and Sullivan, *Patience*, "Dramatis Personæ").[1]

Wilde's task was to speak to audiences in advance of each staging of *Patience* in order to acquaint them with the principal tenets of Aestheticism as well as to offer for them by way of his own image a representation of how an Aesthete looks, moves, and speaks. Much was made of Wilde's novel appearance and manner throughout his American tour, and while there were occasional grumblings about Wilde's apparent lack of manliness, his excessiveness, and his frivolity, Americans generally seemed entranced with Wilde, so much so that his image, his words, and caricatures of his Aesthetic style flooded the advertising market as American manufacturers and storekeepers sought to cash in on the nation's latest curiosity.[2] (See figs. 1-4.)

Despite his increasing fame, by the end of the American tour, some press accounts suggest that Wilde, who upon entering the States had announced to customs officials that "I have nothing to declare except my genius" (qtd. in Ellmann, *Oscar Wilde* 160), had become a figure of growing notoriety: Mary Warner Blanchard argues that although Wilde "was seen as an aesthete" and "was also, to a surprising degree, applauded as 'manly'" (27), "the reaction to Wilde in the popular press indicated an emergent anxiety not only about the new aesthetic ideology but, more dangerously, about the celebrated and stylized masculine self" (3).

Wilde spent much of the year following his return from America lecturing throughout the United Kingdom, further establishing his fame and bolstering the public's perception of his status as a figurehead for the increasingly notorious Aesthetic movement. At the end of 1883, Wilde announced his engagement to Constance Lloyd, whom he married in late May of the next year. Over the ensuing half-decade, Wilde's reputation grew as he regularly contributed reviews to the *Pall Mall Gazette*, assumed editorship of a magazine he renamed *The Woman's World*, and published a series of essays, stories, and children's tales. By this time, the Wildes had become quite famous for entertaining artists in the lavishly decorated home they shared with their two sons in

---

1   Gayden Wren simplifies these characterizations of Bunthorne and Grosvenor, describing them as "a fraud and a fool, respectively, and their followers ... [as] self-indulgent twits" (101).

2   More details about Wilde's American tour as well as about the kind of America Wilde experienced may be found in Blanchard (especially ch. 1, "Oscar Wilde, Aesthetic Style, and the Masculine Self") and throughout Lloyd Lewis and Henry Justin Smith's *Oscar Wilde Discovers America* (excerpted in Appendix G4).

Figure 1: "Strike Me with a Sun Flower." Caricature of Oscar Wilde. Collection of the editor.

Figure 2: Advertisement for "Marie Fontaine's Moth and Freckle Cure." Collection of the editor.

OSCAR WILDE.

Figure 3: Advertisement for Straiton and Storm's Cigars. Collection of the editor.

OSCAR WILDE ON OUR CAST-IRON STOVES.
Another American Institution sat down ee.

Figure 4: Advertisement for a cast-iron stove. Collection of the editor.

the fashionably bohemian neighborhood of Chelsea, a residence designed to showcase Wilde's Aesthetic predilections.[1]

In 1890, Wilde made what many regarded as his first significant misstep by publishing a work entitled *The Picture of Dorian Gray* in the American *Lippincott's Monthly Magazine*. The story of a

---

1  Ellmann provides a fascinating description of the Wildes' "Aesthetic" house on Tite Street; see his *Oscar Wilde*, ch. 10, "Mr. and Mrs. Wilde," especially 255-58.

stunningly beautiful young man, Dorian, and two older gentlemen who variously mentor, woo, adore, and reject him, Wilde's novella offered the best evidence for those who suspected him of secretly harboring same-sex desire. Appearing just a year after the notorious story "The Portrait of Mr. W.H." in which Wilde suggested an erotic relationship between Shakespeare and the dedicatee of his sonnets, *The Picture of Dorian Gray* set off extensive debates among reviewers and the public at large about the nature of desire in Wilde's book as well as about the potentially dangerous influence—indeed, the contagious tendency—that many reviewers perceived as among the book's effects. Speculation about Wilde's private life grew increasingly widespread, and caricatures of Wilde that had depicted the Aesthete in poses of languor and the idle contemplation of beauty now began to appear to the general public also to suggest a certain lack of traditional masculinity easily assigned to the emerging category of the homosexual.[1]

Facing increasingly harsh criticism, Wilde did little to allay society's suspicions. In a series of moves that would come to haunt him around the time of *Earnest*'s première, Wilde inadvertently laid the groundwork for a legal case that would find him guilty of gross indecency, thus hastening the end of his literary career. In 1891, Wilde contributed a set of aphorisms to the Oxford undergraduate magazine *The Chameleon*, "Phrases and Philosophies for the Use of the Young" (excerpted in Appendix H2), which appeared amidst a number of more scandalous works variously hinting at and celebrating outright the pleasures of same-sex eroticism. That Wilde's contribution was offered as a favor to Lord Alfred Douglas, "an Oxonian" (*E* 135) who had become Wilde's lover, only tightened the net that was closing on Wilde, now assumed to be at the center of what many Victorians considered a vile, immoral subculture.

Two years before *The Chameleon* appeared, one of its contributors, J.G.F. Nicholson, published a collection of poetry titled *Love in Earnest* (excerpted in Appendix E), which featured a

---

1 It is beyond the scope of this Introduction to examine the history of the emergence of the category of "the homosexual" in Wilde's culture, and while the use of this term is somewhat anachronistic, it serves to make Wilde's complicated cultural position most easily understandable to twenty-first-century readers. For those interested in the legal history in England for crimes of "gross indecency" (sexual relations between men), see the book-length studies by Joseph Bristow, Ed Cohen, Richard Dellamora, Jonathan Dollimore, Michael S. Foldy, Jonathan Goodman, Neil McKenna, Gary Schmidgall, and Alan Sinfield. See also Appendix G for caricatures of Wilde that suggest a connection between the dandy and the homosexual.

number of *pæans* to youthful male beauty and same-sex desire. That Wilde may have taken the name "Ernest" from Nicholson's poetry provides a tempting basis for reading the double-lives celebrated in Wilde's heterosexual romance as covertly signifying homosexual relationships; and while such an exclusively narrow reading of the play is to be discouraged, one must be struck by the significance the play attaches to names in general and by the significance of the name "Ernest" in particular, just as it is celebrated in Nicholson's poetry.

Another of Wilde's acquaintances who was privy to aspects of Wilde's relationship with Lord Alfred Douglas and who knew of their extensive homosexual social circle was the novelist Robert Hichens. Drawing on his insights into the life Wilde and Douglas shared, in 1894 Hichens published *The Green Carnation*, a thinly veiled account of the Wilde-Douglas *milieu*, which only fueled the flames of controversy raging around Britain's best-known playwright. Wilde acknowledges Hichens's book toward the end of the four-act version of *Earnest* with a characteristically knowing joke: when a copy of Hichens's novel is handed to Lady Brancaster (whom Wilde re-named "Lady Bracknell" in the three-act play), she misunderstands it as having to do with "the culture of exotics" (Wilde, ed. Berggren 190)—that is, horticultural experiments—when in reality the novel examines a truly exotic culture: *fin-de-siècle* homosexuality.

Earlier in his career, Wilde had become a symbol for his culture's debates about art and Aestheticism, but after the publication of *The Picture of Dorian Gray*—and certainly after accounts of his personal life became common knowledge—Wilde emerged as a lightning-rod at the center of his culture's conversations about the self and its pleasures, about men and their desires. All of this came to a head when Lord Alfred Douglas's father, John Sholto Douglas, who was known by his title "The Marquis of Queensberry," launched a series of sometimes very public rebukes of his son and his son's lover, culminating in Queensberry's delivering to Wilde's private club, The Albemarle, a calling card on which he wrote "For Oscar Wilde, Posing as a Somdomite [*sic*]."[1]

---

1   Much has been made of the nearly illegible scrawl on Queensberry's card. Some believe it was meant to say "For Oscar Wilde, Ponce and Sodomite," and all point to the fact that, whether in ignorance, rage, or haste, Queensberry misspelled the key word in his accusation. The original card is now in the British National Archives; see <http://www.nationalarchives.gov.uk/museum/item.asp?item_id=41>.

Motivated to no small degree by his own arrogance, Wilde challenged Queensberry's charge, arguing that by leaving the written accusation with the Porter at The Albemarle, Queensberry had legally libeled him. Wilde brought the case against his opponent on 1 March 1895, merely a fortnight after *Earnest*'s glittering première. The next two months would see Wilde withdraw and thus lose that case, only then to be arrested, charged with crimes of gross indecency, and, after an initial mistrial, found guilty and sentenced to two years of hard labor.[1]

In the midst of Wilde's shame, the German writer Max Nordau's book-length study of the phenomenon known as degeneration was translated into English; *Degeneration* became a best-seller and went through six printings in the year of Wilde's trials alone. That an ostensibly psychological textbook could find such popularity among a general readership indicates the level of anxiety Victorians felt about the falling-apart of their culture as well as their increasing level of awareness regarding matters of same-sex desire, of men "of the Oscar Wilde sort," as a homosexual character in an early twentieth-century novel would describe himself.[2] *Degeneration* cited Wilde as a harbinger of the demise of Victorian culture, essentially in league with the artistic movements Pre-Raphaelitism and Aestheticism, the playwright Henrik Ibsen, the novelists Leo Tolstoy and Émile Zola, and the composer Richard Wagner. In Nordau's view, the degenerate was a symptom of his culture's decline; to cleanse culture, Nordau argued, degenerates must be exposed and corrected, lest the entire Western world fall into chaos. At the end of Wilde's trials, just three months after *Earnest*'s première, such, it seems, was the prevailing cultural attitude toward Wilde, who only a few months before had enjoyed his status as Britain's most celebrated playwright. After serving two years of hard labor in Reading Gaol, Wilde was released from prison, and he spent the remaining three

---

1 The rich history of Wilde's trials forms the subject of a number of studies; key events are reviewed in the Chronology. Readers with interests in Wilde's trials should consult Michael Foldy's *The Trials of Oscar Wilde: Deviance, Morality, and Late-Victorian Society*, Jonathan Goodman's *The Oscar Wilde File*, Merlin Holland's *Irish Peacock and Scarlet Marquess: The Real Trial of Oscar Wilde*, and H. Montgomery Hyde's *The Trials of Oscar Wilde*, as well as Moises Kaufman's drama *Gross Indecency: The Three Trials of Oscar Wilde* and the films *The Trials of Oscar Wilde* and *Wilde*.

2 See E.M. Forster's *Maurice*, 159.

years of his life traveling, residing primarily in and around Paris, that city associated throughout *Earnest* with revolution, vice, superficiality—and pleasure. Wilde died, virtually penniless, at the Hôtel d'Alsace on 30 November 1900.

In light of all of this, the effects of *The Importance of Being Earnest* are difficult to discern. Does Wilde's play suggest that double-lives must cede to more traditional modes of courtship, romance, and marriage, or does the play, as Powell argues ("Algernon's Other Brothers" 151), signal not a correction of behavior but a revolt against Victorian earnestness? One is hard-pressed to assign either of these readings at the expense of the other, suggesting that in its ultimate meanings, *The Importance of Being Earnest* enjoys the same sort of double-life—now conformity, now revolution—that its plot explores.

## Reading *The Importance of Being Earnest*

The critical history of *The Importance of Being Earnest* grows increasingly rich and varied each year. While it is impossible to offer a consideration of each contribution to the critical tradition, a general classification of recent approaches follows in order to guide readers who wish to explore more fully some of the major aspects of the play as well as the composition, performance, and reception histories of *The Importance of Being Earnest*.

General overviews of Wilde's play and the connections between that work and Wilde's *œuvre* include *The Cambridge Companion to Oscar Wilde*, edited by Peter Raby, *Palgrave Advances in Oscar Wilde Studies*, edited by Frederic S. Roden, and *Critical Essays on Oscar Wilde*, edited by Regenia Gagnier. More specifically, Raby's The Importance of Being Earnest: *A Reader's Companion* offers a book-length collection of essays about Wilde's play, each from a specific interpretive perspective, as does *Readings on* The Importance of Being Earnest, edited by Thomas Siebold. Raby's essay "Wilde's Comedies of Society" in the *Cambridge Companion* places *Earnest* in the context of Wilde's "Comedies of Society" and examines closely the play's treatment of late-Victorian culture.

A number of works consider *Earnest* in the context of literary and cultural history. Raby examines the aspects of culture and theatrical tradition that inform Wilde's play in his essay "The Origins of *The Importance of Being Earnest*," as does Powell in "Algernon's Other Brothers" which appears in his book *Oscar*

*Wilde and the Theatre of the 1890s* and, in a slightly revised form, in Gagnier's *Critical Essays*. In a chapter called "The Importance of Being at Terry's," Powell traces the roots of Wilde's play, and Raby examines the significance of the names of Wilde's characters in his essay "'The Persons of the Play': Some Reflections on Wilde's Choice of Names in *The Importance of Being Earnest*," published in the journal *Nineteenth-Century Theatre*.

Joseph Donohue and Ruth Berggren's masterful reconstruction of the first production of *Earnest* provides a rich examination of the play in terms of its specific theatrical and cultural contexts. More broadly, *Oscar Wilde's Profession*, edited by Josephine Guy and Ian Small, examines the relationship between Wilde's work and the culture of writers and writings in the late-Victorian age. Jeremy A. Lalonde considers the connection between Wilde's play and contemporary social debates in "A 'Revolutionary Outrage': *The Importance of Being Earnest* as Social Criticism," which appeared in the periodical *Modern Drama*.

While biographical studies of Wilde and his individual works abound, several book-length treatments establish especially useful contexts for making sense of *Earnest* in terms of Wilde's life and culture. Chief among these is Richard Ellmann's *Oscar Wilde*, still considered by most scholars the authoritative life of the playwright. In *Oscar Wilde: A Certain Genius*, Barbara Belford examines the relationship of Wilde's works to his singular intelligence and psychology. The significance of Wilde's personal relationships and specifically of his sexual relationships with men is traced by Neil McKenna in *The Secret Life of Oscar Wilde: An Intimate Biography* and by Gary Schmidgall in *The Stranger Wilde: Interpreting Oscar*.

Speculation about the significance of Wilde's sexuality to his work has produced scores of books and articles. Many of these treat Wilde's representations of identity in the context of his own trials for gross indecency, which collectively cast Wilde as a novel figure, a "type" to which others might refer in assessing their desires and the desires of those around them. Jonathan Goodman's *The Oscar Wilde File* reproduces newspaper accounts and illustrations of the trial as well as transcripts of significant court exchanges. Michael S. Foldy's *The Trials of Oscar Wilde: Deviance, Morality, and Late-Victorian Society* considers the importance of Wilde's trials not only to Victorian literature and culture but also to the generations to follow. Ed Cohen traces the significance of the Wilde trials in the evolution of a new form of identity, the male homosexual, in *Talk on the Wilde Side: Toward a Genealogy of a Discourse on Male Sexualities*. Similarly, in *The Wilde Century: Effeminacy, Oscar Wilde, and the Queer Moment*, Alan Sinfield examines the long-term effects of the revelation of Wilde's sexuality to more contemporary notions of identity.

In *Sexual Dissidence: Augustine to Wilde, Freud to Foucault*, Jonathan Dollimore locates Wilde in a tradition of writers whose subversive tendencies derive from their own desires. Eve Kosofsky Sedgwick traces the significance of relationships to sexuality in "Tales of the Avunculate: *The Importance of Being Earnest*," a chapter from her collection of essays titled *Tendencies*. Christopher Craft offers a particularly insightful study of the play's treatments of desire and its multiple, complicated codes in his essay "Alias Bunbury: Desire and Termination in *The Importance of Being Earnest*," which appeared in the cultural studies journal *Representations*, and Karl Beckson considers the play's treatment of desire in terms of contemporaneous theories about homosexuality in "Love in Earnest: The Importance of Being Uranian," a chapter from his cultural history *London in the 1890s*.

In addition to those cited above, three sources will prove instructive to any reader of Wilde's play, for each offers an insightful reading of the play's concerns with regard to the theatrical, cultural, and historical concerns that inform it. In *Cosmopolitan Criticism: Oscar Wilde's Philosophy of Art*, Julia Prewitt Brown considers Wilde's attempts to establish the primacy of art in a resolutely industrial world. In *Oscar Wilde and the Poetics of Ambiguity*, Michael Patrick Gillespie examines the histories of reception for Wilde's major works, arguing throughout that a key feature that informs all of Wilde's work is the playwright's interest in multiplicities, in ambiguities—and not only of identity but of meaning, as well. Finally, in *Wilde Style: The Plays and Prose of Oscar Wilde*, Neil Sammells reminds readers that above all else, style animates Wilde's works, and it is to style, to matters of beauty and form, that our attention must always return.

In the pages that follow, I sketch a reading of Wilde's play that focuses on several key themes, a reading that is further and sometimes more specifically articulated in the footnotes to the play itself as well as throughout the appendices. These aspects all coalesce in the play's twin obsessions with language and power, which collude in what I will refer to as the play's "verbal echonomy," a structural and hermeneutic device developed more thoroughly in the six brief sections below.[1]

## Verbal Echonomy: Pre-diction and Echo

> The only thing that can console one for being rich is economy.
> —Wilde, "A Few Maxims for the Instruction
> of the Over-Educated"

*The Importance of Being Earnest* may have been best described by the poet W.H. Auden, who characterized Wilde's ultimate stage triumph as "a verbal opera," "a universe in which the characters are determined by the kinds of things they say, and the plot is nothing but a succession of opportunities to say them" (136). Such an appreciation of Wilde's play helps us see how "each gesture, each rhetorical movement is answered by a symmetrical countermovement of balletic grandeur" (Paglia 553). In considering the relationships between and among the play's characters, the dualities and tensions between life in town and life in the country, and the anxious awaiting for the one-who-knows to reveal the truth of identity at the play's end, *The Importance of Being Earnest* suggests an economy, or a system of exchange, that equalizes knowledge and power, an economy whose currency must be that very tool that enables the keeping or telling of secrets: language. As such, language sets relationships, defines authority, and inscribes, reinscribes, constructs, and deconstructs privilege throughout Wilde's play.

Specifically, the language of *The Importance of Being Earnest* may be understood in terms of twin strategies: pre-diction, the saying of something later to be repeated, and echo, the repetition of something already said. Both linguistic and aural in form, these strategies comprise the play's verbal *echonomy*, a term I borrow from French feminist writer and theorist Luce Irigaray's *Elemental Passions* (55). Throughout *Earnest*, pre-diction aligns or

---

1 Readers who wish to construct a more complete critical history of Wilde's play should consult the following edited collections: Karl Beckson's *Oscar Wilde: The Critical Heritage*, Richard Ellmann's *Oscar Wilde: A Collection of Critical Essays*, Jonathan Freedman's *Oscar Wilde: A Collection of Critical Essays*, Regenia Gagnier's *Critical Essays on Oscar Wilde*, Peter Raby's *The Cambridge Companion to Oscar Wilde*, Frederick S. Roden's *Palgrave Advances in Oscar Wilde Studies*, and Thomas Siebold's *Readings on* The Importance of Being Earnest.

distinguishes characters according to ideological positions—traditional/conservative or forward-thinking/progressive. Such positions may seem obvious from the moment each principal character is introduced, but the trick Wilde plays on us—not unlike the trick at the play's end, where the lie is turned into truth and "the vital Importance of Being Earnest" (*E* 144) is unmasked as the pleasurable rewards of deception—is that pre-diction and echo often allow us to identify connections across ideological lines. Sometimes, for example, Lady Bracknell's re-iterations figure on her side of the battle, but when her words are taken up by her foes, they suggest an implicit—and largely unexamined—alliance. By the same token, echo operates in two distinct ways, either to shore up one's ideological position and, thus, to underscore his or her authority, or to usurp authority from one character when the original phrase gets echoed by an opponent.

An example from Wilde's four-act version best illustrates how the play's verbal economy signals the reversal of power between rivals. Perhaps sensing the threat to her authority posed throughout the play when her words are appropriated by her foes, the character Wilde would later re-name "Lady Bracknell" dismisses echo as little more than magic, as a parlor trick:

> JACK. I really think you must be mistaken about it, Lady Brancaster. There is a sort of echo I believe in this room. I have no doubt it is that.
>
> LADY BRANCASTER [*With a bitter smile*]. In the course of my travels I have visited many of the localities most remarkable for their echoes, both at home and abroad. I am ready to admit that the accuracy of their powers of repetition has been grossly overestimated, no doubt for the sake of gain. (Wilde, ed. Dickson 1: 147)

When Lady Brancaster's pronouncements find an echo in the language of others and her authority proceeds, uninterrupted, she locates in the echoing figure an ideological ally; but when her emphatic language gets taken up by another and echoed back to her in a deliberate mockery of her pompous position, Lady Brancaster finds in the echoing figure a foe to be reckoned with, one who defeats her by way of her own ammunition—language. Two additional examples illustrate the dynamics of such exchanges:

> LADY BRANCASTER. To be born, or at any rate bred, in a hand-bag, whether it had handles or not, seems to me to

display a contempt for family life that reminds one of the worst excesses of the French Revolution. And I presume you know what that unfortunate movement led to? (Wilde, ed. Dickson 1: 30)

MISS PRISM. Cecily, that sounds like Socialism. And I suppose you know where Socialism leads to? (Wilde, ed. Dickson 1: 57)

. . . . . . . . . . . . . . . . . . . . . . . . . . . . . . . . . . . . . . . . . . . . . . . . . . . .

LADY BRANCASTER. But of course, you will clearly understand that all communication between yourself and my daughter must cease immediately. On this point, as indeed on all points, I am firm. (Wilde, ed. Dickson 1: 145)

JACK [*Still smiling and genial*]. I am afraid you don't quite understand me, Lady Brancaster. This engagement is quite out of the question. Nothing could induce me to give my consent. In this matter I am firm, as indeed in all matters I am firm. (Wilde, ed. Dickson 1: 156)

By echoing Lady Brancaster's haughty pronouncements, Jack turns her own speeches against her simply by repeating the pointed phrases she has produced as evidence of her invulnerability: echoing her emphatic language, *he wins*.

Lady Bracknell's intuitive understanding of the verbal echonomy that structures Wilde's play emerges in a moment from the four-act version when she interrupts Jack's speech in order to prevent her enemy from repeating his own words and, thus, underscoring his position of power in their exchange:

LADY BRANCASTER [*Severely*]. I should like to inspect that will.

JACK. It can be seen any day, Lady Brancaster, between the hours of three and five at the offices of Miss Cardew's solicitors, Messrs. Markby, Markby, and Markby, of 149a—

LADY BRANCASTER [*Waving her hand*]. You have already mentioned the address, Mr. Worthing, and even the most interesting pieces of useful information pall a little on repetition. I accept your statement about the will, and I do not see that the proviso you mention need cause us any anxiety. (Wilde, ed. Dickson 1: 162)

Lady Brancaster's interruption provides the most canny instance of echo in the four-act version of Wilde's play: in the exchange above, she understands that allowing a speaker to repeat his own words is tantamount to acknowledging that speaker's power, a power redoubled by the speaker's echo of his own language. Unable to bear such an affront, the usually mannerly Lady Brancaster interrupts, forcing *Earnest*'s verbal echonomy to work in her favor and thus brilliantly preventing her enemy's echo from diminishing the power she so precariously presumes.

Auden's sense of the play's verbal opera and Camille Paglia's description of its movement and countermovement of balletic grandeur take specifically linguistic form in the twin strategies of pre-diction and echo, which together construct the verbal echonomy upon which the play's negotiations of power and privilege turn. It is no surprise, then, that by the play's end, language has moved away from denotative meaning altogether and, in fact, to its own inversion, where a word has come to mean exactly the opposite of itself, to become not itself but its other, just as at the play's conclusion Jack has, finally, become Ernest, that false-self he claimed he was but believed he was not from the beginning. When Jack closes the play by announcing that "On the contrary, Aunt Augusta, I've now realised for the first time in my life the vital Importance of Being Earnest" (*E* 144), Wilde's audiences take delight in knowing that what he says is exactly the opposite of what he means, for at the play's end, language exposes itself, Jack-like, as its own double.

Brown describes *Earnest*'s language as "a labyrinth in which the characters are forever doomed to wander and play" (91); she argues that "[t]he humor of the play depends upon the characters' absolutely terrifying dependence on the power of language and naming" (90). Russell Jackson suggests that language operates in the service of wish-fulfillment, privileging language as the force that allows Wilde's characters to will into reality their individual fantasies of power and pleasure: "[Wilde's] characters do not collide with the real world, but are endowed with an enviable control over it. Their rare moments of helplessness are enjoyed as though they had wished them upon themselves" (xxvii). Noreen Doody recognizes Wilde's skillful deployment of language throughout his *œuvre* in ways that help him negotiate his own identity (252-57), just as Jack and Algernon manage their reputations by way of strategic invocations of their fictional other-selves, Ernest and Bunbury.

Ellmann's characterization of Wilde's use of language as "verbal ricochet" (*Oscar Wilde* 333) offers an apt metaphor for investigating the contentious plots in which language becomes enmeshed. For many of Wilde's readers, among the most pronounced of these is the realm of sexual politics, the negotiations of the place, power, privilege, and pleasure assigned to—and thus allowed for—men and women. Paglia gives the advantage to Wilde's women: "[b]y forcing their suitors to be earnest or sincere, the women ... bind the men by ritual limitations prior to marriage" (561). One is reminded here of Gwendolen's insistence that Jack propose to her in the traditional manner, even though she has alerted him that she has, in effect, already accepted his implied offer of marriage (*E* 84). Ruth Robbins also comments on Wilde's rendering of male characters as utterly powerless in contrast to his women, finding "[i]n the world of the play" a humorous exposure of men as variously ineffective, ridiculous, or absent; but Robbins argues that what takes humorous form on the stage signals a very serious social debate besetting late-Victorian society: "real anxieties about gender reversal" (77).[1]

John Sloan suggests that much of the humor in *Earnest* derives from "the spectacle of domineering women" (119), but he notes that such a portrayal may be regarded as misogynistic, since the play's women are revealed to be as ridiculous as the men they seek to dominate. It does seem in the end that masculinity triumphs, since Jack's discovery of his real name "is grounded entirely in letters, terms, texts ... the book, very simply, of the Names of the Fathers" (Waldrep 25). Indeed, for the whole of his life, Jack/Ernest is circumscribed by language, which is typically associated in feminist criticism with men and masculine power; however, the fact that "he was quite literally exchanged for writing in the cloakroom of Victoria Station" (Fineman 108)—and that the language for which he was exchanged was that of a woman (Miss Prism's manuscript), which took a generic form that many Victorians considered feminine (the novel)—reminds us, as Shelton Waldrep observes, that "[p]hallic power ... does not obey gender roles in this play or, more accurately, does not exist at all" (57).

## Sophistication: The Double-Edged Sword

What may really be at stake in these negotiations of language and power, in the verbal echonomy that structures *Earnest*, is sophistication in the way Joseph Litvak describes it: "a kind of syntax"

---

1 For a trenchant analysis of such anxieties, see Elaine Showalter's *Sexual Anarchy: Gender and Culture at the Fin de Siècle.*

(19), a "double discourse" that "hover[s] between an older construction of the term, meaning 'corruption,' and a newer one, meaning something like 'worldly refinement'" (57). In Litvak's reading, "sophistication offends not only in its artificiality but in its excessiveness: the sophisticate enjoys (himself or herself) too much, which is to say, at the expense of others" (7). Paglia's description of Wilde's play as "inspired by the glamour of the aristocracy alone, divorced from social function" (554) suggests both the excess and the inutility, the corruption-by-doing-nothing at the heart of the play's sophistication, a sparkling world "measured by the rituals of the English version of the tea ceremony" (Raby, "Wilde's Comedies of Society" 145).

Waldrep argues that "Wilde's self-invention has everything to do with his own striving after middle-class—and even upper-class—security and, in many ways, pretension" (63). Waldrep observes that Wilde saw through his culture's elaborate, ritual-driven codes of manners and behavior, and as an outsider looking in, he was especially well-suited to lampoon them. Specifically, Wilde seizes on the image of the dandy, with which he was routinely associated (see Appendix G), and he constructs that figure in telling ways. Wilde's dandies advertise "an image of the cultured as *not for sale*" (Denisoff 119), particularly with regard to their leisurely, languorous, and, as Victorians would increasingly be inclined to argue, feminine pleasures. Nonetheless, Wilde's dandies remain, for most readers, "cross-sex philanderer[s]" (Sinfield 70), primarily heterosexual men, as were the even more rarefied group of Aesthetes that populated late-Victorian culture who were portrayed, as in Gilbert and Sullivan's *Patience*, for example, as "lady-killer[s]," "[desiring] and desired by women" (92). Yet Craft argues that "the object of the play's derision is heterosexual representation itself" and that *Earnest* is, beneath all of its heterosexual horseplay, "a jubilant celebration of male homosexual desire, a trenchant dissection of the supposedly 'legitimate' male heterosexual subject, and a withering critique of the political idea ... that sexuality, inverted or otherwise, could be natural or unnatural at all" (23). What, then, *is* the nature of desire in *The Importance of Being Earnest*, and how does that desire appear—or fail to appear—throughout Wilde's play?

## Displacements: Desire and Food

Waldrep argues provocatively that "[t]he characters in *Earnest* seem already to have begun the process of making themselves into desiring machines" (55). This sense of humans as machines, as mechanically regulated forces over nature, raises questions about what fuels their activity, what keeps them going. Litvak's consideration of sophistication, which is surely one of the aspects of *Earnest*'s world so apparent to all of Wilde's readers both in his day and ours, postulates "the larger operations of culture as a highly elaborated food chain, where, if every act of eating is a speech act and every speech an act of eating, we can mean only in relation to each other's tastes—that is, not just in relation to other people as agents of taste but to our fantasies of what other people taste like" (12). For Litvak, "[i]n talking about sophistication, one needs to keep all these terms—the culinary, the erotic, the linguistic, the economic—in play" (8). In both Litvak's model and Wilde's play, we find "the implicit cannibalism of sophistication," the sense that "to be sophisticated ... is to be more sophisticated than, and to outsophisticate the other ... to incorporate the other: to incorporate, at any rate, the other's way of incorporating" (9), a complicated process hilariously modeled in the tea-time-gone-wrong scene between the suddenly bitchy Cecily and her evenly matched counterpart, Gwendolen (*E* 119-21). In that scene, each tries to outdo—to outsophisticate—the other by overcoming her rival, by consuming her, not least through the ways in which each character expresses her taste as well as through what she is or is not given to eat.

Throughout *Earnest*, food and its consumption pose sophistication in opposition to humdrum domesticity, as an early exchange between Algernon and his manservant suggests:

ALGERNON. Why is it that at a bachelor's establishment the servants invariably drink the champagne? I ask merely for information.

LANE. I attribute it to the superior quality of the wine, sir. I have often observed that in married households the champagne is rarely of a first-rate brand.

ALGERNON. Good heavens! Is marriage so demoralizing as that? (*E* 70)

Elsewhere in *Earnest*, the play's male leads console themselves over the absence or the emotional withdrawal of the beloved by eating—and not just eating anything, but eating foods associated specifically with the absent *amour*. Thus Jack devours bread-and-butter in anticipation of the arrival of Gwendolen, for whom it has been made (*E* 72-73), and Algernon calmly dines on muffins after his dear hostess Cecily dismisses him when she discovers the secret of his true identity (*E* 125).

When food operates as a stand-in for characters not present on the stage, its consumption proceeds according to a logic of relationship:

> ALGERNON. Please don't touch the cucumber sandwiches. They are ordered specially for Aunt Augusta. [*Takes one and eats it.*]
> JACK. Well, you have been eating them all the time.
> ALGERNON. That is quite a different affair. She is my aunt. [*Takes plate from below.*] Have some bread and butter. The bread and butter is for Gwendolen. Gwendolen is devoted to bread and butter.
> JACK [*Advancing to table and helping himself*]. And very good bread and butter it is too.
> ALGERNON. Well, my dear fellow, you need not eat as if you were going to eat it all. You behave as if you were married to her already. (*E* 72-73)

Throughout *Earnest*, food operates as a stand-in, a displacement, for those to whom one is connected and, more often, for those whom one desires. Eating cucumber sandwiches symbolizes Algernon's relationship to his Aunt Augusta, just as devouring bread-and-butter suggests Jack's ravenous desire for Gwendolen. The characters' perpetual hunger suggests that they are, as Waldrep notes, desiring machines, but for the most part, the limits of the play frustrate the satiation of their wants, leaving readers to wonder whether something else may be lurking behind all of these scenes of eating.[1]

James M. Ware finds the precedent for this "appetite-satisfaction motif" in Restoration comedies of manners (17), and Powell notes that such an element of plot was common in Victorian farce, "from pouring tea in a hat in *Charley's Aunt* to throwing bacon and chops out the window in *Box and Cox*" ("The Importance of Being at Terry's" 110). But what *is* this seemingly insatiable appetite that besets Algernon and, to a lesser degree, Jack?

---

1   The excessiveness of the young dandies' consumption of food is even more pronounced in the four-act version of the play, where in act 2, Algernon consumes six lobsters—and during his *second* lunch, at that (Wilde, ed. Dickson 1: 87).

What, or how, do these men want to consume? What, in other words, do they desire?

## Forms of Desire and the Ritual of Pursuit

In his *Reader's Companion* to *The Importance of Being Earnest*, Raby notes that

> [p]art of the strangeness of Wilde's play is that the text itself ... creates the ambiguities of gender and relationship. Jack and Algernon are actually brothers. Cecily, whom Jack addresses as "cousin," is a kind of niece by adoption. Jack addresses Miss Prism as "mother"; when she points him in the direction of Lady Bracknell, there is a moment when it appears that the woman who turns out to be his aunt may in fact be his mother (90)

—and, more shockingly, that his beloved Gwendolen may be his own sister. Yet more than individual identities gets confused throughout *Earnest*: of the scenes in which the men labor under the control or at the mercy of women, Neil Sammells argues that "[t]his inversion of gender roles has encouraged some critics to see *Earnest* as an exercise in gay politics" (111); in a similar vein, Richard A. Kaye reviews key readings of the play that develop what he describes as the "queer history" of Wilde's play (215).

Although not cited by Kaye, one of the most intriguing of these critics reads relationships, particularly those seemingly innocuous connections to aunts and uncles, as indicative of a sexually subversive subtext. Sedgwick approaches *The Importance of Being Earnest* as a play that decenters the specifically empowered social structure of marriage and the home-based family to nominate another model in its place, one predicated neither on marriage nor on cohabitation. Instead, Sedgwick argues, Wilde's play "places the sibling plot in many ways prior to, and hence more tellingly in question than, the marriage plot" (64), in part by "making visible aunts and uncles" (61), creatures not even necessarily related to their nieces and nephews. Jack, for example, is not Cecily's blood-uncle but instead is an adopted member of the family who takes responsibility for her until she grows into adulthood. Sedgwick's reading provides an ideological basis for the productions of *Earnest* that are staged with all-male casts and that construct its "Gorgon," as Jack refers to Lady Bracknell (*E* 90), as the ultimate drag queen: according to Sedgwick, various forms of the term "aunt" "were recognized throughout the nineteenth century ... as terms for (what an 1889 slang dictionary calls) a 'passive sodomist'—or, more likely, for any man who displays a queenly demeanor, whatever he may do with other men in bed" (59). Barbara Belford adds to this the finding that in Wilde's day, "Cecily" was a name often used to refer to male prostitutes (257). So just how earnest *is* Wilde's play in its representation of heterosexual romance? Might this, Wilde's greatest achievement, be far more sophisticated than most of his audience realized? Might *Earnest*'s sophistication point to a combination of Litvak's terms, a "worldly refinement" that traditional Victorians would see not, in fact, as earnestness, but as "corruption" (57)?

## E(a)rnest Bunburying

> JACK. Gwendolen! Can you trust me?
> GWENDOLEN. No, dear. If I could do that, I fear I would find you tedious. (Wilde, ed. Dickson 1: 170)

Kevin Kopelson suggests that "Wilde conceives of truth as a perilous and personal affair," so that in managing his double-life, "Wilde resorts to two time-honored aesthetic solutions: the mask and the lie" (22, 23). In these ways, Wilde operated in a decidedly non-earnest fashion—neither "Ernest"-ly nor earnestly, for that matter: "In the 1830s, when the word 'earnest' began to be used approvingly to denote Victorian devotion to moral and civic duty, the name Ernest became fashionable" (Sloan 117). In Wilde's day and throughout Wilde's play, earnestness assumes a place of similar social function and status, as Craft explains: the homophonic constellation "earnest"/"Ernest" signals

> 1) a plain and proper name (ultimately disclosed as the Name of the Father) that, for obscure reasons, "produces vibrations"; 2) the esteemed high Victorian quality of moral earnestness, repeatedly derided by Wilde; 3) a pun-buried and coded allusion (and here two tongues, German and English, mingle) to a specifically homosexual thematics, to the practices and discourses of the "Urning" and of "Uranian love." (39)

With regard to Craft's third aspect of earnestness/Ernest-ness, Sinfield considers why Wilde's male leads might strike readers in our own day as men so inclined: "Wilde's principal male characters do look and sound like the mid-twentieth-century stereotype of the queer man.... They are effete, camp, leisured or aspiring to be, aesthetic, amoral, witty, insouciant, charming, spiteful, dandified" (vi).

Few terms were available to Wilde and others of his acquaintance to "name" their particular mode of desire, but among these, the word "Urning," derived from "Uraniste" or "Uranian," was one of the most familiar. Coined by the German sexologist Karl Heinrich Ulrichs about thirty years before the staging of *Earnest*, "Uraniste" was one of few names by which the men in Wilde's social/sexual circle might have referred to themselves and to each other. Waldrep follows many late twentieth-century readers of Wilde in reading "'Ernest' (or one who is 'Earnest') [as] a probable pun [on 'Uraniste']" (165n41), therefore connoting same-sex desire. Wilde's play embeds several possible references to such a complicated "mingling" of German and English tongues, to borrow Craft's phrase, particularly in its invocation of the word "German" at significant moments—and in telling ways—throughout the play.[1]

Melanie C. Hawthorne finds that "in the late nineteenth century, ... sexual identity and national identity shared one important common feature: both were thought to be types of person, both were forms of 'incorporation' where inner essence was thought to be manifested through the appearance and behavior of the outer body" (167). Thus, throughout Wilde's play, two terms of nationality, "French" and "German," take on pointed ideological references. While references to France generally invoke the specter of the French Revolution and the consequent bloody chaos into which a once-refined world fell, references to Germany take on specifically homosexual connotations; like the name "Ernest," references to Germany produce (queer) vibrations.

Sedgwick cites the play's invocations of the word "German" in all its forms as "an important switchpoint," although she cautions that "it would be anachronistic to connect the Germanities of *Earnest* fully to the usage in the next decade of 'Do you speak German?' as a pickup line for gay Frenchmen," for "in 1895 homosexuality is not yet referred to as *le vice allemand* ['the German vice']" (65). Nonetheless, Sedgwick argues that Germanness as a metaphor for same-sex desire effectively enters the play at precisely the same moment as Lady Bracknell, who rings

---

1  For references to Germany and explanations of Germanness throughout *Earnest*, see *E* 82n1; see also Appendix I3, 209n1 and 209n2.

Algernon's bell "in that Wagnerian manner" (*E* 79): "Wagner ... crystallized a hypersaturated solution of what were and were becoming homosexual signifiers.... Virtually all of the competing, conflicting figures for understanding same-sex desire ... were coined and circulated in this period in the first place in German, and through German culture, medicine, and politics" (66). Thus, for Sedgwick, "The 'Wagnerian' 'ring' of Aunt Augusta, ... however it may seem to herself a guarantee of perfect sexual rectitude, invokes very different relations in the nephews who attend it as spectators, and who circulate in an urbane world where the very name 'Wagner' is a node of gay recognition and attribution" (65). In Sedgwick's reading, the German-inflected sophistication of Wilde's play "both enables and threatens ... the treatment of fraternal bonds ... as pure alibi" (67).

Just as Jack's covert other-name may operate as a recognizable signifier for same-sex desire, so too may Algernon's: many critics have argued that "Bunbury" suggests an allusion to homosexual eroticism in general and to sodomy in particular. Joel Fineman reports that "bunbury" is "British slang for a male brothel" (113), and Craft suggests that as "[a] screen metaphor for otherwise unspeakable pleasures," "Bunbury ... operates within the heterosexual order as its hidden but irreducible supplement, the fictive and pseudonymous brother whose erotic 'excesses' will be manifested only by continual allusion to their absence" (28, 27). Among the seven functions or meanings for "Bunbury" Craft poses, five of them suggest homosexuality: "a tongue-in-cheek allusion to Wilde's illegal 'sodomitical' practices," "a parody of the contemporaneous medicalization of homosexual desire," "a sly, even chipper allusion to the thanatopolitics of homophobia," "a pragmatics of gay misrepresentation, a nuanced and motile doublespeak, driven both by pleasure and ... 'by the need of self-protection',," and "a pseudonym or alias for the erotic oscillation within the male subject, his fundamental waffling between Jack and Ernest" (28). Like Wilde, whose sexuality could never be reduced to "a bipolar experience" of either this or that (Waldrep 50), E(a)rnest-ness and Bunburying perhaps embed complicated links to a desire and an identity sufficiently well known but not yet clearly articulated by such men at the end of the nineteenth century, men who understood and often operated under the very representational codes that, in Wilde's play, take the form of heterosexual comedy—of straightforward, *earnest* pleasure.

## "Persons Whose Origin Was a Terminus";[1] or, Sophistication Will Eat Itself

ALGERNON. The truth is rarely pure and never simple.
Modern life would be very tedious if it were either, and
modern literature a complete impossibility! (*E* 77)

In the end, there is also great wisdom in reading Bunbury
"straight." To bury oneself in something, as in the proverbial
"burying one's nose in a book," is to express the extreme devotion that marks the play's commitment to earnestness, albeit on
a sheerly superficial level, as Algernon's speech to Jack suggests:
"Have some bread and butter. The bread and butter is for Gwendolen. Gwendolen is devoted to bread and butter" (*E* 72). Like
his words, Algernon's appetite routinely gestures to something
else, to the pursuit of pleasures allowed and disallowed, to what
can and cannot be admitted: Algernon's appetite is, as Ware
observes, "the leitmotif that reminds us of Bunbury" (23). In
Wilde's day, the generic term "bun" stood for a range of sweet
breads, and so in this way "Bunburying" may rather simply
connote an excessive devotion to food, an attitude exemplified by
the perpetual appetites, the conspicuous consumption, and the
suspicious sophistication of *Earnest*'s "young scoundrel[s]" (*E*
109), Jack and Algernon.

On this score, Wilde's treatment of the rarefied world of *The
Importance of Being Earnest* strikes one as rather benign; as
Ellmann remarks, "[t]he substitution of mild gluttony for fearsome lechery renders all vice innocuous" (*Oscar Wilde* 422). Yet
surely one of the most supreme feats of *The Importance of Being
Earnest* is its stunning series of conversions: of Algernon to
Bunbury and then to Ernest, of Jack to Ernest and then *really*
to Ernest, and of course of earnestness to anything other than
what we assumed it was, of earnestness to earnestness *manqué*.
Throughout Wilde's play, earnestness gets interrogated and
exposed as "Victorian solemnity, that kind of false seriousness
which means priggishness, hypocrisy, and lack of irony"
(Bentley 111), a shield for pretension that Gwendolen exposes
most effectively: "What wonderfully blue eyes you have, Ernest!
They are quite, quite blue. I hope you will always look at me
just like that, especially when there are other people present"
(*E* 85).

---

1 Lady Bracknell's pronouncement from act 3 (*E* 132).

Brown argues that "being Ernest and being earnest can never coincide because of the relative insincerity required of us to live in society. When the two are brought together, the play ends" (88). Wilde's play thus strikes some readers as a plunge into an *Alice in Wonderland*-like looking-glass world of reflections and reversals; for Anne Margaret Daniel, *Earnest* is "a story set in the unreal space where illusion and reality can cohabit in bliss in the end" (59). So unprecedented is Wilde's cunning work that Joseph Bristow characterizes *Earnest* as *avant-garde* theatre: "Wilde's comedy marks a radical departure from earlier forms of drama. In fact, in *Earnest*—where everything is exceptionally artificial— there are the beginnings of a theatre of 'alienation' or 'estrangement,' which would become a cornerstone of European modernism, especially in the dramas of Bertolt Brecht" ("Introduction" 23).[1] In the end, Powell observes, "the keystone idea of Victorian earnestness—with its aura of zealous effort, sincerity, and high seriousness—becomes ... a word signifying the opposite of what it means" ("The Importance of Being at Terry's" 121).

For Powell, "[s]uch playing with language—as an antidote to ordinary reality—was for Wilde one of the secrets of life" ("The Importance of Being at Terry's" 121) and, one understands, one of the ways in which Wilde managed his own life's secrets. Ellen Moers's characterization of the play ignores a significant component of the play's subtext, sanitizing what remains, in so many ways, still sexy: *Earnest*, she claims, is "the single work which erases from the mind all the tedious nastiness of the Wilde story" (307). Craft's assessment is much more telling: "*Earnest* deploys inversion as a tropological machine, as a mode of erotic mobility, evasion, play" (37). Throughout *Earnest*'s seemingly limitless instances of inversion, one thing does indeed become another, polite pleasures do stand in for more visceral ones, and a lie finally and ultimately does reveal itself as the truth. "[A]s the last words of the play swallow the first words of its title," Craft cannily observes, *Earnest*'s beginning becomes its end, "its origin ... dutifully assimilated to its terminus" (34).

In the play's final moments, sophistication *seems* to outsophisticate itself, and the play's voracious eaters *seem* to find themselves devoured by the even greater appetites of a culture that *seems* to put an end to Bunbury's earnestness, demanding that the

---

1 For an extended reading of the late-Victorian age as the beginning of Modernism, see Samuel Lyndon Gladden's "Passages: The Long and Difficult Death of the Victorian Era, 1893-1945."

play's leads find out who they are, get married, and get on with it. Nonetheless, through its examinations of the echonomies of pleasure and power, *The Importance of Being Earnest* explores the dynamics of the insatiability of appetite and the negotiations of identity, key strategies for activating the nonsense in which the play delights as well as for avoiding and evading the "most dreadful scrapes" (*E* 77) that are part and parcel of *Earnest*'s—and Ernest's—double-life. Throughout, *Earnest* and Ernest have their cake—and eat it, too.

# Oscar Wilde: A Brief Chronology

1854   Oscar Fingal O'Flahertie Wills Wilde is born (16 October) in Dublin to Sir William Wilde, an oculist and ear surgeon, and Jane Wilde, a poet known as "Speranza."

1855   Baptized at St. Mark's Cathedral in Great Brunswick Street (26 April).

1857   Wilde's sister, Isola, is born (2 April).

1867   Isola dies (23 February), leaving Wilde deeply affected. He keeps a lock of Isola's hair with him for the rest of his life.

1871   Awarded scholarship to Trinity College, Dublin.

1874   Wins Demyship (a Classics scholarship) to Magdalen College, Oxford, where he studies with two of the leading cultural critics of his day, John Ruskin and Walter Pater.

1875   Joins the Oxford University Freemasons (23 February) and achieves the rank of Master Mason (25 May).

1876   Death of Sir William Wilde (19 April).
Wins a first in Moderations in the Honors School (5 July).

1878   Wins a first in Classical Moderations.
Awarded the Newdigate Prize for his poem *Ravenna* (10 June).
Earns first class in *Litterae Humaniores* ("Greats") (19 July).
Receives B.A. (28 November).

1879   Abandons hopes of becoming an academic after his essay "The Rise of Historical Criticism" fails to win the Chancellor's Prize.

1880   *Punch; or, The London Charivari* publishes its first caricature of Wilde by George Du Maurier (4 February).
Publishes *Vera; or, The Nihilists* (September).

1881   Attends the opening of Gilbert and Sullivan's *Patience; or, Bunthorne's Bride* (23 April) (see Appendix D1).
Becomes recognized as the leader of the Aesthetes in London; much caricatured and often lampooned, especially in *Punch*, which characterizes Wilde as the "Aesthete of Aesthetes!" (25 June) (see Appendix G).
Publishes *Poems* (30 June).

Departs for lecture tour of America to accompany Gilbert and Sullivan's *Patience* (24 December) (see Appendices D1 and G4-G7).

1882 Lectures throughout North America, where upon arrival at Customs Wilde states that "I have nothing to declare except my genius" (3 January); meets Walt Whitman, Henry James, and Henry Wadsworth Longfellow, among other notable writers and artists.

Attends an American performance of *Patience* in New York (6 January).

1883 Writes *The Duchess of Padua* (February-May).

Returns to America for the New York première of *Vera; or, The Nihilists* (August and September).

Begins a lecture tour of the United Kingdom (24 September), which lasts throughout the next year.

Announces engagement to Constance Lloyd (26 November).

1884 Marries Constance Lloyd (29 May); honeymoons through June.

1885 The Wildes move to 16 Tite Street in the fashionable Chelsea section of London (1 January), a home to be decorated in Aesthetic style by E.W. Godwin.

Becomes a regular reviewer for the *Pall Mall Gazette* (February through May 1890).

Publishes "Shakespeare and Stage Costume" (later reissued as "The Truth of Masks") in *The Nineteenth Century* (May).

Cyril Wilde is born (5 June).

1886 First meets Robbie Ross, to whom *The Importance of Being Earnest* will be dedicated and who will ultimately serve as executor for Wilde's literary estate.

Vyvyan Wilde is born (3 November).

1887 Publishes "The Canterville Ghost" in *The Court & Society Review* (February/March).

Publishes "The Sphinx Without a Secret" in *The World* (May).

Publishes "Lord Arthur Saville's Crime" in *The Court & Society Review* (May).

Assumes editorship of *The Lady's World*, which Wilde renames *The Woman's World* (18 May).

Publishes "The Model Millionaire" in *The World* (June).

Named as a Fellow of the Society of Authors (17 July).

1888 Publishes *The Happy Prince and Other Tales* (May).

Exchanges barbs with the American painter James McNeill Whistler in *The World* (November).

Publishes "The Young King" in *The Ladies' Pictorial* (December).

Constance Wilde begins editing the *Rational Dress Society Magazine* (through 1889).

1889    Publishes "The Decay of Lying" in *The Nineteenth Century* and "Pen, Pencil, and Poison" in *The Fortnightly Review* (January) (see Appendix H4).

Publishes "The Birthday of the Infanta" in *Paris Illustré* (30 March).

Resigns as editor of *The Woman's World* (July).

Publishes "The Portrait of Mr. W.H." in *Blackwood's Magazine* (July).

Meets John Gray (date uncertain), often cited as Wilde's model for Dorian Gray.

1890    Becomes increasingly enmeshed in a very public and acrimonious exchange with Whistler regarding the latter's charge that Wilde is a plagiarist.

Publishes "The Picture of Dorian Gray" in *Lippincott's Magazine* (20 June).

Publishes in two parts "The True Function and Value of Criticism" (later reissued as "The Critic as Artist") in *The Nineteenth Century* (July and September).

1891    Meets Lord Alfred Douglas (date uncertain).

*The Duchess of Padua* opens anonymously in New York under the title *Guido Ferranti* (26 January).

Publishes "The Soul of Man Under Socialism" in *The Fortnightly Review* (February).

Publishes an extended and somewhat sanitized book-length version of *The Picture of Dorian Gray* and appends a Preface (April) (see Appendix H3).

Publishes *Intentions* (2 May).

Publishes *Lord Arthur Saville's Crime and Other Stories* (July).

Meets Aubrey Beardsley (July).

Publishes *A House of Pomegranates* (November).

Writes *Salomé* in Paris (November and December); while in Paris, meets André Gide, Pierre Louÿs, Stéphane Mallarmé, Marcel Proust, and Paul Verlaine, among others in the *Symboliste* circle.

1892    *Lady Windermere's Fan* premieres (20 February) and proves the first of Wilde's theatrical successes; following the première, Wilde, smoking a cigarette, offers a curtain speech while wearing a green carnation in his buttonhole, as were a number of young men in the audience. Attends the London opening night of a satire on Wilde by Charles Brookfield and J.M. Glover, *The Poet and the Puppets* (19 May).

*Salomé*, in rehearsals starring Sarah Bernhardt, is banned from performance on the stage by the Lord Chamberlain, who cites traditional proscriptions against the depiction of Biblical characters on stage (June).

Composes *A Woman of No Importance* (August and September).

Meets the Marquis of Queensberry, Lord Alfred Douglas's father and Wilde's eventual persecutor, over lunch at the Café Royal (November).

J.G.F. Nicholson's *Love in Earnest*, a collection of homoerotic poetry, is published by Elliot Stock in London (see Appendix E).

1893    Takes rooms at the Savoy Hotel and lives increasingly away from the Tite Street home he shares with his family; occupies these rooms with Lord Alfred Douglas throughout March.

Publishes "The House of Judgment" in *The Spirit Lamp* (February).

Publishes *Salomé* in French (22 February).

Meets Charles and William Parker and Alfred Taylor (13 March); the latter will be indicted as a co-defendant in the second and third of Wilde's three trials of 1895.

Brookfield and Glover's *The Poet and the Puppets* opens in New York (3 April).

*A Woman of No Importance* premieres (19 April).

Publishes "The Disciple" in *The Spirit Lamp* (June).

Composes *An Ideal Husband* (October).

Publishes *Lady Windermere's Fan* (November).

1894    Publishes *Salomé* in English, with drawings by Aubrey Beardsley and the translation credited to Lord Alfred Douglas (9 February).

The Marquis of Queensberry again sees Wilde and Lord Alfred Douglas at the Café Royal and threatens to disown Douglas unless he ceases his relationship with Wilde (1 April).

Max Beerbohm's parody of Wildean Aestheticism, "In Defence of Cosmetics," appears in *The Yellow Book* (April).

Publishes "The Sphinx" (11 June).

The Marquis of Queensberry confronts Wilde at the Wildes' home at 16 Tite Street and threatens to harm him if his relationship with Douglas continues (30 June).

Publishes six "Poems in Prose" in *The Fortnightly Review* (July).

Composes *The Importance of Being Earnest* while at Worthing (August and September).

Publishes *A Woman of No Importance* (9 October).

Publishes "A Few Maxims for the Instruction of the Over-Educated" in *The Saturday Review* (November) (see Appendix H1).

Publishes "Phrases and Philosophies for the Use of the Young" in *The Chameleon* (December) (see Appendix H2).

Robert Hichens's *The Green Carnation*, a thinly veiled account of the homoerotic circle surrounding Wilde, is published in London by W. Heinemann.

1895  *The Green Carnation* is published in New York by D. Appleton.

*An Ideal Husband* premieres (3 January).

Joins André Gide in Algiers while traveling with Lord Alfred Douglas (January and February).

*The Importance of Being Earnest* premieres (14 February).

Receives a calling card from the Marquis of Queensberry at The Albemarle, a private gentlemen's club to which Wilde belonged (28 February; the card was left ten days earlier). The card contains an accusation of sodomy, which leads directly to Wilde's court case for libel against Queensberry and then to the Crown's two trials against Wilde for gross indecency.

Secures an arrest warrant against Queensberry (1 March).

Ada Leverson's affectionate satire "The Advisability of Not Being Brought Up in a Handbag: A Trivial Comedy for Wonderful People" appears in *Punch* (2 March) (see Appendix C).

Attends a performance of *The Importance of Being Earnest* with both Constance and Lord Alfred Douglas; reports claim that Mrs. Wilde is seen with tears in her eyes (7 March).

Vacations in Monte Carlo with Lord Alfred Douglas (mid-March).

Attends another performance of *Earnest* with Constance and Lord Alfred Douglas (1 April).

*Regina (on the prosecution of Oscar Wilde) v. John Douglas (Marquis of Queensberry)*, the trial generally known as *Wilde v. Queensberry*, begins (3 April).

Wilde withdraws his charge against Queensberry. Queensberry is acquitted, and Wilde is subsequently arrested at the Cadogen Hotel (5 April). He is held in custody at Holloway until the first trial for gross indecency.

Wilde's name is removed from the playbills advertising *An Ideal Husband* and *The Importance of Being Earnest* (8 April) (see Appendix A).

An American production of *The Importance of Being Earnest*, produced by Charles Frohman for the Empire Theatre in New York, opens (22 April), only to close one week later.

Auction of Wilde's personal possessions at 16 Tite Street (24 April).

*Regina v. Wilde and [Alfred] Taylor* opens (26 April); both are charged under section eleven of the Criminal Law Amendments Act, which criminalizes "any act of gross indecency" between men.

Hung jury results in a mistrial (1 May).

Wilde is released on £5000 bail (7 May); he resists his friends' urgings to flee into exile before the next trial.

Second trial of *Regina v. Wilde and Taylor* opens (20 May). Taylor is convicted (22 May) and sentenced to two years of hard labor.

Wilde is convicted (25 May) and sentenced to two years of hard labor; he is imprisoned first at Newgate and then at Pentonville.

Publishes *The Soul of Man Under Socialism* (30 May).

Constance and the children move to Bevais, nr Neuchâtel (June).

*The Daily Chronicle* publishes a claim that Wilde has suffered a mental breakdown (5 June).

Wilde is transferred from Pentonville to Wandsworth (4 July).

Constance Wilde legally changes her last name and that of their sons to "Holland" (8 September).

Wilde is declared bankrupt (12 November).

Wilde is transferred from Wandsworth to Reading Gaol (21 November), where he serves the remainder of his sentence.

The English translation of Max Nordau's *Degeneration* is published in London by W. Heinemann, the same firm that published Hichens's *The Green Carnation* a year earlier. *Degeneration* sells out six printings before the year ends.

1896   Wilde's mother dies (3 February).

*Salomé* premieres in Paris (11 February).

Constance visits Wilde in prison to bring the news of his mother's death (19 February); the Wildes will never meet again.

1897   Composes the letter to Lord Alfred Douglas that will become known as *De Profundis* (January through March) (see Appendix H5).

Wilde is released from prison (19 May) and is met by a group of friends, including Ada Leverson, at the home of Stewart Headlam in Bloomsbury. On the same day, Bram Stoker's novel *Dracula*, often considered a demonization of Wilde, is published. Soon after, Wilde travels to Dieppe and for the rest of his life lives on the Continent, often under the name "Sebastian Melmoth."

Entrusts to Robbie Ross the manuscript of the letter to Douglas, which Ross will title *De Profundis* upon its expurgated publication (20 May).

Composes *The Ballad of Reading Gaol* (July through October).

Reunites with Lord Alfred Douglas (August or September).

Mrs. Humphrey's *Manners for Men* is published by James Bowden in London (see Appendix F1).

1898   Publishes *The Ballad of Reading Gaol* (13 February).

Constance Wilde dies (7 April); her tombstone does not include her married name.

1899   Publishes *The Importance of Being Earnest* in three-act form, as it appeared on the stage, through Leonard Smithers and Company of London (February).

Publishes *An Ideal Husband* (July).

Wilde's older brother, Willie, dies (13 March).

1900   Undergoes surgery on his ear in his room at the Hôtel d'Alsace (10 October); shortly afterwards, he becomes increasingly frail and incoherent.

Dies at 1:50 p.m. at the Hôtel d'Alsace (30 November). Among Wilde's last words was the celebrated quip, "My wallpaper and I are fighting a duel to the death. One or the other of us has to go." Extensive debate has grown around Wilde's decision to be received into the Catholic Church before he died, some pointing to a sincere desire for conversion and others suggesting that Wilde was too delirious to make rational decisions.

Interred at Bagneaux, Paris (3 December).

1905 Robbie Ross publishes portions of *De Profundis* (February), excising all references to Lord Alfred Douglas.

1906 Under Ross's direction, Wilde's estate is released from bankruptcy (28 May).

1908 Publication by Methuen of the first edition of the *Complete Works of Oscar Wilde*, edited by Robbie Ross.

1909 Wilde's remains are moved from Bagneaux to Père Lachaise beneath a monument by Jacob Epstein that bears an epitaph taken from *The Ballad of Reading Gaol*: "And alien tears will fill for him / Pity's long-broken urn, / For his mourners will be outcast men, / And outcasts always mourn" (20 July).

Ross entrusts the complete manuscript of *De Profundis* to the British Museum under the condition that it remain sealed for fifty years.

1918 Ross dies (5 October); as per his request, his ashes are placed inside Wilde's tomb at Père Lachaise.

1945 Lord Alfred Douglas dies (20 March).

1949 Vyvyan Holland publishes the suppressed portions of *De Profundis*.

1956 Publication of the four-act version of *The Importance of Being Earnest*, edited by Sarah Augusta Dickson, by the New York Public Library, Arents Tobacco Collection.

1962 Publication of Wilde's collected letters, edited by Vyvyan Holland and Rupert Hart-Davis, containing the first unabridged version of *De Profundis*.

# A Note on the Text

Composed in 1894 and first staged, to great success, in 1895, *The Importance of Being Earnest* was not published until 1899, two years after Wilde's release from Reading Gaol. By that time, Wilde had served two years of hard labor, the result of the series of trials for gross indecency that began shortly after *Earnest*'s première on 14 February 1895 and rocked all of London, if not the whole of the Western world. Wilde's sudden and shocking reversal of fortune not only prevented him from overseeing the publication of his works during the years of his incarceration but also precipitated a seismic shift in attitudes toward the once-beloved playwright, so that the popularity and profitability of his *œuvre* were thrown into question.

Wilde's typescript of the play bears his working title *Lady Lancing: A Serious Comedy for Trivial People.*[1] Following his release from prison in 1897, Wilde prepared *The Importance of Being Earnest* for publication, drawing from the shortened, three-act version of the play as staged in 1895 by George Alexander and relying heavily on Alexander's notes to the first production. That version, published in 1899 by Leonard Smithers and Company of London, is generally considered the authoritative text of the play, although some scholars prefer the one authorized by the dedicatee of *Earnest*, Wilde's friend and literary executor Robbie Ross, which was published by Wyman-Fogg Company in 1909 and which drew from the Smithers edition of 1899 as well as from a German translation published by Verlag von M. Spohr in 1903 (Jackson xliii-xliv).

The textual history of *The Importance of Being Earnest* proves endlessly complicated. The licensing copy of the play, which reflects Alexander's reduction of Wilde's four acts to three, was registered under the title *Lady Lancing* and dated 30 January 1895 by the Lord Chamberlain's stamp. Yet an altered main title, *The Importance of Being Earnest*, was added to the typescript by way of a gummed label that mis-identifies the work as a four-act play, not the three-act version Alexander submitted for licensing purposes (Donohue and Berggren 73). Thus, even in its officially

---

1 The manuscript and typescript for *Lady Lancing* are held by the New York Public Library as part of the Arents Tobacco Collection. These documents were edited by Sarah Augusta Dickson and published by the NYPL in 1956.

registered version, the status of Wilde's play remains radically indeterminate, replicating in miniature the play's larger textual history, not to mention echoing the play's own interests in identity, texts, truth, and the ambiguities that plague them.

In sorting through this textual morass, one must remain ever mindful that *The Importance of Being Earnest* consists not of one text but of at least three, none of which alone may truly be called "authoritative" and all of which participate in the unfolding, process-oriented nature of Wilde's writing: Wilde's original four-act version of the play, which he completed in 1894; the play's three-act performance version of 1895; and the 1899 published version, which includes Wilde's modifications to the three-act performance text according to Alexander's notes. Despite the successful staging of the play, Wilde remained ambivalent about the alterations to his original four-act script made at Alexander's insistence: following a dress rehearsal of *Earnest*, Wilde remarked to Alexander that "it is a quite good play. I remember I wrote one very like it myself, but that was even more brilliant than this" (qtd. in Ellmann, *Oscar Wilde* 430). Wilde's decision to publish the three-act version of *Earnest* may have reflected less his preference than his status in exile, without access to his original notes and with only a copy of the three-act script sent to him by Alexander as a working text. Whether Wilde would have preferred to have published the four-act version is a question that can never truly be resolved; instead, one is left to choose between a tight performance piece and a longer, more complicated original version.

As a whole, this Broadview edition seeks to make accessible not only the so-called canonical three-act version of the play but also key exchanges that appear in the four-act *Lady Lancing*, which collectively provide a more complete and complex understanding of the play's relationship to Wilde's life, his career, and the culture the play lampoons. The present edition takes as its source the three-act text published by Leonard Smithers and Company in London in 1899, copies of which are held by the Harry Ransom Humanities Research Center at the University of Texas at Austin. Throughout, there are a few silent corrections to that edition, primarily in capitalization, but major alterations have been noted. Significant exchanges from the original four-act *Lady Lancing*, including the lengthy scene involving Ernest's near-arrest for debts at the Savoy, usually referred to as "the Gribsby Scene," have been preserved in Appendix I, which includes extensive notes that indicate the relevance of those excised lines to a larger understanding of the many and complicated resonances of Wilde's work. The present edition seeks to make Wilde's play and its cultural relevance, both in his day and ours, accessible to a wide range of readers, and thus it includes commentary, a chronology, notes, and contemporaneous documents that illuminate cultural, autobiographical, thematic, and theoretical insights relevant to such a readership.

In their masterful reconstruction of the first performance text of *The Importance of Being Earnest*, Joseph Donohue and Ruth Berggren combine several texts to produce what they believe to be the most complete representation of Alexander's opening-night staging. Donohue and Berggren describe their edition as "a syncretized one, formed by a comparative treatment intended to reconcile differences occurring in four texts, none of which has sufficient authority to represent by itself the text of opening night" (82). They acknowledge that theirs is "at best an approximation of opening night, the nearest that can be made, given evidence that is circumstantial, implicative, and suggestive, not definitive" (82). In a similar way, this Broadview edition seeks to illuminate aspects of *Earnest* that speak with particular immediacy to its contexts of production as well as to the conditions of life at the waning of the Victorian era.

# THE IMPORTANCE OF BEING EARNEST:
## A TRIVIAL COMEDY FOR SERIOUS PEOPLE[1]

## BY OSCAR WILDE

---

1   The first published version of the play, issued in 1899 by Leonard
    Smithers and Company of London, was dedicated to Wilde's friend and
    eventual literary executor, Robbie Ross, as follows: "*To* / ROBERT
    BALDWIN ROSS / *in Appreciation* / *in Affection*". Wilde inscribed Ross's
    own copy even more personally: "To the Mirror of Perfect Friendship:
    Robbie: whose name I have written on the portal of this little play.
    Oscar. February '99" (Jackson 2n). See the Note on the Text for a more
    complete discussion of the history of *Earnest* from its original, four-act
    version as *Lady Lancing: A Serious Comedy for Trivial People* to the final,
    published three-act text of 1899.

# THE PERSONS OF THE PLAY

JOHN WORTHING, J.P.[1]
ALGERNON MONCRIEFF[2]
REV. CANON CHASUBLE, D.D.[3]
MERRIMAN, Butler
LANE, Manservant
LADY BRACKNELL[4]
HON. GWENDOLEN FAIRFAX[5]

---

1   In his edition of *Earnest*, Peter Raby notes that Worthing was the name
    of the seaside town where Wilde wrote most of *Lady Lancing*; Raby
    observes as well that "Worthing" is "an appropriately upright name for a
    Justice of the Peace" (*The Importance of Being Earnest and Other Plays*
    [hereafter *EOP*] 356n).

2   Algernon Moncrieff was originally named Lord Alfred Rufford and,
    later, Algernon Montford. The character's original name was altered,
    Raby argues, given its obvious link to the name of Wilde's lover, Lord
    Alfred Douglas (*EOP* 356n).

3   *Divinitatus Doctor*, or "Doctor of Divinity," indicating Chasuble's
    achievement of what in the United Kingdom has traditionally been
    regarded as the highest academic degree.

4   The surname "Bracknell" appears in two other works by Wilde, *A
    Woman of No Importance*, staged in 1893, and *An Ideal Husband*, which
    was playing when *Earnest* opened. Raby notes that Bracknell was the
    name of the town where Lord Alfred Douglas's mother lived (*EOP*
    357n). "Bracknell" was a late revision to the character's name, which
    had originally been "Lady Brancaster" in the four-act text.

5   As H. Montgomery Hyde notes, Gwendolen's title of "Hon." (Honor-
    able) "indicates that she is the daughter of a Viscount or Baron in the
    British peerage. [Such a title] is never used colloquially so that she is
    formally and correctly addressed in the play as Miss Fairfax" (*The
    Annotated Oscar Wilde* 327n1).

Cecily Cardew[1]
Miss Prism,[2] Governess

---

1    In Wilde's *A Woman of No Importance*, Lady Hunstanton observes that
"Politics are in a sad way, everywhere.... Dear Mr. Cardew is ruining the
country. I wonder Mrs. Cardew allows him" (471). There and throughout *Earnest*, the Cardew *femmes* control their men, allowing or not
allowing them to do or even to *be* this or that. Later in *A Woman*, Mrs.
Allonby laments the state of her marriage to Ernest, by whom she has
been "horribly deceived," a man who "talks all the time," yet "what he
talks about I don't know. I haven't listened to him for years" (479). Pre-
dating *Earnest* by two years, *A Woman* introduces "Ernest" into Wilde's
emerging cast of characters as a man who fails to meet women's expec-
tations—an exact counter to the kind of man Gwendolen and Cecily, in
the present play, fantasize "Ernest" will be.

2    Miss Prism's name "is a near-pun on the word misprision, meaning misunderstanding" (Robbins 27) and describing "someone very affected
and precise" (Raby, *EOP* 357n). Her name was obviously important to
Wilde, as it is the only name not altered from the original four-act manuscript draft of the play. Wilde repeatedly poked fun at the sincerity and
uprightness Miss Prism embodied, attacking earnestness in particular in
"The Decay of Lying" by saying that "a short primer, 'When to Lie and
How,' ... would no doubt command a large sale, and would prove of real
practical service to many earnest and deep-thinking people" (1090). In
*The Picture of Dorian Gray*, Wilde describes Mrs. Vandeleur as "convers-
ing in that intensely earnest manner which is the one unpardonable
error ... that all really good people fall into, and from which none of
them quite ever escape" (35). Upon hearing Dorian described as "very
earnest," Lord Henry reports that he "at once pictured to [himself] a
creature with spectacles and lank hair, horribly freckled, and tramping
about on huge feet" (183).

# THE SCENES OF THE PLAY

Act I    *Algernon Moncrieff's Flat in Half-Moon Street, W.*[1]
Act II   *The Garden at the Manor House, Woolton.*
Act III  *Drawing-Room*[2] *at the Manor House, Woolton.*

*Time*
*The Present.*[3]

---

1  The postal code "W" indicates Westminster, in the western part of
   London. Half-Moon Street lies in the general vicinity of such posh surroundings as Kensington and Notting Hill.
2  The stage directions for act 3 indicate that it is set in the morning-
   room, an inconsistency Wilde left uncorrected in the play's page proofs.
3  *Earnest* opened at the St. James's Theatre in London on 14 February
   1895 and played concurrently with *An Ideal Husband*, which had been
   running at the Haymarket Theatre since 3 January. Bowing to public
   outrage over the revelations of Wilde's trials for gross indecency, George
   Alexander, the producer of *Earnest*, closed the play after only 89 performances (see the Introduction 12-13 and 16-18).

# FIRST ACT

SCENE—*Morning-room in* ALGERNON's *flat in Half-Moon Street. The room is luxuriously and artistically furnished. The sound of a piano is heard in the adjoining room.*

[LANE *is arranging afternoon tea on the table, and after the music has ceased,* ALGERNON *enters.*]

ALGERNON. Did you hear what I was playing, Lane?

LANE. I didn't think it polite to listen, sir.

ALGERNON. I'm sorry for that, for your sake. I don't play accurately—anyone can play accurately—but I play with wonderful expression. As far as the piano is concerned, sentiment is my forte. I keep science for Life.[1]

LANE. Yes, sir.

ALGERNON. And, speaking of the science of Life, have you got the cucumber sandwiches cut for Lady Bracknell?

LANE. Yes, sir. [*Hands them on a salver.*]

ALGERNON [*Inspects them, takes two, and sits down on the sofa*]. Oh! ... by the way, Lane, I see from your book that on Thursday night, when Lord Shoreham and Mr. Worthing were dining with me, eight bottles of champagne are entered as having been consumed.[2]

LANE. Yes, sir; eight bottles and a pint.

ALGERNON. Why is it that at a bachelor's establishment the servants invariably drink the champagne? I ask merely for information.

---

1  Joseph Donohue and Ruth Berggren (102n) suggest that Algernon's musicianship may serve as Wilde's acknowledgement of a moment in *The Green Carnation*, a novel that described in scarcely veiled detail the scandalous, male-centered private life of its Wilde-like hero: Hichens writes that "Lord Reggie and Mr. Amarinth [Douglas and Wilde, essentially] both played the piano in an easy, tentative sort of way, making excess of expression do duty for deficiencies of execution, and covering occasional mistakes with the soft rather than with the loud pedal" (70). See Appendix I1, 201n4.

2  Lord Shoreham is the father of Lady Lancing, whose name serves as the main title of the four-act manuscript and typescript.

LANE. I attribute it to the superior quality of the wine, sir. I have often observed that in married households the champagne is rarely of a first-rate brand.[1]

ALGERNON. Good heavens! Is marriage so demoralizing as that?

LANE. I believe it *is* a very pleasant state, sir. I have had very little experience of it myself up to the present. I have only been married once. That was in consequence of a misunderstanding between myself and a young person.

ALGERNON [*Languidly*]. I don't know that I am much interested in your family life, Lane.

LANE. No, sir; it is not a very interesting subject. I never think of it myself.

ALGERNON. Very natural, I am sure. That will do, Lane, thank you.

LANE. Thank you, sir.

[LANE *goes out.*]

ALGERNON. Lane's views on marriage seem somewhat lax. Really, if the lower orders don't set us a good example, what on earth is the use of them? They seem, as a class, to have absolutely no sense of moral responsibility.

[*Enter* LANE.]

LANE. Mr. Ernest Worthing.

[*Enter* JACK. LANE *goes out.*]

ALGERNON. How are you, my dear Ernest? What brings you up to town?

JACK. Oh, pleasure, pleasure! What else should bring one anywhere? Eating as usual, I see, Algy!

---

1   Wilde's thoughts about the irresponsible pleasures of bachelorhood are illuminated by one of Jack's speeches near the end of the four-act *Lady Lancing*: "More young men are ruined now-a-days by paying their bills than by anything else. I know many fashionable young men ... whose rooms are absolutely littered with receipts, and who ... have no hesitation in paying ready money for the mere luxuries of life. Such conduct seems to me to strike at the very foundation of things.... Why is it that we all despise the middle classes? Simply because they invariably pay what they owe" (Wilde, ed. Dickson 1: 159).

ALGERNON [*Stiffly*]. I believe it is customary in good society to take some slight refreshment at five o'clock. Where have you been since last Thursday?

JACK [*Sitting down on the sofa*]. In the country.

ALGERNON. What on earth do you do there?

JACK [*Pulling off his gloves*]. When one is in town one amuses oneself. When one is in the country one amuses other people. It is excessively boring.[1]

ALGERNON. And who are the people you amuse?

JACK [*Airily*]. Oh, neighbours, neighbours.

ALGERNON. Got nice neighbours in your part of Shropshire?

JACK. Perfectly horrid! Never speak to one of them.

ALGERNON. How immensely you must amuse them! [*Goes over and takes sandwich.*] By the way, Shropshire is your county, is it not?

JACK. Eh? Shropshire? Yes, of course. Hallo! Why all these cups? Why cucumber sandwiches? Why such reckless extravagance in one so young? Who is coming to tea?

ALGERNON. Oh! merely Aunt Augusta and Gwendolen.

JACK. How perfectly delightful!

ALGERNON. Yes, that is all very well; but I am afraid Aunt Augusta won't quite approve of your being here.

JACK. May I ask why?

ALGERNON. My dear fellow, the way you flirt with Gwendolen is perfectly disgraceful. It is almost as bad as the way Gwendolen flirts with you.

JACK. I am in love with Gwendolen. I have come up to town expressly to propose to her.

ALGERNON. I thought you had come up for pleasure? ... I call that business.

JACK. How utterly unromantic you are!

---

1 Jack's speech and Algernon's preceding it introduce the notion of country life and city life as resolutely divergent aspects of a larger existence, as binary oppositions that function as each place's "other." In *Lady Lancing*, Jack describes his country house as "just on the borders" (Wilde, ed. Dickson 1: 6). Borders function both to separate and to connect, linking-points where things imagined to be distinct—city and country life, sophistication and earnestness—are in fact joined, making the division between the one and the other difficult to discern, ultimately underscoring Wilde's belief that identity is not a single, unified construct but a much more diverse, multi-faceted constellation.

ALGERNON. I really don't see anything romantic in proposing. It is very romantic to be in love. But there is nothing romantic about a definite proposal. Why, one may be accepted. One usually is, I believe. Then the excitement is all over. The very essence of romance is uncertainty. If I ever get married, I'll certainly try to forget the fact.[1]

JACK. I have no doubt about that, dear Algy. The Divorce Court was specially invented for people whose memories are so curiously constituted.[2]

ALGERNON. Oh! there is no use speculating on that subject. Divorces are made in Heaven—[3] [JACK *puts out his hand to take a sandwich.* ALGERNON *at once interferes.*] Please don't touch the cucumber sandwiches. They are ordered specially for Aunt Augusta. [*Takes one and eats it.*]

JACK. Well, you have been eating them all the time.

ALGERNON. That is quite a different matter. She is my aunt. [*Takes plate from below.*] Have some bread and butter. The bread and butter is for Gwendolen. Gwendolen is devoted to bread and butter.

JACK [*Advancing to table and helping himself*]. And very good bread and butter it is too.

ALGERNON. Well, my dear fellow, you need not eat as if you were going to eat it all. You behave as if you were married to

---

1 Wilde's take on marriage proves frequently skeptical, if not cynical: in *The Picture of Dorian Gray*, Lord Henry reminds the bachelor painter Basil Hallward that "you seem to forget that I am married, and the one charm of marriage is that it makes a life of deception necessary for both parties. I never know where my wife is, and my wife never knows what I am doing" (175).

2 The word "curious" circulated in Wilde's day as a euphemism for same-sex desire (see *E* 118n1; also Appendix I1, 201n4). Jack's statement would thus have resonated quite comically among those in Wilde's audience who would find in the single, dandified, "musical" Algernon a secretly gay man (for "musical," like "curious," was a similarly coded signifier), the very type so "constituted" that his marriage would likely end in divorce.

3 One of many examples of the play's deployments of "verbal echonomy" (see the Introduction 38-42), achieved here by Wilde's reversal of the well-known saying "Marriages are made in heaven." Such doublespeak reminds readers of the play's strategy of invoking mainstays of traditional wisdom and behavior only to overturn them, always to great comic effect.

her already.[1] You are not married to her already, and I don't think you ever will be.

JACK. Why on earth do you say that?

ALGERNON. Well, in the first place girls never marry the men they flirt with. Girls don't think it right.

JACK. Oh, that is nonsense!

ALGERNON. It isn't. It is a great truth. It accounts for the extraordinary number of bachelors that one sees all over the place. In the second place, I don't give my consent.

JACK. Your consent!

ALGERNON. My dear fellow, Gwendolen is my first cousin. And before I allow you to marry her, you will have to clear up the whole question of Cecily. [*Rings bell.*]

JACK. Cecily! What on earth do you mean? What do you mean, Algy, by Cecily? I don't know anyone of the name of Cecily.

[*Enter* LANE.]

ALGERNON. Bring me that cigarette case Mr. Worthing left in the smoking-room the last time he dined here.[2]

LANE. Yes, sir.

[LANE *goes out.*]

JACK. Do you mean to say you have had my cigarette case all this time? I wish to goodness you had let me know. I have been writing frantic letters to Scotland Yard about it. I was very nearly offering a large reward.

---

1 Algernon's observation introduces one of the play's metaphoric substitutions of food for desire (see the Introduction 43-46). By eating the food intended for the one desired (bread and butter, made for Gwendolen), Jack expresses that desire by symbolically ingesting Gwendolen herself. In this way, one's appetite for food symbolizes one's appetite for a romantic connection. More generally, food may also stand for other kinds of established, legitimate relationships: when Algernon eats the cucumber sandwiches, for example, he justifies such an action by remarking that they were made for *his* Aunt Augusta.

2 Donohue and Berggren remind readers that Wilde frequently presented silver cigarette cases to his beautiful young male friends, and so this moment in the play "might have held autobiographical significance for intimates of Wilde who could have been in the St. James's audience" (116n). See also Appendix I3, 208n1.

ALGERNON. Well, I wish you would offer one. I happen to be more than usually hard up.

JACK. There is no good offering a large reward now that the thing is found.

[*Enter* LANE *with the cigarette case on a salver.* ALGERNON *takes it at once.* LANE *goes out.*][1]

ALGERNON. I think that is rather mean of you, Ernest, I must say. [*Opens case and examines it.*] However, it makes no matter, for, now that I look at the inscription inside, I find that the thing isn't yours after all.

JACK. Of course it is mine. [*Moving to him.*] You have seen me with it a hundred times, and you have no right whatsoever to read what is written inside. It is a very ungentlemanly thing to read a private cigarette case.

ALGERNON. Oh! it is absurd to have a hard-and-fast rule about what one should read and what one shouldn't. More than half of modern culture depends on what one shouldn't read.

JACK. I am quite aware of the fact, and I don't propose to discuss modern culture. It isn't the sort of thing one should talk of in private. I simply want my cigarette case back.

ALGERNON. Yes; but this isn't your cigarette case. This cigarette case is a present from someone of the name of Cecily, and you said you didn't know anyone of that name.

JACK. Well, if you want to know, Cecily happens to be my aunt.

ALGERNON. Your aunt!

JACK. Yes. Charming old lady she is, too. Lives at Tunbridge Wells.[2] Just give it back to me, Algy.

---

1   Presenting a calling card on a silver salver was a late-Victorian common-place in houses of this social standing; but here and throughout the play, the use of the salver signals a moment when power is about to shift, when those certain of their pleasure and security are about to come under fire. A similar moment occurs in Wilde's controversial play *Salomé* (1894), the climax of which sees the title character, newly empowered, demanding that the decapitated head of Iokanaan (John the Baptist) be brought to her on a silver charger, a plate or small tray thus akin to the salver here.

2   In her notes to the Methuen Student Edition of *Earnest*, Glenda Leeming indicates that Tunbridge Wells is a quiet town in Southern England known for its mineral waters and, thus, as "the resort of wealthy invalids" (75). Raby adds that Tunbridge Wells was a "tradi-tional residence for respectable old aunts" (*EOP* 358).

ALGERNON [*Retreating to back of sofa*]. But why does she call herself little Cecily if she is your aunt and lives at Tunbridge Wells? [*Reading.*] "From little Cecily with her fondest love."

JACK [*Moving to sofa and kneeling upon it*]. My dear fellow, what on earth is there in that? Some aunts are tall, some aunts are not tall. That is a matter that surely an aunt may be allowed to decide for herself. You seem to think that every aunt should be exactly like your aunt! That is absurd! For Heaven's sake give me back my cigarette case. [*Follows* ALGERNON[1] *round the room.*]

ALGERNON. Yes. But why does your aunt call you her uncle? "From little Cecily, with her fondest love to her dear Uncle Jack." There is no objection, I admit, to an aunt being a small aunt, but why an aunt, no matter what her size may be, should call her own nephew her uncle, I can't quite make out. Besides, your name isn't Jack at all; it is Ernest.

JACK. It isn't Ernest; it's Jack.

ALGERNON. You have always told me it was Ernest. I have introduced you to everyone as Ernest. You answer to the name of Ernest. You look as if your name was Ernest. You are the most earnest looking person I ever saw in my life.[2] It is perfectly absurd your saying your name isn't Ernest. It's on your cards. Here is one of them. [*Taking it from case.*] "Mr. Ernest Worthing, B.4, The Albany."[3] I'll keep this as a proof that your name is Ernest if you ever attempt to deny it to me, or to Gwendolen, or to anyone else. [*Puts the card in his pocket.*]

---

1  While Smithers's edition mistakenly places the name "Ernest" here, subsequent editions correct that error to "Algernon," as above.

2  Algernon's comment acknowledges the widely held nineteenth-century belief in physiognomy, that notion that the face may be read as a text telling the truth of the person's soul.

3  In *Lady Lancing*, Wilde designated Jack's address as "E.4, The Albany" (Wilde, ed. Dickson 1: 8). An exclusive residence near Picadilly, The Albany was inhabited primarily by bachelors (Hyde, *The Annotated Oscar Wilde* 330n7). Jack's original address, "E.4", was actually the apartment of George Ives, a homosexual acquaintance of Wilde's, as well as the apartment in which Wilde met John Francis ("Jack") Bloxam, founder and editor of the notorious Oxford journal *The Chameleon* (Raby, *EOP* 358-59), to which Wilde contributed his "Phrases and Philosophies for the Use of the Young" (see Appendix H2), a witty set of epigrams that would be entered into evidence against Wilde during his trials for gross indecency.

JACK. Well, my name is Ernest in town and Jack in the country, and the cigarette case was given to me in the country.

ALGERNON. Yes, but that does not account for the fact that your small Aunt Cecily, who lives at Tunbridge Wells, calls you her dear uncle. Come, old boy, you had much better have the thing out at once.

JACK. My dear Algy; you talk exactly as if you were a dentist. It is very vulgar to talk like a dentist when one isn't a dentist. It produces a false impression.[1]

ALGERNON. Well, that is exactly what dentists always do. Now, go on! Tell me the whole thing. I may mention that I have always suspected you of being a confirmed and secret Bunburyist;[2] and I am quite sure of it now.

JACK. Bunburyist? What on earth do you mean by a Bunburyist?

ALGERNON. I'll reveal to you the meaning of that incomparable expression as soon as you are kind enough to inform me why you are Ernest in town and Jack in the country.

JACK. Well, produce my cigarette case first.

ALGERNON. Here it is. [*Hands cigarette case.*] Now produce your explanation, and pray make it improbable. [*Sits on sofa.*]

JACK. My dear fellow, there is nothing improbable about my explanation at all. In fact it's perfectly ordinary. Old Mr. Thomas Cardew, who adopted me when I was a little boy, made me in his will guardian to his grand-daughter, Miss Cecily Cardew. Cecily, who addresses me as her uncle from motives of respect that you could not possibly appreciate, lives at my place in the country under the charge of her admirable governess, Miss Prism.

ALGERNON. Where is that place in the country, by the way?

JACK. That is nothing to you, dear boy. You are not going to be

---

1  As Leeming notes, Wilde plays on the dental use of the term "impression" to name an object taken in preparation for the manufacture of false teeth—devices of deception, not at all so far removed from the devices of false names, alternate addresses, and "Bunbury suits" (*E* 95n1) celebrated throughout Wilde's play.

2  For more about the term "Bunbury," see the Introduction 19, 25, and 47–49. Wilde did know someone by that name, Henry S. Bunbury, a classmate at Trinity College (Raby, *EOP* 359). Donohue and Berggren suggest that the name may have been lifted from F.C. Philips and Charles Brookfield's *Godpapa*, a comedy produced in 1891, which featured "an old widower named John Bunbury who unwittingly plays into the subterfuge of the hero, Reginald, to marry Bunbury's daughter Violet" (123).

invited.... I may tell you candidly that the place is not in Shropshire.

ALGERNON. I suspected that, my dear fellow! I have Bunburyed all over Shropshire on two separate occasions. Now, go on. Why are you Ernest in town and Jack in the country?

JACK. My dear Algy, I don't know whether you will be able to understand my real motives. You are hardly serious enough. When one is placed in the position of guardian, one has to adopt a very high moral tone on all subjects. It's one's duty to do so. And as a high moral tone can hardly be said to conduce very much to either one's health or one's happiness, in order to get up to town I have always pretended to have a younger brother of the name of Ernest, who lives in The Albany, and gets into the most dreadful scrapes. That, my dear Algy, is the whole truth pure and simple.

ALGERNON. The truth is rarely pure and never simple. Modern life would be very tedious if it were either, and modern literature a complete impossibility!

JACK. That wouldn't be at all a bad thing.

ALGERNON. Literary criticism is not your forte, my dear fellow. Don't try it. You should leave that to people who haven't been at a University. They do it so well in the daily papers. What you really are is a Bunburyist. I was quite right in saying you were a Bunburyist. You are one of the most advanced Bunburyists I know.[1]

JACK. What on earth do you mean?

ALGERNON. You have invented a very useful younger brother called Ernest, in order that you may be able to come up to town as often as you like. I have invented an invaluable permanent invalid called Bunbury, in order that I may be able to go down[2] into the country whenever I choose. Bunbury is perfectly invaluable. If it wasn't for Bunbury's extraordinary bad

---

1 Algernon's characterization of Jack as an "advanced" Bunburyist remarks on the various levels of sophistication or refinement of such a duplicitous lifestyle; at the same time, his comment introduces what Victorians would have recognized as a medical language that pathologizes differences in desire, so that an "advanced" Bunburyist might, for Wilde's readers, be akin to an advanced case of a disorder or a disease, such as Degeneration (see the Introduction 35, and Appendix I3, 175n1).

2 In Victorian England, "up" meant toward London and "down" meant away from London.

health, for instance, I wouldn't be able to dine with you at Willis's[1] to-night, for I have been really engaged to Aunt Augusta for more than a week.

JACK. I haven't asked you to dine with me anywhere to-night.

ALGERNON. I know. You are absurdly careless about sending out invitations. It is very foolish of you. Nothing annoys people so much as not receiving invitations.

JACK. You had much better dine with your Aunt Augusta.

ALGERNON. I haven't the smallest intention of doing anything of the kind. To begin with, I dined there on Monday, and once a week is quite enough to dine with one's own relations. In the second place, whenever I do dine there I am always treated as a member of the family, and sent down[2] with either no woman at all, or two. In the third place, I know perfectly well whom she will place me next to, to-night. She will place me next [to][3] Mary Farquhar, who always flirts with her own husband across the dinner-table. That is not very pleasant. Indeed, it is not even decent ... and that sort of thing is enormously on the increase. The amount of women in London who flirt with their own husbands is perfectly scandalous. It looks so bad. It is simply washing one's clean linen in public.[4] Besides, now that I know you to be a confirmed Bunburyist I naturally want to talk to you about Bunburying. I want to tell you the rules.[5]

JACK. I'm not a Bunburyist at all. If Gwendolen accepts me, I am going to kill my brother, indeed I think I'll kill him in any

---

1 Wilde dithered quite a bit about the location of the men's evening entertainment, going back and forth from Willis's to the Savoy; see Appendix I1, 201n1 for a discussion of the significance of The Savoy to the earlier four-act version of Wilde's play. Willis's, located near the St. James's Theatre, was one of Wilde's favorite restaurants.

2 In the Victorian era, hostesses typically assigned seating, sending individuals downstairs from the parlor into the dining room to sit as instructed.

3 The word "to" appears in neither the *Lady Lancing* manuscript nor the Smithers edition of *Earnest* but has been inserted here for clarity.

4 Here, as Leeming notes, Wilde comically inverts the common expression "washing one's dirty linen in public" (76).

5 That there are "rules" to Bunburying suggests not only that such a double-life is a well-established alternative to Victorian earnestness, complete with its own set of alternative behavioral codes, but also that it is a recognized subculture among those-in-the-know. See *E* 77n1 and Appendix I3, 206n2.

case. Cecily is a little too much interested in him. It is rather a bore. So I am going to get rid of Ernest. And I strongly advise you to do the same with Mr. ... with your invalid friend who has the absurd name.

ALGERNON. Nothing will induce me to part with Bunbury, and if you ever get married, which seems to me extremely problematic, you will be very glad to know Bunbury. A man who marries without knowing Bunbury has a very tedious time of it.

JACK. That is nonsense. If I marry a charming girl like Gwendolen, and she is the only girl I ever saw in my life that I would marry, I certainly won't want to know Bunbury.

ALGERNON. Then your wife will. You don't seem to realize, that in married life three is company and two is none.[1]

JACK [*Sententiously*]. That, my dear young friend, is the theory that the corrupt French Drama has been propounding for the last fifty years.[2]

ALGERNON. Yes; and that the happy English home has proved in half the time.

JACK. For heaven's sake, don't try to be cynical. It's perfectly easy to be cynical.

ALGERNON. My dear fellow, it isn't easy to be anything now-a-days. There's such a lot of beastly competition about. [*The sound of an electric bell is heard.*] Ah! that must be Aunt Augusta. Only relatives, or creditors, ever ring in that Wagnerian[3] manner. Now, if I get her out of the way for ten minutes, so that you can have an opportunity for proposing to Gwendolen, may I dine with you to-night at Willis's?

---

1  Leeming observes that "the proverb is that '*two* is company and *three* is none,' implying that lovers preferred not to be interrupted by others" (76). By altering this well-known maxim, Wilde lampoons traditional notions about courtship and romance.

2  Jack's language pre-dicts Lady Bracknell's later in act 1 when she observes that "To be born, or at any rate bred, in a hand-bag, whether it had handles or not, seems to me to display a contempt for the ordinary decencies of family life that remind one of the worst excesses of the French Revolution. And I presume you know what that unfortunate movement led to?" (*E* 39-40).

3  An allusion to the operas of Richard Wagner (1813-83), whose dramatic music—and dramatic heroines—were often considered excessive and were even identified as a threat to traditional culture in Max Nordau's *Degeneration*, a book that similarly demonized Wilde. See the Introduction 34.

JACK. I suppose so, if you want to.

ALGERNON. Yes, but you must be serious about it. I hate people who are not serious about meals. It is so shallow of them.

[*Enter* LANE.]

LANE. Lady Bracknell and Miss Fairfax.

[ALGERNON *goes forward to meet them. Enter* LADY BRACK-NELL *and* GWENDOLEN.]

LADY BRACKNELL. Good afternoon, dear Algernon, I hope you are behaving very well.

ALGERNON. I'm feeling very well, Aunt Augusta.

LADY BRACKNELL. That's not quite the same thing. In fact the two things rarely go together. [*Sees* JACK *and bows to him with icy coldness.*]

ALGERNON [*To* GWENDOLEN]. Dear me, you are smart!

GWENDOLEN. I am always smart! Aren't I, Mr. Worthing?

JACK. You're quite perfect, Miss Fairfax.

GWENDOLEN. Oh! I hope I am not that. It would leave no room for developments, and I intend to develop in many directions. [GWENDOLEN *and* JACK *sit down together in the corner.*]

LADY BRACKNELL. I'm sorry if we are a little late, Algernon, but I was obliged to call on dear Lady Harbury. I hadn't been there since her poor husband's death. I never saw a woman so altered; she looks quite twenty years younger. And now I'll have a cup of tea, and one of those nice cucumber sandwiches you promised me.

ALGERNON. Certainly, Aunt Augusta. [*Goes over to tea-table.*]

LADY BRACKNELL. Won't you come and sit here, Gwendolen?

GWENDOLEN. Thanks, mamma, I'm quite comfortable where I am.

ALGERNON [*Picking up empty plate in horror*]. Good heavens! Lane! Why are there no cucumber sandwiches? I ordered them specially.

LANE [*Gravely*]. There were no cucumbers in the market this morning, sir. I went down twice.

ALGERNON. No cucumbers!

LANE. No, sir. Not even for ready money.

ALGERNON. That will do, Lane, thank you.

LANE. Thank you, sir. [*Goes out.*]

ALGERNON. I am greatly distressed, Aunt Augusta, about there being no cucumbers, not even for ready money.

LADY BRACKNELL. It really makes no matter, Algernon. I had some crumpets with Lady Harbury, who seems to me to be living entirely for pleasure now.

ALGERNON. I hear her hair has turned quite gold from grief.[1]

LADY BRACKNELL. It certainly has changed its colour. From what cause I, of course, cannot say. [ALGERNON *crosses and hands tea.*] Thank you. I have quite a treat for you to-night, Algernon. I am going to send you down with Mary Farquhar. She is such a nice woman, and so attentive to her husband. It's delightful to watch them.

ALGERNON. I am afraid, Aunt Augusta, I shall have to give up the pleasure of dining with you to-night, after all.

LADY BRACKNELL [*Frowning*]. I hope not, Algernon. It would put my table completely out. Your uncle would have to dine upstairs. Fortunately he is accustomed to that.

ALGERNON. It is a great bore, and, I need hardly say, a terrible disappointment to me, but the fact is I have just had a telegram to say that my poor friend Bunbury is very ill again. [*Exchanges glances with* JACK.] They seem to think I should be with him.

LADY BRACKNELL. It is very strange. This Mr. Bunbury seems to suffer from curiously bad health.

ALGERNON. Yes; poor Bunbury is a dreadful invalid.

LADY BRACKNELL. Well, I must say, Algernon, that I think it is high time that Mr. Bunbury made up his mind whether he was going to live or to die. This shilly-shallying with the question is absurd. Nor do I in any way approve of the modern sympathy with invalids. I consider it morbid. Illness of any kind is hardly a thing to be encouraged in others. Health is the primary duty of life. I am always telling that to your poor uncle, but he never seems to take much notice ... as far as any improvement in his ailments goes. I should be very much obliged if you would ask Mr. Bunbury, from me, to be kind enough not to have a relapse on Saturday, for I rely on you to arrange my music for me. It is my last reception, and one wants

---

1 Wilde recycles another of his witticisms: in *The Picture of Dorian Gray*, Henry Wotton remarks of Lady Narborough that "Her capacity for family affection is extraordinary. When her third husband died, her hair turned quite gold from grief" (137).

something that will encourage conversation, particularly at the end of the season when everyone has practically said whatever they had to say, which, in most cases, was probably not much.

ALGERNON. I'll speak to Bunbury, Aunt Augusta, if he is still conscious, and I think I can promise you he'll be all right by Saturday. Of course the music is a great difficulty. You see, if one plays good music, people don't listen, and if one plays bad music people don't talk. But I'll run over the programme I've drawn out, if you will kindly come into the next room for a moment.

LADY BRACKNELL. Thank you, Algernon. It is very thought-ful of you. [*Rising, and following* ALGERNON.] I'm sure the programme will be delightful, after a few expurgations. French songs I cannot possibly allow. People always seem to think that they are improper, and either look shocked, which is vulgar, or laugh, which is worse. But German sounds a thoroughly respectable language, and indeed, I believe is so.[1] Gwendolen, you will accompany me.

GWENDOLEN. Certainly, mamma.

[LADY BRACKNELL *and* ALGERNON *go into the music-room.* GWENDOLEN *remains behind.*]

JACK. Charming day it has been, Miss Fairfax.

GWENDOLEN. Pray don't talk to me about the weather, Mr. Worthing. Whenever people talk to me about the weather, I always feel that they mean something else. And that makes me so nervous.

---

1  See the Introduction 48-49 on the symbolic connections between nations and types of desire. Just as Lady Bracknell invokes "France" as a symbolic term for political and social unrest, for the toppling of all things she considers traditional and, thus, respectable (see *E* 89n1), some read "German" as Wilde's coded reference to homosexuality (see Eve Kosofsky Sedgwick, "Tales of the Avunculate," especially 65-67). In "The Critic as Artist," Ernest's speech anticipates Lady Bracknell's in its resistance to German music: "No; I don't want music just at present. It is far too indefinite [...]. Now, whatever music sounds like, I am glad to say it does not sound in the smallest degree like German. There are forms of patriotism that are really quite degrading" (1109). In *An Ideal Husband*, Mabel Chiltern remarks "severely" to Lord Goring that "The music is in German. You would not understand it" (522), a particularly comic moment for readers who understand Lord Goring not only as a dandy (see the Introduction 14) but also, perhaps, as gay.

JACK. I do mean something else.

GWENDOLEN. I thought so. In fact, I am never wrong.

JACK. And I would like to be allowed to take advantage of Lady Bracknell's temporary absence ...

GWENDOLEN. I would certainly advise you to do so. Mamma has a way of coming back suddenly into a room that I have often had to speak to her about.

JACK [*Nervously*]. Miss Fairfax, ever since I met you I have admired you more than any girl ... I have ever met since ... I met you.

GWENDOLEN. Yes, I am quite aware of the fact. And I often wish that in public, at any rate, you had been more demonstrative. For me you have always had an irresistible fascination. Even before I met you I was far from indifferent to you. [*JACK looks at her in amazement.*] We live, as I hope you know, Mr. Worthing, in an age of ideals. The fact is constantly mentioned in the more expensive monthly magazines, and has reached the provincial pulpits I am told: and my ideal has always been to love some one of the name of Ernest. There is something in that name that inspires absolute confidence.[1] The moment Algernon first mentioned to me that he had a friend called Ernest, I knew I was destined to love you.

JACK. You really love me, Gwendolen?[2]

GWENDOLEN. Passionately!

JACK. Darling! You don't know how happy you've made me.

GWENDOLEN. My own Ernest!

JACK. But you don't really mean to say that you couldn't love me if my name wasn't Ernest?

GWENDOLEN. But your name is Ernest.

JACK. Yes, I know it is. But supposing it was something else? Do you mean to say you couldn't love me then?

GWENDOLEN [*Glibly*]. Ah! that is clearly a metaphysical spec-

---

1 In a line cut from the third act of *Lady Lancing*, Gwendolen underscores this sentiment: "To one whose name is Ernest deception of any kind would be impossible" (Wilde, ed. Dickson 1: 124).

2 Jack's first use of Gwendolen's Christian name signals a shift in relationship from formality to affection; this shift, however, reverses suddenly when Gwendolen demands a formal proposal and once again addresses her beloved as "Mr. Worthing." Such an observation should also be made of the initial conversation between Cecily and Gwendolen in act 2, where the formalities of "Miss Cardew" and "Miss Fairfax" get discarded only to be reinvoked when each wishes to distance herself from the other once the women discover they are rivals.

ulation, and like most metaphysical speculations has very little reference at all to the actual facts of real life, as we know them.

JACK. Personally, darling, to speak quite candidly, I don't much care about the name of Ernest ... I don't think the name suits me at all.

GWENDOLEN. It suits you perfectly. It is a divine name. It has a music of its own. It produces vibrations.

JACK. Well, really, Gwendolen, I must say that I think there are lots of other much nicer names. I think Jack, for instance, a charming name.

GWENDOLEN. Jack? ... No, there is very little music in the name Jack, if any at all, indeed. It does not thrill. It produces absolutely no vibrations.... I have known several Jacks, and they all, without exception, were more than usually plain. Besides, Jack is a notorious domesticity for John! And I pity any woman who is married to a man called John. She would probably never be allowed to know the entrancing pleasure of a single moment's solitude. The only really safe name is Ernest.

JACK. Gwendolen, I must get christened at once—I mean we must get married at once. There is no time to be lost.

GWENDOLEN. Married, Mr. Worthing?

JACK [*Astounded*]. Well ... surely. You know that I love you, and you led me to believe, Miss Fairfax, that you were not absolutely indifferent to me.

GWENDOLEN. I adore you. But you haven't proposed to me yet. Nothing has been said at all about marriage. The subject has not even been touched on.

JACK. Well ... may I propose to you now?

GWENDOLEN. I think it would be an admirable opportunity. And to spare you any possible disappointment, Mr. Worthing, I think it only fair to tell you quite frankly beforehand that I am fully determined to accept you.

JACK. Gwendolen!

GWENDOLEN. Yes, Mr. Worthing, what have you got to say to me?

JACK. You know what I have got to say to you.

GWENDOLEN. Yes, but you don't say it.

JACK. Gwendolen, will you marry me? [*Goes on his knees.*]

GWENDOLEN. Of course I will, darling. How long you have been about it! I am afraid you have had very little experience in how to propose.

JACK. My own one, I have never loved anyone in the world but you.

GWENDOLEN. Yes, but men often propose for practice. I know my brother Gerald does. All my girl-friends tell me so. What wonderfully blue eyes you have, Ernest! They are quite, quite blue. I hope you will always look at me just like that, especially when there are other people present.

[*Enter* LADY BRACKNELL.]

LADY BRACKNELL. Mr. Worthing! Rise, sir, from this semi-recumbent posture. It is most indecorous.

GWENDOLEN. Mamma! [*He tries to rise; she restrains him.*] I must beg you to retire. This is no place for you. Besides, Mr. Worthing has not quite finished yet.

LADY BRACKNELL. Finished what, may I ask?

GWENDOLEN. I am engaged to Mr. Worthing, mamma. [*They rise together.*]

LADY BRACKNELL. Pardon me, you are not engaged to anyone. When you do become engaged to some one, I, or your father, should his health permit him, will inform you of the fact. An engagement should come on a young girl as a surprise, pleasant or unpleasant, as the case may be. It is hardly a matter that she could be allowed to arrange for herself.... And now I have a few questions to put to you, Mr. Worthing. While I am making these inquiries, you, Gwendolen, will wait for me below in the carriage.

GWENDOLEN [*Reproachfully*]. Mamma!

LADY BRACKNELL. In the carriage, Gwendolen! [GWEN-DOLEN *goes to the door. She and* JACK *blow kisses to each other behind* LADY BRACKNELL's *back.* LADY BRACKNELL *looks vaguely about as if she could not understand what the noise was. Finally turns round.*] Gwendolen, the carriage!

GWENDOLEN. Yes, mamma. [*Goes out, looking back at* JACK.]

LADY BRACKNELL [*Sitting down*]. You can take a seat, Mr. Worthing. [*Looks in her pocket for note-book and pencil.*]

JACK. Thank you, Lady Bracknell, I prefer standing.

LADY BRACKNELL [*Pencil and note-book in hand*]. I feel bound to tell you that you are not down on my list of eligible young men, although I have the same list as the dear Duchess of

Bolton has.[1] We work together, in fact. However, I am quite ready to enter your name, should your answers be what a really affectionate mother requires. Do you smoke?

JACK. Well, yes, I must admit I smoke.

LADY BRACKNELL. I am glad to hear it. A man should always have an occupation of some kind.[2] There are far too many idle men in London as it is. How old are you?

JACK. Twenty-nine.

LADY BRACKNELL. A very good age to be married at. I have always been of opinion that a man who desires to get married should know either everything or nothing.[3] Which do you know?

JACK [*After some hesitation*]. I know nothing, Lady Bracknell.

LADY BRACKNELL. I am pleased to hear it. I do not approve of anything that tampers with natural ignorance.[4] Ignorance is like a delicate exotic fruit; touch it and the bloom is gone. The whole theory of modern education is radically unsound. Fortunately in England, at any rate, education produces no effect whatsoever.[5] If it did, it would prove a serious danger to the upper classes, and probably lead to acts of violence in

---

1 Like many of Wilde's characters, the Duchess of Bolton appears in more than one work—here and in "The Canterville Ghost." As Donohue and Berggren suggest, many contemporary associations with the name "Bolton" would have amused Wilde's audience: Bolton was an important manufacturing town, making the notion of a "Duchess of Bolton" preposterous to Wilde's class-aware audience. "Boulton" was also the last name of one of the men arrested for transvestitism and homosexual prostitution in the notorious "Cleveland Street" scandal of 1871—and Boulton's first name was Ernest (155).

2 Again, Wilde recycles a line from *A Woman of No Importance* in which Lord Alfred, in reflecting on the expensive, monogrammed cigarettes he purchases (as did Wilde), laments that "One must have some occupation nowadays" (473). Wilde also recycles an observation about idleness here, this time recalling 1894's "Phrases and Philosophies for the Use of the Young" (excerpted in Appendix H2): "The condition of perfection is idleness: the aim of perfection is youth" (1245).

3 Russell Jackson (27n) observes that, once again, Wilde recycles a line from *Dorian Gray*'s Lord Henry Wotton: "There are only two kinds of people who are really fascinating—people who know absolutely everything, and people who know absolutely nothing" (213).

4 Another example of Wilde's reversals of traditional logic: Lady Bracknell's statement would be expected to focus on innocence, not ignorance.

5 Lady Bracknell's sarcasm echoes a line from Wilde's essay "The Decay of Lying," published four years before the premiere of *Earnest*, in which the character Cyril observes that "Thinking is the most unhealthy thing

Grosvenor Square.[1] What is your income?

JACK. Between seven and eight thousand a year.[2]

LADY BRACKNELL [*Makes a note in her book*]. In land, or in investments?

JACK. In investments, chiefly.

LADY BRACKNELL. That is satisfactory. What between the duties expected of one during one's lifetime, and the duties exacted from one after one's death, land has ceased to be either a profit or a pleasure.[3] It gives one position, and prevents one from keeping it up. That's all that can be said about land.

JACK. I have a country house with some land, of course, attached to it, about fifteen hundred acres, I believe; but I don't depend on that for my real income. In fact, as far as I can make out, the poachers are the only people who make anything out of it.

LADY BRACKNELL. A country house! How many bedrooms? Well, that point can be cleared up afterwards. You have a town house, I hope? A girl with a simple, unspoiled nature, like Gwendolen, could hardly be expected to reside in the country.[4]

JACK. Well, I own a house in Belgrave Square, but it is let by the year to Lady Bloxham.[5] Of course, I can get it back whenever I like, at six months' notice.

---

in the world, and people die of it just as they die of any other disease. Fortunately, in England at any rate, thought is not catching" (1071-72).

1 One of several fashionable neighborhoods in the city, home to many affluent and, for the most part, politically conservative Londoners.

2 Jackson notes that this amount is "quite a fortune, at a time when a working man was lucky if he was paid 20 shillings a week and [when] £1,000 a year [would have placed one in the upper middle classes]" (28n). Readers who wish to convert the play's amounts to present-day dollars or pounds based on a variety of indices such as retail price index, average earnings, and so on should consult the currency calculators at <www.measuringworth.com>.

3 Leeming points out (77) that the Finance Act, mandating so-called death duties or after-death estate taxes, had been passed into law in 1894, the year before Wilde's play debuted, making Lady Bracknell's observation particularly timely and, thus, especially comic.

4 By setting "the country" and girlish innocence in contrast, Wilde comically dismantles the long-held myth of the pastoral, which associates natural settings with purity and truth.

5 Belgrave forms one of the grand squares in London and borders the equally posh neighborhood of Knightsbridge. In Wilde's day, Belgrave Square was occupied by many well-known aristocrats and was home to a number of national embassies. Jackson (29n) notes that "Bloxham is a village in Oxfordshire, but Wilde may have recalled John Francis Bloxam, editor of *The Chameleon*" (see *E* 75n3).

LADY BRACKNELL. Lady Bloxham? I don't know her.

JACK. Oh, she goes about very little. She is a lady considerably advanced in years.

LADY BRACKNELL. Ah, now-a-days that is no guarantee of respectability of character. What number in Belgrave Square?

JACK. 149.

LADY BRACKNELL [*Shaking her head*]. The unfashionable side. I thought there was something. However, that could easily be altered.

JACK. Do you mean the fashion, or the side?

LADY BRACKNELL [*Sternly*]. Both, if necessary, I presume. What are your politics?

JACK. Well, I am afraid I really have none. I am a Liberal Unionist.[1]

LADY BRACKNELL. Oh, they count as Tories. They dine with us. Or come in the evening, at any rate. Now to minor matters. Are your parents living?

JACK. I have lost both my parents.

LADY BRACKNELL. Both? ... That seems like carelessness.[2] Who was your father? He was evidently a man of some wealth. Was he born in what the Radical papers call the purple of commerce, or did he rise from the ranks of the aristocracy?[3]

JACK. I am afraid I really don't know. The fact is, Lady Bracknell, I said I had lost my parents. It would be nearer the truth to say that my parents seem to have lost me ... I don't actually know who I am by birth. I was ... well, I was found.

LADY BRACKNELL. Found!

JACK. The late Mr. Thomas Cardew, an old gentleman of a very charitable and kindly disposition, found me, and gave me the name of Worthing, because he happened to have a first-class

---

1 Liberal Unionists formed an unofficial third party in the British political system, resulting from divisions among members of Parliament over Irish Home Rule. Liberal Unionists adopted the Conservative position on this issue and thus counted as Tories, as Lady Bracknell notes in the following speech (Donohue and Berggren 163).

2 Smithers's edition renders the line as indicated, but in many subsequent editions the speech begins: "Both? ... To lose one parent may be regarded as a misfortune ... to lose both looks like carelessness" (Wilde, *Complete Works* 369).

3 Wilde's audience would have appreciated his ironic acknowledgement of the rise of the middle class in the Victorian era: "born to the purple" traditionally refers to members of royal or aristocratic families, but in the decades following the Industrial Revolution, even the most lowly born might rise to the highest levels of society by working their way to wealth.

ticket for Worthing in his pocket at the time. Worthing is a place in Sussex. It is a seaside resort.

LADY BRACKNELL. Where did the charitable gentleman who had a first-class ticket for this seaside resort find you?

JACK [*Gravely*]. In a hand-bag.

LADY BRACKNELL. A hand-bag?

JACK [*Very seriously*]. Yes, Lady Bracknell, I was in a hand-bag— a somewhat large, black leather hand-bag, with handles to it— an ordinary hand-bag in fact.

LADY BRACKNELL. In what locality did this Mr. James, or Thomas, Cardew come across this ordinary hand-bag?

JACK. In the cloak-room at Victoria Station. It was given to him in mistake for his own.

LADY BRACKNELL. The cloak-room at Victoria Station?

JACK. Yes. The Brighton line.

LADY BRACKNELL. The line is immaterial. Mr. Worthing, I confess I feel somewhat bewildered by what you have just told me. To be born, or at any rate bred, in a hand-bag, whether it had handles or not, seems to me to display a contempt for the ordinary decencies of family life that remind one of the worst excesses of the French Revolution. And I presume you know what that unfortunate movement led to?[1] As for the particular locality in which the hand-bag was found, a cloak-room at a railway station might serve to conceal a social indiscretion[2]— has probably, indeed, been used for that purpose before now —but it could hardly be regarded as an assured basis for a recognized position in good society.[3]

---

1 Lady Bracknell aligns Jack's origin with a place associated with sexual license and liberty, implying his wanton, disrespectable heritage and, in a manner consistent with her pronouncements throughout the play, connecting that heritage with France in general and with the French Revolution in particular. For more on the symbolic associations of nations throughout *Earnest*, see *E* 82n1 and the Introduction 48-49.

2 A violation of traditional modes of conduct, especially of a romantic or erotic sort.

3 One of the speeches from *Lady Lancing* emphasizes this point, as Lady Brancaster (whom Wilde later renamed Lady Bracknell) observes that "Wickedness may go unpunished; usually does indeed—but a social indiscretion never" (Wilde, ed. Dickson 1: 176). These lines suggest that Lady Brancaster may subscribe to the philosophy Wilde associates with the younger leads in his play, which acknowledges the superiority of society over morality. Similar arguments appear in "Phrases and Philosophies for the Use of the Young" and *The Picture of Dorian Gray*; see Appendices H2 and H3.

JACK. May I ask you then what you would advise me to do? I need hardly say I would do anything in the world to ensure Gwendolen's happiness.

LADY BRACKNELL. I would strongly advise you, Mr. Worthing, to try and acquire some relations as soon as possible, and to make a definite effort to produce at any rate one parent, of either sex, before the season is quite over.

JACK. Well, I don't see how I could possibly manage to do that. I can produce the hand-bag at any moment. It is in my dressing-room at home. I really think that should satisfy you, Lady Bracknell.

LADY BRACKNELL. Me, sir! What has it to do with me? You can hardly imagine that I and Lord Bracknell would dream of allowing our only daughter—a girl brought up with the utmost care—to marry into a cloak-room, and form an alliance with a parcel? Good morning, Mr. Worthing!

[LADY BRACKNELL *sweeps out in majestic indignation.*]

JACK. Good morning! [ALGERNON, *from the other room, strikes up the Wedding March.* JACK *looks perfectly furious, and goes to the door.*] For goodness' sake don't play that ghastly tune, Algy! How idiotic you are!

[*The music stops, and* ALGERNON *enters cheerily.*]

ALGERNON. Didn't it go off all right, old boy? You don't mean to say Gwendolen refused you? I know it is a way she has. She is always refusing people. I think it is most ill-natured of her.

JACK. Oh, Gwendolen is right as a trivet. As far as she is concerned, we are engaged. Her mother is perfectly unbearable. Never met such a Gorgon ... I don't really know what a Gorgon is like, but I am quite sure that Lady Bracknell is one. In any case, she is a monster, without being a myth, which is rather unfair ... I beg your pardon, Algy, I suppose I shouldn't talk about your own aunt in that way before you.

ALGERNON. My dear boy, I love hearing my relations abused. It is the only thing that makes me put up with them at all. Relations are simply a tedious pack of people, who haven't got the remotest knowledge of how to live, nor the smallest instinct about when to die.

JACK. Oh, that is nonsense!

ALGERNON. It isn't!

JACK. Well, I won't argue about the matter. You always want to argue about things.

ALGERNON. That is exactly what things were originally made for.

JACK. Upon my word, if I thought that, I'd shoot myself ... [*A pause.*] You don't think there is any chance of Gwendolen becoming like her mother in about a hundred and fifty years, do you Algy?

ALGERNON. All women become like their mothers. That is their tragedy. No man does. That's his.

JACK. Is that clever?

ALGERNON. It is perfectly phrased! and quite as true as any observation in civilized life should be.

JACK. I am sick to death of cleverness. Everybody is clever now-a-days. You can't go anywhere without meeting clever people. The thing has become an absolute public nuisance. I wish to goodness we had a few fools left.

ALGERNON. We have.

JACK. I should extremely like to meet them. What do they talk about?

ALGERNON. The fools? Oh! about the clever people, of course.

JACK. What fools!

ALGERNON. By the way, did you tell Gwendolen the truth about your being Ernest in town, and Jack in the country?

JACK [*In a very patronising manner*]. My dear fellow, the truth isn't quite the sort of thing one tells to a nice sweet refined girl. What extraordinary ideas you have about the way to behave to a woman![1]

ALGERNON. The only way to behave to a woman is to make love to her, if she is pretty, and to someone else if she is plain.

JACK. Oh, that is nonsense.

ALGERNON. What about your brother? What about the profligate Ernest?[2]

JACK. Oh, before the end of the week I shall have got rid of him. I'll say he died in Paris of apoplexy. Lots of people die of apoplexy, quite suddenly, don't they?

---

1 Jack's comment reminds readers of the connection between Bunburying and illicit activity, emphasizing his belief that Bunburying may well be antithetical to traditional, heterosexual romance.

2 In *Talk on the Wilde Side*, Ed Cohen connects "profligacy" to male sexual wantonness, to the careless "spending" of one's "seed"—an activity clearly inimical to the maintenance of an upstanding household, as three of Miss Prism's speeches in *Lady Lancing* acknowledge:    (Continued)

ALGERNON. Yes, but it's hereditary, my dear fellow. It's a sort of thing that runs in families. You had much better say a severe chill.

JACK. You are sure a severe chill isn't hereditary, or anything of that kind?

ALGERNON. Of course it isn't!

JACK. Very well, then. My poor brother Ernest is carried off suddenly in Paris, by a severe chill. That gets rid of him.

ALGERNON. But I thought you said that ... Miss Cardew was a little too much interested in your poor brother Ernest? Won't she feel his loss a good deal?

JACK. Oh, that is all right. Cecily is not a silly romantic girl, I am glad to say. She has got a capital appetite, goes [on][1] long walks, and pays no attention at all to her lessons.

ALGERNON. I would rather like to see Cecily.

JACK. I will take very good care you never do. She is excessively pretty, and she is only just eighteen.

ALGERNON. Have you told Gwendolen yet that you have an excessively pretty ward[2] who is only just eighteen?

JACK. Oh! one doesn't blurt these things out to people. Cecily and Gwendolen are perfectly certain to be extremely great friends. I'll bet you anything you like that half an hour after they have met, they will be calling each other sister.

ALGERNON. Women only do that when they have called each other a lot of other things first. Now, my dear boy, if we want to get a good table at Willis's, we really must go and dress. Do you know it is nearly seven?

JACK [*Irritably*]. Oh! it is always nearly seven.

---

she observes that "I trust that unhappy young profligate will never desecrate with his presence the quiet precincts of this refined home. I would not feel safe"; she laments that "We have already to-day had a sad but vivid object-lesson of the inevitable results of profligacy and extravagance"; and she opines that "Profligacy is apt to dull the senses, Mr. Worthing" (Wilde, ed. Dickson 1: 53, 1: 97, and 1: 98). See Cohen's Chapter Three, "Marking Social Dis-Ease"; see *E* 106n3 and Appendix I, 199n2, and 205n1.

1 The word "on" appears neither in the *Lady Lancing* manuscript nor in the Smithers edition of *Earnest* but was inserted in the typescript of Dickson's edition, as it is here.

2 Richard Allen Cave notes the potential *double entendre*, saying that "it was not unknown for an older man to pass off his mistress in public as his ward; and it was not uncommon for genuine wards to be wedded in time to their guardians" (427n17).

ALGERNON. Well, I'm hungry.

JACK. I never knew you when you weren't....[1]

ALGERNON. What shall we do after dinner? Go to a theatre?

JACK. Oh no! I loathe listening.

ALGERNON. Well, let us go to the Club?[2]

JACK. Oh no! I hate talking.

ALGERNON. Well, we might trot round to the Empire at ten?[3]

JACK. Oh no! I can't bear looking at things. It is so silly.

ALGERNON. Well, what shall we do?

JACK. Nothing!

ALGERNON. It is awfully hard work doing nothing. However, I don't mind hard work where there is no definite object of any kind.[4]

[*Enter* LANE.]

LANE. Miss Fairfax.

[*Enter* GWENDOLEN. LANE *goes out*.]

ALGERNON. Gwendolen, upon my word!

GWENDOLEN. Algy, kindly turn your back. I have something very particular to say to Mr. Worthing.

---

1   As before, hunger functions both literally and metaphorically, in the latter case suggesting a specifically carnal appetite: Jack knows Algernon to be one who lives for pleasures, among them the pleasures of eroticism, a term unspoken here but surely and powerfully present in this dandy's life; see the Introduction 43-46.

2   Raby observes that Algernon is clearly talking about an all-male club "such as White's or Boodle's, near the St. James's Theatre" (*EOP* 362).

3   The Empire, a music hall in Leicester Square, became notorious for the many prostitutes who plied their trade in its promenade. Leeming notes that a year before Wilde's play debuted, the Empire had come under siege as part of a purity campaign led by a woman named Mrs. Chant (78). Raby suggests that if the men had indeed arrived at The Empire by ten o'clock, "they would have seen the 'Grand Ballet' featuring the *première danseuse* Helene Cornalba in 'Round the Town'" (*EOP* 363).

4   This insistence that the dandy's life, his "doing nothingness," is in fact *real work* reminds us of Wilde's particularly "Decadent" perspective as well as of the tongue-in-cheek send-up of the so-called Decadence that Algernon and Jack embody, especially when they are bunburying. Donohue and Berggren note that in his *Daily Maxims*, Wilde wrote that "'It is more painful to do nothing than something'" (qtd. in Donohue and Berggren 185). See also *E* 126n1.

ALGERNON. Really, Gwendolen, I don't think I can allow this at all.

GWENDOLEN. Algy, you always adopt a strictly immoral attitude towards life. You are not quite old enough to do that.

[ALGERNON *retires to the fireplace.*]

JACK. My own darling!

GWENDOLEN. Ernest, we may never be married. From the expression on mamma's face I fear we never shall. Few parents now-a-days pay any regard to what their children say to them. The old-fashioned respect for the young is fast dying out. Whatever influence I ever had over mamma, I lost at the age of three. But although she may prevent us from becoming man and wife, and I may marry someone else, and marry often, nothing that she can possibly do can alter my eternal devotion to you.[1]

JACK. Dear Gwendolen!

GWENDOLEN. The story of your romantic origin, as related to me by mamma, with unpleasing comments, has naturally stirred the deeper fibres of my nature. Your Christian name has an irresistible fascination. The simplicity of your character makes you exquisitely incomprehensible to me. Your town address at the Albany I have. What is your address in the country?

JACK. The Manor House, Woolton, Hertfordshire.

[ALGERNON, *who has been carefully listening, smiles to himself, and writes the address on his shirt-cuff. Then picks up the Railway Guide.*]

GWENDOLEN. There is a good postal service, I suppose? It may be necessary to do something desperate. That of course

---

1  In his 1885 *Pall Mall Gazette* review of Reverend Edward J. Hardy's *How to Be Happy Though Married: Being a Handbook to Marriage*, Wilde celebrates the book's collection of unintentionally amusing and subversive replies intoned during the marriage vows, all of which undermine marriage by exposing it as a ridiculous institution ripe for parody, fertile ground for countless arguments between the sexes. As Wilde observes, "indeed, marriage is the one subject on which all women agree and all men disagree" ("A Handbook to Marriage" 10)—a double-view consistent with the different attitudes to love represented by *Earnest*'s male and female leads.

will require serious consideration. I will communicate with you daily.

JACK. My own one!

GWENDOLEN. How long do you remain in town?

JACK. Till Monday.

GWENDOLEN. Good! Algy, you may turn round now.

ALGERNON. Thanks, I've turned round already.

GWENDOLEN. You may also ring the bell.

JACK. You will let me see you to your carriage, my own darling?

GWENDOLEN. Certainly.

JACK [*To* LANE, *who now enters*]. I will see Miss Fairfax out.

LANE. Yes, sir. [JACK *and* GWENDOLEN *go off*.]

[LANE *presents several letters on a salver to* ALGERNON. *It is to be surmised that they are bills, as* ALGERNON, *after looking at the envelopes, tears them up*.]

ALGERNON. A glass of sherry, Lane.

LANE. Yes, sir.

ALGERNON. To-morrow, Lane, I'm going Bunburying.

LANE. Yes, sir.

ALGERNON. I shall probably not be back till Monday. You can put up my dress clothes, my smoking jacket, and all the Bunbury suits ...[1]

LANE. Yes, sir. [*Handing sherry.*]

ALGERNON. I hope to-morrow will be a fine day, Lane.

LANE. It never is, sir.

ALGERNON. Lane, you're a perfect pessimist.

LANE. I do my best to give satisfaction, sir.

[*Enter* JACK. LANE *goes off.*]

JACK. There's a sensible, intellectual girl! The only girl I ever cared for in my life. [ALGERNON *is laughing immoderately*.] What on earth are you so amused at?

ALGERNON. Oh, I'm a little anxious about poor Bunbury, that is all.

---

1 Algernon's indication that he has "Bunbury suits" reminds us that Bunbury is a role he plays; like an actor on the stage, first he must be costumed appropriately. Such a recognition underscores the old truism that "clothes make the man" and, thus, that Algernon in fact *becomes* an entirely different person simply by dressing as one. See also *E* 76n1.

JACK. If you don't take care, your friend Bunbury will get you into a serious scrape some day.

ALGERNON. I love scrapes. They are the only things that are never serious.

JACK. Oh, that's nonsense, Algy. You never talk anything but nonsense.[1]

ALGERNON. Nobody ever does.

[JACK *looks indignantly at him, and leaves the room.* ALGERNON *lights a cigarette, reads his shirt-cuff, and smiles.*]

## ACT DROP.

---

1 The last several speeches align Algernon's pet attitude, "nonsense," with one of his preferred activities, "scrapes," suggesting the dark aspects of the very real forms nonsense may take. However, in the four-act version of the play, Algy's more playful take on the ridiculous returns, and he remarks, for example, that "I hate seriousness of any kind" (Wilde, ed. Berggren 131). See Appendix I1, 201n4.

# SECOND ACT

SCENE—*Garden at the Manor House. A flight of gray stone steps leads up to the house. The garden, an old-fashioned one, full of roses. Time of year, July. Basket chairs, and a table covered with books, are set under a large yew tree.*

[MISS PRISM *discovered seated at the table.* CECILY *is at the back watering flowers.*]

MISS PRISM [*Calling*]. Cecily, Cecily! Surely such a utilitarian occupation as the watering of flowers is rather Moulton's duty than yours? Especially at a moment when intellectual pleasures await you. Your German grammar is on the table. Pray open it at page fifteen. We will repeat yesterday's lesson.

CECILY [*Coming over very slowly*]. But I don't like German. It isn't at all a becoming language. I know perfectly well that I look quite plain after my German lesson.

MISS PRISM. Child, you know how anxious your guardian is that you should improve yourself in every way. He laid particular stress on your German, as he was leaving for town yesterday.[1] Indeed, he always lays stress on your German when he is leaving for town.

CECILY. Dear Uncle Jack is so very serious! Sometimes he is so serious that I think he cannot be quite well.

MISS PRISM [*Drawing herself up*]. Your guardian enjoys the best of health, and his gravity of demeanour is especially to be commended in one so comparatively young as he is. I know no one who has a higher sense of duty and responsibility.

CECILY. I suppose that is why he often looks a little bored when we three are together.

MISS PRISM. Cecily! I am surprised at you. Mr. Worthing has many troubles in his life. Idle merriment and triviality would be out of place in his conversation. You must remember his constant anxiety about that unfortunate young man, his brother.

---

1  Miss Prism's words are telling: before Jack leaves the country for the pleasures of the city, where he is not his real but his false self, "Ernest"/earnest self, he apparently has things "German" on his mind; see *E* 82n1.

CECILY. I wish Uncle Jack would allow that unfortunate young man, his brother, to come down here sometimes. We might have a good influence over him, Miss Prism. I am sure you certainly would. You know German, and geology, and things of that kind influence a man very much.

[CECILY *begins to write in her diary*.]

MISS PRISM [*Shaking her head*]. I do not think that even I could produce any effect on a character that according to his own brother's admission is irretrievably weak and vacillating. Indeed I am not sure that I would desire to reclaim him. I am not in favour of this modern mania for turning bad people into good people at a moment's notice. As a man sows so let him reap.[1] You must put away your diary, Cecily. I really don't see why you should keep a diary at all.

CECILY. I keep a diary in order to enter the wonderful secrets of my life. If I didn't write them down I should probably forget all about them.

MISS PRISM. Memory, my dear Cecily, is the diary that we all carry about with us.

CECILY. Yes, but it usually chronicles the things that have never happened, and couldn't possibly have happened. I believe that Memory is responsible for nearly all the three-volume novels that Mudie sends us.

MISS PRISM. Do not speak slightingly of the three-volume novel, Cecily. I wrote one myself in earlier days.[2]

CECILY. Did you really, Miss Prism? How wonderfully clever

---

1  As an embodiment of conventional morality, Miss Prism proved much more Lady Brancaster's equal in the four-act version of the play, where Miss Prism makes clear how opposed she is to fluidity of character, to flux and change; to her, reform is revolutionary and leads to the sort of "excesses" about which Lady Brancaster complains in act 1 (Wilde, ed. Dickson 1: 30). The final line of that speech survives in the three-act version but loses the context Wilde originally provides: in *Lady Lancing*, Prism's comment "as a man sows, so let him reap" reinforces her moral inflexibility, whereas in *Earnest*, the line makes Prism seem simply short-sighted and discriminatory.

2  Here, Wilde makes Miss Prism look ridiculous by aligning her with a popular yet much-derided form, the three-volume novel, about which he observed in "The Critic as Artist" that "anybody can write a three-volume novel. It merely requires a complete ignorance of both life and literature" (1120).

you are! I hope it did not end happily? I don't like novels that end happily. They depress me so much.

MISS PRISM. The good ended happily, and the bad unhappily. That is what Fiction means.

CECILY. I suppose so. But it seems very unfair. And was your novel ever published?

MISS PRISM. Alas! no. The manuscript unfortunately was abandoned. I use the word in the sense of lost or mislaid.[1] To your work, child, these speculations are profitless.

CECILY [*Smiling*]. But I see dear Dr. Chasuble coming up through the garden.[2]

MISS PRISM [*Rising and advancing*]. Dr. Chasuble! This is indeed a pleasure.

[*Enter* CANON CHASUBLE.]

CHASUBLE. And how are we this morning? Miss Prism, you are, I trust, well?

CECILY. Miss Prism has just been complaining of a slight headache. I think it would do her so much good to have a short stroll with you in the Park, Dr. Chasuble.

MISS PRISM. Cecily, I have not mentioned anything about a headache.

CECILY. No, dear Miss Prism, I know that, but I felt instinctively that you had a headache. Indeed I was thinking about that, and not about my German lesson, when the Rector came in.

CHASUBLE. I hope, Cecily, you are not inattentive.

CECILY. Oh, I am afraid I am.

CHASUBLE. That is strange. Were I fortunate enough to be

---

1 Raby notes that Miss Prism's use of the word "abandoned" also connotes something "licentious," thus exposing one of the play's many *double-entendres* (*EOP* 364). Throughout this scene, characters' clarifications of their intended meanings of words accentuate the play's interest in the slippery significance of language, in any word's definitional insufficiency: one can never be sure what words mean, the play seems to argue, and thus it may be by way of language that deception—Bunburying—proceeds.

2 "Chasuble" names not only the character in question but also the garment he wears when dispatching his duties; thus, Wilde reminds his audience that one is (only) what one wears, that identity is merely a garment, ultimately to be removed, discarded. Dr. Chasuble's name evinces the play's investment in the superficiality of truth, in identities one can, so to speak, put on and take off at will (see also *E* 95n1).

Miss Prism's pupil, I would hang upon her lips. [MISS PRISM *glares*.] I spoke metaphorically.—My metaphor was drawn from bees. Ahem! Mr. Worthing, I suppose, has not returned from town yet?

MISS PRISM. We do not expect him till Monday afternoon.

CHASUBLE. Ah yes, he usually likes to spend his Sunday in London. He is not one of those whose sole aim is enjoyment, as, by all accounts, that unfortunate young man his brother seems to be. But I must not disturb Egeria[1] and her pupil any longer.

MISS PRISM. Egeria? My name is Lætitia, Doctor.

CHASUBLE [*Bowing*]. A classical allusion merely, drawn from the Pagan authors. I shall see you both no doubt at Evensong?

MISS PRISM. I think, dear Doctor, I will have a stroll with you. I find I have a headache after all, and a walk might do it good.

CHASUBLE. With pleasure, Miss Prism, with pleasure. We might go as far as the schools and back.

MISS PRISM. That would be delightful. Cecily, you will read your Political Economy in my absence. The chapter on the Fall of the Rupee you may omit. It is somewhat too sensational. Even these metallic problems have their melodramatic side. [*Goes down the garden with* DR. CHASUBLE.]

CECILY [*Picks up books and throws them back on table*]. Horrid Political Economy! Horrid Geography! Horrid, horrid German!

[*Enter* MERRIMAN *with a card on a salver*.]

MERRIMAN. Mr. Ernest Worthing has just driven over from the station. He has brought his luggage with him.

CECILY [*Takes the card and reads it*]. "Mr. Ernest Worthing, B.4, The Albany, W." Uncle Jack's brother! Did you tell him Mr. Worthing was in town?

MERRIMAN. Yes, Miss. He seemed very much disappointed. I mentioned that you and Miss Prism were in the garden. He said he was anxious to speak to you privately for a moment.

---

1   In Roman mythology, Egeria was a water nymph who conveyed the secrets of wisdom to the second King of Rome, who used them to build the Empire; it was also the name of a fourth-century Christian woman who wrote about her travels to the Holy Land. Wilde's use of mythological names signals the double role Miss Prism occupies: like Egeria, she functions as a font of wisdom, as an inspiration and a muse. Her real name, Lætitia, is Latin for "joy" or "happiness" (Jackson 44n).

CECILY. Ask Mr. Ernest Worthing to come here. I suppose you had better talk to the housekeeper about a room for him.

MERRIMAN. Yes, Miss. [MERRIMAN *goes off.*]

CECILY. I have never met any really wicked person before. I feel rather frightened. I am so afraid he will look just like everyone else.

[*Enter* ALGERNON, *very gay and debonnair.*[1]]

He does!

ALGERNON [*Raising his hat*]. You are my little cousin Cecily, I'm sure.

CECILY. You are under some strange mistake. I am not little. In fact, I believe I am more than usually tall for my age. [ALGERNON *is rather taken aback.*] But I am your cousin Cecily. You, I see from your card, are Uncle Jack's brother, my cousin Ernest, my wicked cousin Ernest.

ALGERNON. Oh! I am not really wicked at all, cousin Cecily. You mustn't think that I am wicked.

CECILY. If you are not, then you have certainly been deceiving us all in a very inexcusable manner. I hope you have not been leading a double life, pretending to be wicked and being really good all the time. That would be hypocrisy.[2]

ALGERNON [*Looks at her in amazement*]. Oh! of course I have been rather reckless.

CECILY. I am glad to hear it.

ALGERNON. In fact, now you mention the subject, I have been very bad in my own small way.

CECILY. I don't think you should be so proud of that, though I am sure it must have been very pleasant.

---

1 The misspelling is Smithers's.

2 In *Lady Windermere's Fan*, Lord Darlington remarks that "nowadays so many conceited people go about Society pretending to be good, and I think it shows rather a sweet and modest disposition to pretend to be bad" (422). Later, Darlington dismisses these terms altogether: "It is absurd to divide people into good and bad. People are either charming or tedious" (423). Wilde's investigation of these dualities echoes the Preface to *The Picture of Dorian Gray*, in which he shifts the register of literary criticism from ethics (the moral/the amoral) to aesthetics (the beautiful/the ugly): "There is no such thing as a moral or an immoral book. Books are well written, or badly written. That is all"(3).

ALGERNON. It is much pleasanter being here with you.[1]

CECILY. I can't understand how you are here at all. Uncle Jack won't be back till Monday afternoon.

ALGERNON. That is a great disappointment. I am obliged to go up by the first train on Monday morning. I have a business appointment that I am anxious ... to miss.

CECILY. Couldn't you miss it anywhere but in London?

ALGERNON. No: the appointment is in London.

CECILY. Well, I know, of course, how important it is not to keep a business engagement, if one wants to retain any sense of the beauty of life, but still I think you had better wait till Uncle Jack arrives. I know he wants to speak to you about your emigrating.

ALGERNON. About my what?

CECILY. Your emigrating. He has gone up to buy your outfit.

ALGERNON. I certainly wouldn't let Jack buy my outfit. He has no taste in neckties at all.

CECILY. I don't think you will require neckties. Uncle Jack is sending you to Australia.

ALGERNON. Australia! I'd sooner die.[2]

CECILY. Well, he said at dinner on Wednesday night, that you would have to choose between this world, the next world, and Australia.[3]

---

1 Although his exchange with Cecily might seem to suggest that Algernon distinguishes wickedness from pleasure, these terms in fact remain conflated, since in being with Cecily while pretending to be Ernest—and thus experiencing pleasure—Algernon continues to engage in the wickedness of deception. Like nonsense, wickedness emerges as one of Algernon's favorite activities; for him, both nonsense and wickedness lead to the same end: pleasure. Thus the play that seems often to be devoted to correcting bad behavior also, and at the same time, celebrates it, reminding readers of the play's own Bunbury-like nature, its tendency to compartmentalize without canceling out two very different sorts of lives.

2 Raby notes that Australia was "a common Victorian destination for wayward younger sons" (*EOP* 364). Australia's reputation as a prison colony—and thus the very antithesis of the pampered life of the dandy to which Algy has become accustomed—would surely have amused Wilde's audience.

3 Both Cecily's speech and the notion of a foreign location as a place for the convenient depositing of difficult characters, not to mention criminals, echoes a similar passage in *The Picture of Dorian Gray*, when Lord Henry speculates about Basil Hallward's disappearance that "'I suppose in about a fortnight we will be told that he has been seen in San Francisco. It must be a delightful city, and possess all the attractions of the next world'" (275). Like Paris, the city into which Jack's Ernest will

ALGERNON. Oh, well! The accounts I have received of Australia and the next world are not particularly encouraging. This world is good enough for me, cousin Cecily.

CECILY. Yes, but are you good enough for it?

ALGERNON. I'm afraid I'm not that. That is why I want you to reform me. You might make that your mission, if you don't mind, cousin Cecily.

CECILY. I'm afraid I've no time, this afternoon.

ALGERNON. Well, would you mind my reforming myself this afternoon?

CECILY. It is rather Quixotic[1] of you. But I think you should try.

ALGERNON. I will. I feel better already.

CECILY. You are looking a little worse.

ALGERNON. That is because I am hungry.

CECILY. How thoughtless of me. I should have remembered that when one is going to lead an entirely new life, one requires regular and wholesome meals. Won't you come in?

ALGERNON. Thank you. Might I have a button-hole[2] first? I never have any appetite unless I have a button-hole first.

CECILY. A Maréchal Niel?[3] [*Picks up scissors.*]

ALGERNON. No, I'd sooner have a pink rose.

CECILY. Why? [*Cuts a flower.*]

ALGERNON. Because you are like a pink rose, cousin Cecily.

CECILY. I don't think it can be right for you to talk to me like that. Miss Prism never says such things to me.

ALGERNON. Then Miss Prism is a short-sighted old lady. [CECILY *puts the rose in his button-hole.*] You are the prettiest girl I ever saw.

CECILY. Miss Prism says that all good looks are a snare.

ALGERNON. They are a snare that every sensible man would like to be caught in.

---

vanish, San Francisco has long been associated with taboo-flaunting behavior, particularly of an erotic sort.

1 Impulsive, well-meaning, and unpredictable; derived from the depiction of Don Quixote, the title character in the early seventeenth-century novel by Miguel de Cervantes.

2 A boutonnière, usually an individual flower or bud worn in the button-hole of the lapel of a gentleman's suit coat.

3 As Hyde notes, the Maréchal Niel was "a yellow noisette rose called after the French minister of war and army reformer Marshal Adolphe Niel"; it was introduced to England in the 1860s (*The Annotated Oscar Wilde* 342n41).

CECILY. Oh! I don't think I would care to catch a sensible man. I shouldn't know what to talk to him about.

[*They pass into the house.* MISS PRISM *and* DR. CHASUBLE *return.*]

MISS PRISM. You are too much alone, dear Dr. Chasuble. You should get married. A misanthrope I can understand—a womanthrope, never![1]

CHASUBLE [*With a scholar's shudder*]. Believe me, I do not deserve so neologistic a phrase. The precept as well as the practice of the Primitive Church was distinctly against matrimony.

MISS PRISM [*Sententiously*]. That is obviously the reason why the Primitive Church has not lasted up to the present day. And you do not seem to realize, dear Doctor, that by persistently remaining single, a man converts himself into a permanent public temptation. Men should be more careful; this very celibacy leads weaker vessels astray.

CHASUBLE. But is a man not equally attractive when married?[2]

MISS PRISM. No married man is ever attractive except to his wife.

CHASUBLE. And often, I've been told, not even to her.

MISS PRISM. That depends on the intellectual sympathies of the woman. Maturity can always be depended on. Ripeness can be trusted. Young women are green. [DR. CHASUBLE *starts*.] I spoke horticulturally. My metaphor was drawn from fruits. But where is Cecily?

CHASUBLE. Perhaps she followed us to the schools.

[*Enter* JACK *slowly from the back of the garden. He is dressed in the deepest mourning, with crape hat-band and black gloves.*]

---

1 Many editors of *Earnest* have pointed out that "womanthrope," Wilde's term for "misogynist," first appeared in his essay "The Critic as Artist," in which the phrase is facetiously said to have been "borrow[ed] ... from one of the pretty Newnham graduates" (1120). Newnham, the women's college at Cambridge University, was founded in 1871 and suffered many such barbs from a public slow to accept the higher education of women.

2 Chasuble's remark makes much more explicit the bachelor's erotic appeal, despite his apparent rejection of eroticism. In this way, Wilde's play offers one more example of doubleness, where the presence of one thing (erotic desirability) is marked by its very absence (celibacy).

MISS PRISM. Mr. Worthing!

CHASUBLE. Mr. Worthing?

MISS PRISM. This is indeed a surprise. We did not look for you till Monday afternoon.

JACK [*Shakes* MISS PRISM*'s hand in a tragic manner*]. I have returned sooner than I expected. Dr. Chasuble, I hope you are well?

CHASUBLE. Dear Mr. Worthing, I trust this garb of woe does not betoken some terrible calamity?

JACK. My brother.

MISS PRISM. More shameful debts and extravagance?

CHASUBLE. Still leading his life of pleasure?

JACK [*Shaking his head*]. Dead!

CHASUBLE. Your brother Ernest dead?

JACK. Quite dead.[1]

MISS PRISM. What a lesson for him! I trust he will profit by it.

CHASUBLE. Mr. Worthing, I offer you my sincere condolence. You have at least the consolation of knowing that you were always the most generous and forgiving of brothers.

JACK. Poor Ernest! He had many faults, but it is a sad, sad blow.

CHASUBLE. Very sad indeed. Were you with him at the end?

JACK. No. He died abroad; in Paris, in fact. I had a telegram last night from the manager of the Grand Hotel.

CHASUBLE. Was the cause of death mentioned?

JACK. A severe chill, it seems.

MISS PRISM. As a man sows, so shall he reap.

CHASUBLE [*Raising his hand*]. Charity, dear Miss Prism, charity! None of us are perfect. I myself am peculiarly susceptible to draughts. Will the interment take place here?

JACK. No. He seemed to have expressed a desire to be buried in Paris.

CHASUBLE. In Paris! [*Shakes his head.*] I fear that hardly points to any very serious state of mind at the last.[2] You would no

---

1 Donohue and Berggren (226) cite Kerry Powell's claim that Wilde may have drawn this moment from John Maddison Morton's *A Husband to Order*, in which the male lead, disguised as his brother, announces his own death, there as here for duplicitous purposes.

2 The death of Ernest in Paris points to that character's connection to the flaunting of taboos, to selfish pleasures, and to all manner of vice. This is not the first time Wilde located in Paris the end of a problematic character who questions society's norms: four years earlier in *The Picture of Dorian Gray*, Basil Hallward planned to catch the train to leave for Paris just after he admitted his unrequited love for Dorian.

doubt wish me to make some slight allusion to this tragic domestic affliction next Sunday. [JACK *presses his hand convulsively*.] My sermon on the meaning of the manna in the wilderness can be adapted to almost any occasion, joyful, or, as in the present case, distressing.[1] [*All sigh*.] I have preached it at harvest celebrations, christenings, confirmations, on days of humiliation and festal days. The last time I delivered it was in the Cathedral, as a charity sermon on behalf of the Society for the Prevention of Discontent among the Upper Orders. The Bishop, who was present, was much struck by some of the analogies I drew.[2]

JACK. Ah! that reminds me, you mentioned christenings I think, Dr. Chasuble? I suppose you know how to christen all right? [DR. CHASUBLE *looks astounded*.] I mean, of course, you are continually christening, aren't you?

MISS PRISM. It is, I regret to say, one of the Rector's most constant duties in this parish.[3] I have often spoken to the poorer classes on the subject. But they don't seem to know what thrift is.

CHASUBLE. But is there any particular infant in whom you are interested, Mr. Worthing? Your brother was, I believe, unmarried, was he not?

JACK. Oh yes.

MISS PRISM [*Bitterly*]. People who live entirely for pleasure usually are.[4]

JACK. But it is not for any child, dear Doctor. I am very fond of

---

1 For more on "manna in the wilderness," see Exodus 16.13-15.

2 Chasuble's admission of the obvious meaninglessness of his sermons—they make sense to anyone, anywhere, anytime, and thus they say nothing—reminds readers of the life this play describes: in each of these cases, all talk is *double-entendre*, both meaninglessness and an excess of meaning, at once everything and nothing. A similar note rings throughout Lady Bracknell's description of Algernon in act 3 when she insists that "he has nothing, but he looks everything" (*E* 135).

3 Wilde deleted an additional sentence from the four-act version of the play, in which Miss Prism observes that "The amount of christenings that seem necessary every year point clearly to a certain recklessness of living, and a sad lack of thrift" (Wilde, ed. Dickson 1: 69). Raby flags "thrift" as a *double entendre*, suggesting that the term operates as "a euphemism for sexual continence" (Raby, ed., *Importance* 365). See also *E* 91n2.

4 Donohue and Berggren read Prism's "bitter comment" as "[reflecting] a widely held conviction about marriage as an obligatory, not a pleasurable, state" (233).

children. No! the fact is, I would like to be christened myself, this afternoon, if you have nothing better to do.

CHASUBLE. But surely, Mr. Worthing, you have been christened already?

JACK. I don't remember anything about it.

CHASUBLE. But have you any grave doubts on the subject?

JACK. I certainly intend to have. Of course I don't know if the thing would bother you in any way, or if you think I am a little too old now.

CHASUBLE. Not at all. The sprinkling, and, indeed, the immersion of adults is a perfectly canonical practice.

JACK. Immersion!

CHASUBLE. You need have no apprehensions. Sprinkling is all that is necessary, or indeed I think advisable. Our weather is so changeable. At what hour would you wish the ceremony performed?

JACK. Oh, I might trot round about five if that would suit you.

CHASUBLE. Perfectly, perfectly! In fact I have two similar ceremonies to perform at that time. A case of twins that occurred recently in one of the outlying cottages on your own estate. Poor Jenkins the carter,[1] a most hard-working man.

JACK. Oh! I don't see much fun in being christened along with other babies. It would be childish. Would half-past five do?

CHASUBLE. Admirably! Admirably! [*Takes out watch.*] And now, dear Mr. Worthing, I will not intrude any longer into a house of sorrow. I would merely beg you not to be too much bowed down by grief. What seem to us bitter trials are often blessings in disguise.

MISS PRISM. This seems to me a blessing of an extremely obvious kind.

[*Enter* CECILY *from the house.*]

CECILY. Uncle Jack! Oh, I am pleased to see you back. But what horrid clothes you have got on! Do go and change them.

MISS PRISM. Cecily!

CHASUBLE. My child! my child! [CECILY *goes towards* JACK; *he kisses her brow in a melancholy manner.*]

CECILY. What is the matter, Uncle Jack? Do look happy! You look as if you had toothache, and I have got such a surprise for you. Who do you think is in the dining-room? Your brother!

---

1 A laborer who moves things around in a cart; a farmhand.

JACK. Who?

CECILY. Your brother Ernest. He arrived about half an hour ago.

JACK. What nonsense! I haven't got a brother.

CECILY. Oh, don't say that. However badly he may have behaved to you in the past he is still your brother. You couldn't be so heartless as to disown him. I'll tell him to come out. And you will shake hands with him, won't you, Uncle Jack? [*Runs back into the house.*]

CHASUBLE. These are very joyful tidings.

MISS PRISM. After we had all been resigned to his loss, his sudden return seems to me peculiarly distressing.

JACK. My brother is in the dining-room? I don't know what it all means. I think it is perfectly absurd.

[*Enter* ALGERNON *and* CECILY *hand in hand. They come slowly up to* JACK.]

JACK. Good heavens! [*Motions* ALGERNON *away.*]

ALGERNON. Brother John, I have come down from town to tell you that I am very sorry for all the trouble I have given you, and that I intend to lead a better life in the future. [JACK *glares at him and does not take his hand.*]

CECILY. Uncle Jack, you are not going to refuse your own brother's hand?

JACK. Nothing will induce me to take his hand. I think his coming down here disgraceful. He knows perfectly well why.

CECILY. Uncle Jack, do be nice. There is some good in everyone. Ernest has been just telling me about his poor invalid friend Mr. Bunbury whom he goes to visit so often. And surely there must be much good in one who is kind to an invalid, and leaves the pleasures of London to sit by a bed of pain.

JACK. Oh! he has been talking about Bunbury, has he?

CECILY. Yes, he has told me all about poor Mr. Bunbury, and his terrible state of health.

JACK. Bunbury! Well, I won't have him talk to you about Bunbury or about anything else. It is enough to drive one perfectly frantic.

ALGERNON. Of course I admit that the faults were all on my side. But I must say that I think that Brother John's coldness to me is peculiarly painful. I expected a more enthusiastic welcome, especially considering it is the first time I have come here.

CECILY. Uncle Jack, if you don't shake hands with Ernest I will never forgive you.

JACK. Never forgive me?

CECILY. Never, never, never!

JACK. Well, this is the last time I shall ever do it. [*Shakes hands with* ALGERNON *and glares.*]

CHASUBLE. It's pleasant, is it not, to see so perfect a reconciliation? I think we might leave the two brothers together.

MISS PRISM. Cecily, you will come with us.

CECILY. Certainly, Miss Prism. My little task of reconciliation is over.

CHASUBLE. You have done a beautiful action to-day, dear child.

MISS PRISM. We must not be premature in our judgments.

CECILY. I feel very happy. [*They all go off.*]

JACK. You young scoundrel, Algy, you must get out of this place as soon as possible. I don't allow any Bunburying here.

[*Enter* MERRIMAN.]

MERRIMAN. I have put Mr. Ernest's things in the room next to yours, sir. I suppose that is all right?

JACK. What?

MERRIMAN. Mr. Ernest's luggage, sir. I have unpacked it and put it in the room next to your own.

JACK. His luggage?

MERRIMAN. Yes, sir. Three portmanteaus, a dressing-case, two hat-boxes, and a large luncheon-basket.

ALGERNON. I am afraid I can't stay more than a week this time.

JACK. Merriman, order the dog-cart[1] at once. Mr. Ernest has been suddenly called back to town.

MERRIMAN. Yes, sir. [*Goes back into the house.*]

ALGERNON. What a fearful liar you are, Jack. I have not been called back to town at all.

JACK. Yes, you have.

ALGERNON. I haven't heard anyone call me.

JACK. Your duty as a gentleman calls you back.

ALGERNON. My duty as a gentleman has never interfered with my pleasures in the smallest degree.

JACK. I can quite understand that.

ALGERNON. Well, Cecily is a darling.

JACK. You are not to talk of Miss Cardew like that. I don't like it.

---

1  A lightweight, two-wheeled carriage with back-to-back seats.

ALGERNON. Well, I don't like your clothes. You look perfectly ridiculous in them. Why on earth don't you go up and change? It is perfectly childish to be in deep mourning for a man who is actually staying for a whole week with you in your house as a guest. I call it grotesque.

JACK. You are certainly not staying with me for a whole week as a guest or anything else. You have got to leave ... by the four-five train.

ALGERNON. I certainly won't leave you so long as you are in mourning. It would be most unfriendly. If I were in mourning you would stay with me, I suppose. I should think it very unkind if you didn't.

JACK. Well, will you go if I change my clothes?

ALGERNON. Yes, if you are not too long.[1] I never saw anybody take so long to dress, and with such little result.

JACK. Well, at any rate, that is better than being always over-dressed as you are.

ALGERNON. If I am occasionally a little over-dressed, I make up for it by being always immensely over-educated.[2]

JACK. Your vanity is ridiculous, your conduct is an outrage, and your presence in my garden utterly absurd. However, you have got to catch the four-five, and I hope you will have a pleasant journey back to town. This Bunburying, as you call it, has not been a great success for you. [*Goes into the house.*]

ALGERNON. I think it has been a great success. I'm in love with Cecily, and that is everything.

[*Enter* CECILY *at the back of the garden. She picks up the can and begins to water the flowers.*]

But I must see her before I go, and make arrangements for another Bunbury. Ah, there she is.

---

1  Algernon's speech pre-dicts Gwendolen's language in act 3: "If you are not too long, I will wait here for you all my life" (*E* 140).

·  2  Jackson notes that Wilde recycles these lines from Lord Henry's description of Lord Grotrian in *The Picture of Dorian Gray*: "He atones for being occasionally somewhat overdressed, by being always absolutely overeducated" (140). Donohue and Berggren trace Wilde's line to "Phrases and Philosophies for the Use of the Young," in which he writes that "The only way to atone for being occasionally a little overdressed is by being always absolutely overeducated" (1245).

CECILY. Oh, I merely came back to water the roses. I thought you were with Uncle Jack.

ALGERNON. He's gone to order the dog-cart for me.

CECILY. Oh, is he going to take you for a nice drive?

ALGERNON. He's going to send me away.

CECILY. Then have we got to part?

ALGERNON. I am afraid so. It's a very painful parting.

CECILY. It is always painful to part from people whom one has known for a very brief space of time. The absence of old friends one can endure with equanimity. But even a momentary separation from anyone to whom one has just been introduced is almost unbearable.

ALGERNON. Thank you.

[*Enter* MERRIMAN.]

MERRIMAN. The dog-cart is at the door, sir.

[ALGERNON *looks appealingly at* CECILY.]

CECILY. It can wait, Merriman ... for ... five minutes.

MERRIMAN. Yes, Miss. [*Exit* MERRIMAN.]

ALGERNON. I hope, Cecily, I shall not offend you if I state quite frankly and openly that you seem to me to be in every way the visible personification of absolute perfection.

CECILY. I think your frankness does you great credit, Ernest. If you will allow me I will copy your remarks into my diary. [*Goes over to table and begins writing in diary.*]

ALGERNON. Do you really keep a diary? I'd give anything to look at it. May I?

CECILY. Oh, no. [*Puts her hand over it.*] You see, it is simply a very young girl's record of her own thoughts and impressions, and consequently meant for publication. When it appears in volume form I hope you will order a copy. But pray, Ernest, don't stop. I delight in taking down from dictation. I have reached "absolute perfection." You can go on. I am quite ready for more.

ALGERNON [*Somewhat taken aback*]. Ahem! Ahem!

CECILY. Oh, don't cough, Ernest. When one is dictating one should speak fluently and not cough. Besides, I don't know how to spell a cough. [*Writes as* ALGERNON *speaks.*]

ALGERNON [*Speaking very rapidly*]. Cecily, ever since I first looked upon your wonderful and incomparable beauty, I have dared to love you wildly, passionately, devotedly, hopelessly.[1]

CECILY. I don't think that you should tell me that you love me wildly, passionately, devotedly, hopelessly. Hopelessly doesn't seem to make much sense, does it?

ALGERNON. Cecily!

[*Enter* MERRIMAN.]

MERRIMAN. The dog-cart is waiting, sir.

ALGERNON. Tell it to come round next week, at the same hour.

MERRIMAN [*Looks at* CECILY, *who makes no sign*]. Yes, sir. [MERRIMAN *retires*.]

CECILY. Uncle Jack would be very much annoyed if he knew you were staying on till next week, at the same hour.

ALGERNON. Oh, I don't care about Jack. I don't care for anybody in the world but you. I love you, Cecily. You will marry me, won't you?

CECILY. You silly boy! Of course. Why, we have been engaged for the last three months.

ALGERNON. For the last three months?

CECILY. Yes, it will be exactly three months on Thursday.

ALGERNON. But how did we become engaged?

CECILY. Well, ever since dear Uncle Jack first confessed to us that he had a younger brother who was very wicked and bad, you of course have formed the chief topic of conversation between myself and Miss Prism. And of course a man who is much talked about is always very attractive. One feels there must be something in him after all. I daresay it was foolish of me, but I fell in love with you, Ernest.

ALGERNON. Darling! And when was the engagement actually settled?

CECILY. On the 14th of February last. Worn out by your entire

---

1 Algernon's declaration of love to Cecily contributes to a homosexual subtext by echoing Basil Hallward's confession of deep feelings for the title character of *The Picture of Dorian Gray*: "Well, from the moment I met you, your personality had the most extraordinary influence over me. I quite admit that I adored you madly, extravagantly, absurdly" (232). Donohue and Berggren trace a (heterosexual) precedent for this line in *Lady Windermere's Fan*, when Lord Darlington admits to Lady Windermere that "I love you—love you as I have never loved any living thing. From the moment I met you I loved you blindly, adoringly, madly!" (439).

ignorance of my existence, I determined to end the matter one way or the other, and after a long struggle with myself I accepted you one evening under this dear old tree here. The next day I bought this little ring in your name, and this is the little bangle with the true lovers' knot I promised you always to wear.

ALGERNON. Did I give you this? It's very pretty, isn't it?

CECILY. Yes, you've wonderfully good taste, Ernest. It's the excuse I've always given for your leading such a bad life. And this is the box in which I keep all your dear letters. [*Kneels at table, opens box, and produces letters tied up with blue ribbon.*]

ALGERNON. My letters! But my own sweet Cecily, I have never written you any letters.

CECILY. You need hardly remind me of that, Ernest. I remember only too well that I was forced to write your letters for you. I wrote always three times a week, and sometimes oftener.

ALGERNON. Oh, do let me read them, Cecily?

CECILY. Oh, I couldn't possibly. They would make you far too conceited. [*Replaces box.*] The three you wrote me after I had broken off the engagement are so beautiful, and so badly spelled, that even now I can hardly read them without crying a little.

ALGERNON. But was our engagement ever broken off?

CECILY. Of course it was. On the 22nd of last March. You can see the entry if you like. [*Shows diary.*] "To-day I broke off my engagement with Ernest. I feel it is better to do so. The weather still continues charming."

ALGERNON. But why on earth did you break it off? What had I done? I had done nothing at all. Cecily, I am very much hurt indeed to hear you broke it off. Particularly when the weather was so charming.

CECILY. It would hardly have been a really serious engagement if it hadn't been broken off at least once. But I forgave you before the week was out.

ALGERNON [*Crossing to her, and kneeling*]. What a perfect angel you are, Cecily.

CECILY. You dear romantic boy. [*He kisses her, she puts her fingers through his hair.*] I hope your hair curls naturally, does it?

ALGERNON. Yes, darling, with a little help from others.

CECILY. I am so glad.

ALGERNON. You'll never break off our engagement again, Cecily?

CECILY. I don't think I could break it off now that I have actually met you. Besides, of course, there is the question of your name.

ALGERNON. Yes, of course. [*Nervously.*]

CECILY. You must not laugh at me, darling, but it had always been a girlish dream of mine to love some one whose name was Ernest. [ALGERNON *rises*, CECILY *also*.] There is something in the name that seems to inspire absolute confidence. I pity any poor married woman whose husband is not called Ernest.

ALGERNON. But, my dear child, do you mean to say you could not love me if I had some other name?

CECILY. But what name?

ALGERNON. Oh, any name you like—Algernon—for instance ...

CECILY. But I don't like the name of Algernon.

ALGERNON. Well, my own dear, sweet, loving little darling, I really can't see why you should object to the name of Algernon. It is not at all a bad name. In fact, it is rather an aristocratic name. Half of the chaps who get into the Bankruptcy Court are called Algernon. But seriously, Cecily ... [*Moving to her*] ... if my name was Algy, couldn't you love me?

CECILY [*Rising*]. I might respect you, Ernest, I might admire your character, but I fear that I should not be able to give you my undivided attention.

ALGERNON. Ahem! Cecily! [*Picking up hat.*] Your Rector here is, I suppose, thoroughly experienced in the practice of all the rites and ceremonials of the Church?

CECILY. Oh, yes. Dr. Chasuble is a most learned man. He has never written a single book, so you can imagine how much he knows.

ALGERNON. I must see him at once on a most important christening—I mean on most important business.

CECILY. Oh!

ALGERNON. I shan't be away more than half an hour.

CECILY. Considering that we have been engaged since February the 14th, and that I only met you to-day for the first time, I think it is rather hard that you should leave me for so long a period as half an hour. Couldn't you make it twenty minutes?

ALGERNON. I'll be back in no time. [*Kisses her and rushes down the garden.*]

CECILY. What an impetuous boy he is! I like his hair so much. I must enter his proposal in my diary.

[*Enter* MERRIMAN.]

MERRIMAN. A Miss Fairfax has just called to see Mr. Worthing. On very important business Miss Fairfax states.

CECILY. Isn't Mr. Worthing in his library?

MERRIMAN. Mr. Worthing went over in the direction of the Rectory some time ago.

CECILY. Pray ask the lady to come out here; Mr. Worthing is sure to be back soon. And you can bring tea.

MERRIMAN. Yes, Miss. [*Goes out.*]

CECILY. Miss Fairfax! I suppose one of the many good elderly women who are associated with Uncle Jack in some of his philanthropic work in London. I don't quite like women who are interested in philanthropic work. I think it is so forward of them.

[*Enter* MERRIMAN.]

MERRIMAN. Miss Fairfax.

[*Enter* GWENDOLEN. *Exit* MERRIMAN.]

CECILY [*Advancing to meet her*]. Pray let me introduce myself to you. My name is Cecily Cardew.

GWENDOLEN. Cecily Cardew? [*Moving to her and shaking hands.*] What a very sweet name! Something tells me that we are going to be great friends. I like you already more than I can say. My first impressions of people are never wrong.[1]

CECILY. How nice of you to like me so much after we have known each other such a comparatively short time. Pray sit down.

GWENDOLEN [*Still standing up*]. I may call you Cecily, may I not?

CECILY. With pleasure!

GWENDOLEN. And you will always call me Gwendolen, won't you.

---

1   In the fourth act of *Lady Lancing*, Gwendolen repeats her final remark from this speech in an exchange that proves telling, declaring that "Cecily is a perfect darling! The moment I met her I said to myself: 'There is the wife of my cousin Algernon.' My first impressions of people are never wrong" (Wilde, ed. Dickson 1: 153).

CECILY. If you wish.

GWENDOLEN. Then that is all quite settled, is it not?

CECILY. I hope so.

[*A pause. They both sit down together.*]

GWENDOLEN. Perhaps this might be a favourable opportunity for my mentioning who I am. My father is Lord Bracknell. You have never heard of papa, I suppose?

CECILY. I don't think so.

GWENDOLEN. Outside the family circle, papa, I am glad to say, is entirely unknown. I think that is quite as it should be. The home seems to me to be the proper sphere for the man.[1] And certainly once a man begins to neglect his domestic duties he becomes painfully effeminate, does he not? And I don't like that. It makes men so very attractive.[2] Cecily, mamma, whose views on education are remarkably strict, has brought me up to be extremely short-sighted; it is part of her system; so do you mind my looking at you through my glasses?

CECILY. Oh! not at all, Gwendolen. I am very fond of being looked at.

GWENDOLEN [*After examining* CECILY *carefully through a lorgnette*]. You are here on a short visit I suppose.

CECILY. Oh no! I live here.

GWENDOLEN [*Severely*]. Really? Your mother, no doubt, or some female relative of advanced years, resides here also?

CECILY. Oh no! I have no mother, nor, in fact, any relations.

GWENDOLEN. Indeed?

CECILY. My dear guardian, with the assistance of Miss Prism, has the arduous task of looking after me.

GWENDOLEN. Your guardian?

---

1 Wilde again reverses a well-known maxim, here substituting "man" for "woman" (Leeming 81). In so doing, Wilde engages contemporary conversations and controversies about the shifting roles of women and men, the so-called masculinization of women who leave the home to enter the public sphere and the emasculated men who are left to assume women's traditional roles in their absence. This line thus connects *Earnest* to many of Wilde's works in its critique of gender, nature, and behavior, and it also participates in the so-called Decadent commitment to revealing all "truths" as mere social constructions, as behavioral conventions with no real basis in truth itself.

2 Cave observes that the equation of male effeminacy and attractiveness is a "gibe by Wilde at the Victorian cult of manliness" (427n16).

CECILY. Yes, I am Mr. Worthing's ward.[1]

GWENDOLEN. Oh! it is strange he never mentioned to me that he had a ward. How secretive of him! He grows more interesting hourly. I am not sure, however, that the news inspires me with feelings of unmixed delight. [*Rising and going to her.*] I am very fond of you, Cecily; I have liked you ever since I met you! But I am bound to state that now that I know that you are Mr. Worthing's ward, I cannot help expressing a wish you were— well, just a little older than you seem to be—and not quite so very alluring in appearance. In fact, if I may speak candidly—
_____[2]

CECILY. Pray do! I think that whenever one has anything unpleasant to say, one should always be quite candid.

GWENDOLEN. Well, to speak with perfect candour, Cecily, I wish that you were fully forty-two, and more than usually plain for your age. Ernest has a strong upright nature.[3] He is the very soul of truth and honour. Disloyalty would be as impossible to him as deception. But even men of the noblest possible moral character are extremely susceptible to the influence of the physical charms of others. Modern, no less than Ancient History, supplies us with many most painful examples of what I refer to. If it were not so, indeed, History would be quite unreadable.

CECILY. I beg your pardon, Gwendolen, did you say Ernest?

GWENDOLEN. Yes.

CECILY. Oh, but it is not Mr. Ernest Worthing who is my guardian. It is his brother—his elder brother.

GWENDOLEN [*Sitting down again*]. Ernest never mentioned to me that he had a brother.

---

1 Given the *double-entendre* of the term "ward" (see *E* 92n2), Cecily's announcement would do little to allay Gwendolen's fears, thus heightening the tension between the women as well as the amusement of the audience.

2 Ruth Robbins argues that Gwendolen's announcement that she will "speak candidly" signals a complete breakdown of order in the play, underscoring the success of Wilde's satire of privileged British life: "To speak plainly ... is to break up the social game-playing on which this society is based. To speak one's mind, or to call a spade a spade, would represent a failure of upper-class manners, and a slanging match, especially in front of the servants, would be most inappropriate" (60).

3 By referring to her intended as Ernest rather than as Mr. Worthing, Gwendolen indicates to Cecily the intimate nature of their relationship.

CECILY. I am sorry to say they have not been on good terms for a long time.

GWENDOLEN. Ah! that accounts for it. And now that I think of it I have never heard any man mention his brother. The subject seems distasteful to most men. Cecily, you have lifted a load from my mind. I was growing almost anxious. It would have been terrible if any cloud had come across a friendship like ours, would it not? Of course you are quite, quite sure that it is not Mr. Ernest Worthing who is your guardian?

CECILY. Quite sure. [*A pause.*] In fact, I am going to be his.

GWENDOLEN [*Enquiringly*]. I beg your pardon?

CECILY [*Rather shy and confidingly*]. Dearest Gwendolen, there is no reason why I should make a secret of it to you. Our little county newspaper is sure to chronicle the fact next week. Mr. Ernest Worthing and I are engaged to be married.

GWENDOLEN [*Quite politely, rising*]. My darling Cecily, I think there must be some slight error. Mr. Ernest Worthing is engaged to me. The announcement will appear in the "Morning Post" on Saturday at the latest.

CECILY [*Very politely, rising*]. I am afraid you must be under some misconception. Ernest proposed to me exactly ten minutes ago. [*Shows diary.*]

GWENDOLEN [*Examines diary through her lorgnette carefully*]. It is certainly very curious,[1] for he asked me to be his wife yesterday afternoon at 5.30. If you would care to verify the incident, pray do so. [*Produces diary of her own.*] I never travel without my diary. One should always have something sensational to read in the train.[2] I am so sorry, dear Cecily, if it is

---

1 Wilde introduced the adjective "curious" in the three-act version, and while the term's resonances clearly fit this context, they may also embed references to non-normative sexual desires and practices—in short, to homosexuality. Like many other slang words of the day, "curious" was one of several terms by which Victorians alluded to suspected homosexual practices.

2 The word "sensational" links Gwendolen's diary to the "sensation fiction" so popular and so controversial in the Victorian era, works that were imagined to take physical, sensual form: for the most traditional of Victorian readers, "sensation fiction" was akin to soft-core pornography. Wilde's characterization of Gwendolen's diary reminds readers that the mannerly courting we see on stage may not, in fact, be the whole story of these characters' lives, just as the lives Jack and Algernon live in the country and in the town, respectively, are not the entirety of their lives, which are expanded and doubled through the sensational false-selves of "Ernest" and "Bunbury."

any disappointment to you, but I am afraid *I* have the prior claim.

CECILY. It would distress me more than I can tell you, dear Gwendolen, if it caused you any mental or physical anguish, but I feel bound to point out that since Ernest proposed to you he clearly has changed his mind.

GWENDOLEN [*Meditatively*]. If the poor fellow has been entrapped into any foolish promise I shall consider it my duty to rescue him at once, and with a firm hand.

CECILY [*Thoughtfully and sadly*]. Whatever unfortunate entanglement my dear boy may have got into, I will never reproach him with it after we are married.

GWENDOLEN. Do you allude to me, Miss Cardew, as an entanglement? You are presumptuous. On an occasion of this kind it becomes more than a moral duty to speak one's mind. It becomes a pleasure.

CECILY. Do you suggest, Miss Fairfax, that I entrapped Ernest into an engagement? How dare you? This is no time for wearing the shallow mask of manners. When I see a spade I call it a spade.[1]

GWENDOLEN [*Satirically*]. I am glad to say that I have never seen a spade. It is obvious that our social spheres have been widely different.

[*Enter* MERRIMAN, *followed by the* FOOTMAN. *He carries a salver, table cloth, and plate stand.* CECILY *is about to retort. The presence of the servants exercises a restraining influence, under which both girls chafe.*]

MERRIMAN. Shall I lay tea here as usual, Miss?

CECILY [*Sternly, in a calm voice*]. Yes, as usual. [MERRIMAN *begins to clear and lay cloth. A long pause.* CECILY *and* GWENDOLEN *glare at each other.*]

GWENDOLEN. Are there many interesting walks in the vicinity, Miss Cardew?

CECILY. Oh! yes! a great many. From the top of one of the hills quite close one can see five counties.

---

1 Donohue and Berggren find a real-life precedent for this line in Wilde's speech to members of the Royal General Theatrical Fund in 1892: when he "responded to being praised for calling a spade a spade and lashing vice in *Lady Windermere's Fan*," Wilde replied that "'I would like to protest against the statement that I have ever called a spade a spade. The man who did so should be condemned to use one'" (273).

GWENDOLEN. Five counties! I don't think I should like that. I hate crowds.

CECILY [*Sweetly*]. I suppose that is why you live in town?

[GWENDOLEN *bites her lip, and beats her foot nervously with her parasol.*]

GWENDOLEN [*Looking round*]. Quite a well-kept garden this is, Miss Cardew.

CECILY. So glad you like it, Miss Fairfax.

GWENDOLEN. I had no idea there were any flowers in the country.

CECILY. Oh, flowers are as common here, Miss Fairfax, as people are in London.[1]

GWENDOLEN. Personally I cannot understand how anybody manages to exist in the country, if anybody who is anybody does. The country always bores me to death.

CECILY. Ah! This is what the newspapers call agricultural depression, is it not?[2] I believe the aristocracy are suffering very much from it just at present. It is almost an epidemic amongst them, I have been told. May I offer you some tea, Miss Fairfax?

GWENDOLEN [*With elaborate politeness*]. Thank you. [*Aside.*] Detestable girl! But I require tea!

CECILY [*Sweetly*]. Sugar?

GWENDOLEN [*Superciliously*]. No, thank you. Sugar is not fashionable any more.

[CECILY *looks angrily at her, takes up the tongs and puts four lumps of sugar into the cup.*]

CECILY [*Severely*]. Cake or bread and butter?

GWENDOLEN [*In a bored manner*]. Bread and butter, please.

---

1 The success of Cecily's sarcasm derives from the double meaning of "common": of flowers, it suggests abundance; of people, a lack of refinement.

2 Agricultural depression gripped Britain from about 1870 through the first third or so of the twentieth century, during which time the fortunes of many British landowners remained in a state of constant peril. Cecily's quip makes much of city-dweller Gwendolen's unhappiness in the country by suggesting that the well-being of the rich depends upon what happens in the country, thereby giving country-girl Cecily some measure of power and control over city-dweller Gwendolen.

Cake is rarely seen at the best houses nowadays.

CECILY [*Cuts a very large slice of cake, and puts it on the tray*]. Hand that to Miss Fairfax.[1]

[MERRIMAN *does so, and goes out with* FOOTMAN. GWENDOLEN *drinks the tea and makes a grimace. Puts down cup at once, reaches out her hand to the bread and butter, looks at it, and finds it is cake. Rises in indignation.*]

GWENDOLEN. You have filled my tea with lumps of sugar, and though I asked most distinctly for bread and butter, you have given me cake. I am known for the gentleness of my disposition, and the extraordinary sweetness of my nature, but I warn you, Miss Cardew, you may go too far.

CECILY [*Rising*]. To save my poor, innocent, trusting boy from the machinations of any other girl there are no lengths to which I would not go.

GWENDOLEN. From the moment I saw you I distrusted you. I felt that you were false and deceitful. I am never deceived in such matters. My first impressions of people are invariably right.[2]

CECILY. It seems to me, Miss Fairfax, that I am trespassing on your valuable time. No doubt you have many other calls of a similar character to make in the neighbourhood.[3]

[*Enter* JACK.]

GWENDOLEN. [*Catching sight of him.*] Ernest! My own Ernest!

JACK Gwendolen! Darling! [*Offers to kiss her.*]

GWENDOLEN [*Drawing back*]. A moment! May I ask if you are engaged to be married to this young lady? [*Points to* CECILY.]

JACK [*Laughing*]. To dear little Cecily! Of course not! What could have put such an idea into your pretty little head?

---

1   Wilde's stage directions and Cecily's speech prove significant for two reasons: first, because they re-invoke the use of the salver, which functioned to announce an imminent reversal of power in act 1; second, Cecily's defiant, emphatic sentence acknowledges her recognition that she is now in a war with Gwendolen and that she must turn to whatever devices are at hand to gain dominance over her opponent.

2   Here Gwendolen echoes her initial remark upon meeting Cecily, exemplifying the play's "verbal echonomy," as described in the Introduction (38-42).

3   Cecily's retort implies that Gwendolen has stolen the affections of many men and that she is therefore morally disreputable.

GWENDOLEN. Thank you. You may! [*Offers her cheek.*]

CECILY [*Very sweetly*]. I knew there must be some misunderstanding, Miss Fairfax. The gentleman whose arm is at present round your waist is my dear guardian, Mr. John Worthing.

GWENDOLEN. I beg your pardon?

CECILY. This is Uncle Jack.

GWENDOLEN [*Receding*]. Jack! Oh!

[*Enter* ALGERNON.]

CECILY. Here is Ernest.

ALGERNON [*Goes straight over to* CECILY *without noticing anyone else*]. My own love! [*Offers to kiss her.*]

CECILY [*Drawing back*]. A moment, Ernest! May I ask you—are you engaged to be married to this young lady?

ALGERNON [*Looking round*]. To what young lady? Good heavens! Gwendolen!

CECILY. Yes! to good heavens, Gwendolen, I mean to Gwendolen.

ALGERNON [*Laughing*]. Of course not! What could have put such an idea into your pretty little head?

CECILY. Thank you. [*Presenting her cheek to be kissed.*] You may. [ALGERNON *kisses her.*]

GWENDOLEN. I felt there was some slight error, Miss Cardew. The gentleman who is now embracing you is my cousin, Mr. Algernon Moncrieff.

CECILY [*Breaking away from* ALGERNON]. Algernon Moncrieff! Oh!

[*The two girls move towards each other and put their arms round each other's waists as if for protection.*]

CECILY. Are you called Algernon?

ALGERNON. I cannot deny it.

CECILY. Oh!

GWENDOLEN. Is your name really John?

JACK [*Standing rather proudly*]. I could deny it if I liked. I could deny anything if I liked. But my name certainly is John. It has been John for years.

CECILY [*To* GWENDOLEN]. A gross deception has been practiced on both of us.

GWENDOLEN. My poor wounded Cecily!

CECILY. My sweet wronged Gwendolen!

GWENDOLEN [*Slowly and seriously*]. You will call me sister, will you not?

[*They embrace.* JACK *and* ALGERNON *groan and walk up and down.*]

CECILY [*Rather brightly*]. There is just one question I would like to be allowed to ask my guardian.

GWENDOLEN. An admirable idea! Mr. Worthing, there is just one question I would like to be permitted to put to you.[1] Where is your brother Ernest? We are both engaged to be married to your brother Ernest, so it is a matter of some importance to us to know where your brother Ernest is at present.

JACK [*Slowly and hesitatingly*]. Gwendolen—Cecily—it is very painful for me to be forced to speak the truth. It is the first time in my life that I have ever been reduced to such a painful position, and I am really quite inexperienced in doing anything of the kind. However, I will tell you quite frankly that I have no brother Ernest. I have no brother at all. I never had a brother in my life, and I certainly have not the smallest intention of ever having one in the future.

CECILY [*Surprised*]. No brother at all?

JACK [*Cheerily*]. None!

GWENDOLEN [*Severely*]. Had you never a brother of any kind?

JACK [*Pleasantly*]. Never. Not even of any kind.

GWENDOLEN. I am afraid it is quite clear, Cecily, that neither of us is engaged to be married to anyone.

CECILY. It is not a very pleasant position for a young girl suddenly to find herself in. Is it?

GWENDOLEN. Let us go into the house. They will hardly venture to come after us there.

CECILY. No, men are so cowardly, aren't they?

[*They retire into the house with scornful looks.*]

JACK. This ghastly state of things is what you call Bunburying, I suppose?

ALGERNON. Yes, and a perfectly wonderful Bunbury it is. The most wonderful Bunbury I have ever had in my life.

JACK. Well, you've no right whatsoever to Bunbury here.

---

1 Again, Wilde invokes a surname to call attention to Gwendolen's assertion of something other than an intimate relationship with Jack/Ernest and, thus, to mark her emotional distance from the man to whom she only recently declared her love and her intention to marry.

ALGERNON. That is absurd. One has a right to Bunbury anywhere one chooses. Every serious Bunburyist knows that.

JACK. Serious Bunburyist! Good heavens!

ALGERNON. Well, one must be serious about something, if one
wants to have any amusement in life. I happen to be serious
about Bunburying. What on earth you are serious about I
haven't got the remotest idea. About everything, I should
fancy. You have such an absolutely trivial nature.[1]

JACK. Well, the only small satisfaction I have in the whole of this
wretched business is that your friend Bunbury is quite
exploded.[2] You won't be able to run down to the country quite
so often as you used to do, dear Algy. And a very good thing
too.

ALGERNON. Your brother is a little off colour, isn't he, dear
Jack? You won't be able to disappear to London quite so frequently as your wicked custom was. And not a bad thing either.

JACK. As for your conduct towards Miss Cardew, I must say that
your taking in a sweet, simple, innocent girl like that is quite
inexcusable. To say nothing of the fact that she is my ward.

ALGERNON. I can see no possible defence at all for your deceiving a brilliant, clever, thoroughly experienced young lady like
Miss Fairfax. To say nothing of the fact that she is my cousin.[3]

JACK. I wanted to be engaged to Gwendolen, that is all. I love
her.

ALGERNON. Well, I simply wanted to be engaged to Cecily. I
adore her.

JACK. There is certainly no chance of your marrying Miss Cardew.

---

1  As suggested in the Introduction and throughout the notes to the play,
   *Earnest* depends upon the logic of inversion, of reversal: here seriousness
   equals amusement. Equally significant is the fact that Jack's trivial
   nature echoes the play's subtitle, especially with regard to Wilde's observation about the members of the audience: those "serious people" are,
   in many ways, as trivial as Jack, and thus Wilde's audiences recognize in
   Jack a stand-in for themselves, adding to the satirical effects of the play's
   comic appeal.

2  Donohue and Berggren note that while by "exploded" "Jack of course
   means 'discredited,' [...] the eighteenth-century sense of the word
   meaning 'hissed off the stage' seems amusingly appropriate (*OED*)"
   (292).

3  Together, this speech and the one preceding it offer another example of
   the play's verbal echonomy: Algernon's final line repeats Jack's almost
   exactly, but in its "twist" it takes power away from Jack, its original
   speaker, and invests it instead in Algernon.

ALGERNON. I don't think there is much likelihood, Jack, of you and Miss Fairfax being united.

JACK. Well, that is no business of yours.

ALGERNON. If it was my business, I wouldn't talk about it. [*Begins to eat muffins.*] It is very vulgar to talk about one's business. Only people like stockbrokers do that, and then merely at dinner parties.

JACK. How can you sit there, calmly eating muffins when we are in this horrible trouble, I can't make out. You seem to me to be perfectly heartless.

ALGERNON. Well, I can't eat muffins in an agitated manner. The butter would probably get on my cuffs. One should always eat muffins quite calmly. It is the only way to eat them.

JACK. I say it's perfectly heartless your eating muffins at all, under the circumstances.

ALGERNON. When I am in trouble, eating is the only thing that consoles me. Indeed, when I am in really great trouble, as anyone who knows me intimately will tell you, I refuse everything except food and drink. At the present moment I am eating muffins because I am unhappy. Besides, I am particularly fond of muffins. [*Rising.*]

JACK [*Rising*]. Well, that is no reason why you should eat them all in that greedy way. [*Takes muffins from* ALGERNON.]

ALGERNON [*Offering tea-cake*]. I wish you would have tea-cake instead. I don't like tea-cake.[1]

JACK. Good heavens! I suppose a man may eat his own muffins in his own garden.

ALGERNON. But you have just said it was perfectly heartless to eat muffins.

JACK. I said it was perfectly heartless of you, under the circumstances. That is a very different thing.

ALGERNON. That may be. But the muffins are the same. [*He seizes the muffin-dish from* JACK.]

JACK. Algy, I wish to goodness you would go.

ALGERNON. You can't possibly ask me to go without having some dinner. It's absurd. I never go without my dinner. No one ever does, except vegetarians and people like that. Besides I have just made arrangements with Dr. Chasuble to be christened at a quarter to six under the name of Ernest.

JACK. My dear fellow, the sooner you give up that nonsense the better. I made arrangements this morning with Dr. Chasuble

---

1  More verbal echonomy, here echoing Jack and Algernon's negotiations of food throughout act 1.

to be christened myself at 5.30, and I naturally will take the name of Ernest. Gwendolen would wish it. We can't both be christened Ernest. It's absurd. Besides, I have a perfect right to be christened if I like. There is no evidence at all that I ever have been christened by anybody. I should think it extremely probable I never was, and so does Dr. Chasuble. It is entirely different in your case. You have been christened already.

ALGERNON. Yes, but I have not been christened for years.

JACK. Yes, but you have been christened. That is the important thing.

ALGERNON. Quite so. So I know my constitution can stand it. If you are not quite sure about your ever having been christened, I must say I think it rather dangerous your venturing on it now. It might make you very unwell. You can hardly have forgotten that someone very closely connected with you was very nearly carried off this week in Paris by a severe chill.

JACK. Yes, but you said yourself that a severe chill was not hereditary.

ALGERNON. It usen't to be, I know—but I daresay it is now. Science is always making wonderful improvements in things.

JACK [*Picking up the muffin-dish*]. Oh, that is nonsense; you are always talking nonsense.[1]

ALGERNON. Jack, you are at the muffins again! I wish you wouldn't. There are only two left. [*Takes them.*] I told you I was particularly fond of muffins.

JACK. But I hate tea-cake.

ALGERNON. Why on earth then do you allow tea-cake to be served up for your guests? What ideas you have of hospitality!

JACK. Algernon! I have already told you to go. I don't want you here. Why don't you go!

ALGERNON. I haven't quite finished my tea yet! and there is still one muffin left.

[JACK *groans, and sinks into a chair.* ALGERNON *still continues eating.*][2]

## ACT DROP.

---

1   As Jack asserts here, Algernon remains thoroughly devoted to nonsense, to play, whereas Jack consistently claims to reject such a position. Of the two, Algernon is clearly the more dandiacal, since he recasts idleness as industry (see *E* 86n2 and 93n4), whereas Jack urges for a more productive mode of life, his own version of Bunburying notwithstanding.

2   This act drop concludes the exchanges that cast Algernon as the consummate dandy and Jack as one suffering from internalized dandy-

# THIRD ACT

SCENE—*Morning-room at the Manor House.*

[GWENDOLEN *and* CECILY *are at the window, looking out into the garden.*]

GWENDOLEN. The fact that they did not follow us at once into the house, as anyone else would have done, seems to me to show that they have some sense of shame left.

CECILY. They have been eating muffins. That looks like repentance.

GWENDOLEN [*After a pause*]. They don't seem to notice us at all. Couldn't you cough?

CECILY. But I haven't got a cough.[1]

GWENDOLEN. They're looking at us. What effrontery!

CECILY. They're approaching. That's very forward of them.

GWENDOLEN. Let us preserve a dignified silence.

CECILY. Certainly. It's the only thing to do now.

---

phobia. Although twenty-first-century readers might easily align dandyism and homosexuality, such an equation would not have occurred to most of the members of Wilde's audience, for it was not until his trials that Wilde's looks, personality, and various poses came to be aligned with what his culture demonized as sexually deviant. For more on the meaning and significance of the dandy, see Cohen's *Talk on the Wilde Side*, ch. 5, and Alan Sinfield's *The Wilde Century*, especially chs. 3 and 4.

1   Another instance of verbal echonomy: cf. Cecily to Algernon in act 2: "Besides, I don't know how to spell a cough" (*E* 111). In that case, such a protest gave Cecily power, as it guaranteed the exactitude of Algernon's protestations of love to her, which she recorded in her diary; here, Cecily's near-repetition of the same concept and phrase disempowers her, making her seem simple-minded and overly literal.

[*Enter* JACK *followed by* ALGERNON. *They whistle some dreadful popular air from a British Opera.*[1]]

GWENDOLEN. This dignified silence seems to produce an unpleasant effect.

CECILY. A most distasteful one.

GWENDOLEN. But we will not be the first to speak.

CECILY. Certainly not.

GWENDOLEN. Mr. Worthing, I have something very particular to ask you. Much depends on your reply.

CECILY. Gwendolen, your common sense is invaluable. Mr. Moncrieff, kindly answer me the following question. Why did you pretend to be my guardian's brother?

ALGERNON. In order that I might have an opportunity of meeting you.

CECILY [*To* GWENDOLEN]. That certainly seems a satisfactory explanation, does it not?

GWENDOLEN. Yes, dear, if you can believe him.

CECILY. I don't. But that does not affect the wonderful beauty of his answer.

GWENDOLEN. True. In matters of grave importance, style, not sincerity is the vital thing. Mr. Worthing, what explanation can you offer to me for pretending to have a brother? Was it in order that you might have an opportunity of coming up to town to see me as often as possible?

JACK. Can you doubt it, Miss Fairfax?[2]

GWENDOLEN. I have the gravest doubts upon the subject. But

---

1   Critics generally agree that this is Wilde's not-so-subtle yet playfully affectionate barb at the popular pieces by W.S. Gilbert and Arthur Sullivan, whose comic opera *Patience; or, Bunthorne's Bride* made fun of Wilde and the Aesthetic movement he had come to represent (see Appendix D1 and the Introduction 26-27). However, Donohue and Berggren take issue with this assumption and identify the song as "Home Sweet Home" by Henry Bishop and J.H. Payne (304n).

2   Jack's addressing of Gwendolen as "Miss Fairfax" marks the stiff formality that deception has introduced into their relationship. In an early version of the performance text, Wilde's stage directions described Jack and Algernon moving throughout these exchanges "*à la dude*" (Jackson 84n33). The pejorative "dude" described "a man affecting an exaggerated fastidiousness in dress, speech, and deportment, and very particular about what is aesthetically 'good form'; hence, extended to an exquisite, a dandy, 'a swell'" (*OED*, s.v. "dude"), a physical manifestation of the arch formality Jack's language to Gwendolen intones.

I intend to crush them. This is not the moment for German scepticism.[1] [*Moving to* CECILY.] Their explanations appear to be quite satisfactory, especially Mr. Worthing's. That seems to me to have the stamp of truth on it.

CECILY. I am more than content with what Mr. Moncrieff said. His voice alone inspires one with absolute credulity.

GWENDOLEN. Then you think we should forgive them?

CECILY. Yes. I mean no.

GWENDOLEN. True! I had forgotten. There are principles at stake that one cannot surrender. Which of us should tell them? The task is not a pleasant one.

CECILY. Could we not both speak at the same time?

GWENDOLEN. An excellent idea! I nearly always speak at the same time as other people. Will you take the time from me?

CECILY. Certainly. [GWENDOLEN *beats time with uplifted finger.*]

GWENDOLEN and CECILY [*Speaking together*]. Your Christian names are still an insuperable barrier! That is all.

JACK and ALGERNON [*Speaking together*]. Our Christian names! Is that all? But we are going to be christened this afternoon.[2]

GWENDOLEN [*To* JACK]. For my sake you are prepared to do this terrible thing?

JACK. I am.

CECILY [*To* ALGERNON]. To please me you are ready to face this fearful ordeal?

ALGERNON. I am!

GWENDOLEN. How absurd to talk of the equality of the sexes! Where questions of self-sacrifice are concerned, men are infinitely beyond us.

JACK. We are. [*Clasps hands with* ALGERNON.]

---

1 Here too is a possible allusion to *Earnest*'s "gay" subtext and humor: Gwendolen's disinclination to treat her suitor's claims skeptically saves their relationship, for were she to give in to her "German scepticism" (see *E* 82n1), their relationship could well be compromised, perhaps exposing something inimical to their romantic career—something, indeed, rather "German."

2 That Jack and Algernon speak together immediately following Gwendolen and Cecily's speaking in unison reminds us that the four are all of a sort: youthful, superficial, and somewhat rash in their emotional attachments, the young lovers offer a strong and unified counterpoint to the embodiments of traditional morality represented by the older characters in the play.

CECILY. They have moments of physical courage of which we women know absolutely nothing.

GWENDOLEN [*To* JACK]. Darling!

ALGERNON [*To* CECILY]. Darling! [*They fall into each other's arms.*]

[*Enter* MERRIMAN. *When he enters he coughs loudly, seeing the situation.*[1]]

MERRIMAN. Ahem! Ahem! Lady Bracknell!

JACK. Good heavens!

[*Enter* LADY BRACKNELL. *The couples separate in alarm. Exit* MERRIMAN.]

LADY BRACKNELL. Gwendolen! What does this mean?

GWENDOLEN. Merely that I am engaged to be married to Mr. Worthing, mamma.

LADY BRACKNELL. Come here. Sit down. Sit down immediately. Hesitation of any kind is a sign of mental decay in the young, of physical weakness in the old. [*Turns to* JACK.] Apprised, sir, of my daughter's sudden flight by her trusty maid, whose confidence I purchased by means of a small coin, I followed her at once by a luggage train. Her unhappy father is, I am glad to say, under the impression that she is attending a more than usually lengthy lecture by the University Extension Scheme on the Influence of a permanent income on Thought. I do not propose to undeceive him. Indeed I have never undeceived him on any question. I would consider it wrong. But of course, you will clearly understand that all communication between yourself and my daughter must cease

---

1 Merriman's cough echoes Algernon's throughout his dictation to Cecily when he first assumed the false role of Ernest. While Algernon's coughing probably indicates a nervous acknowledgement that he is doing something wrong, Merriman's cough reminds the young lovers that they are misbehaving. Like other incidents of echo (see the Introduction 38-42), Merriman's cough calls into sharp relief the difference between Algernon's amorous behavior with Cecily and the "earnestness" that Algernon, as Ernest, ought to embody. See also Appendix I3, 205n2 and 212n1.

immediately from this moment. On this point, as indeed on all points, I am firm.[1]

JACK. I am engaged to be married to Gwendolen, Lady Bracknell!

LADY BRACKNELL. You are nothing of the kind, sir. And now, as regards Algernon! ... Algernon!

ALGERNON. Yes, Aunt Augusta.

LADY BRACKNELL. May I ask if it is in this house that your invalid friend Mr. Bunbury resides?

ALGERNON [*Stammering*]. Oh! No! Bunbury doesn't live here. Bunbury is somewhere else at present. In fact, Bunbury is dead.

LADY BRACKNELL. Dead! When did Mr. Bunbury die? His death must have been extremely sudden.

ALGERNON [*Airily*]. Oh! I killed Bunbury this afternoon. I mean poor Bunbury died this afternoon.

LADY BRACKNELL. What did he die of?

ALGERNON. Bunbury? Oh, he was quite exploded.

LADY BRACKNELL. Exploded! Was he the victim of a revolutionary outrage?[2] I was not aware that Mr. Bunbury was interested in social legislation. If so, he is well punished for his morbidity.

ALGERNON. My dear Aunt Augusta, I mean he was found out! The doctors found out that Bunbury could not live, that is what I mean—so Bunbury died.

LADY BRACKNELL. He seems to have had great confidence in the opinion of his physicians. I am glad, however, that he made up his mind at the last to some definite course of action, and acted under proper medical advice. And now that we have finally got rid of this Mr. Bunbury, may I ask, Mr. Worthing, who is that young person whose hand my nephew Algernon is

---

1   In lines excised from the four-act version of the play, Lady Bracknell's apparent authority here would be undercut later in this same act when Jack, mocking her, exactly repeats her final phrase; see Appendix I1, 212n1.

2   Lady Bracknell's query plays into *Earnest*'s symbolic associations of nations with morals (see *E* 82n1): in aligning Bunbury with revolution (which throughout the nineteenth century usually connotes the French Revolution), Lady Bracknell casts him as colluding with chaos, with subversion, and thus she rejects him for his "morbidity," a term that suggests both ill health as well as that which inspires disgust, just as Bunbury clearly does for her.

now holding in what seems to me a peculiarly unnecessary manner?

JACK. That lady is Miss Cecily Cardew, my ward.

[LADY BRACKNELL *bows coldly to* CECILY.]

ALGERNON. I am engaged to be married to Cecily, Aunt Augusta.

LADY BRACKNELL. I beg your pardon?

CECILY. Mr. Moncrieff and I are engaged to be married, Lady Bracknell.

LADY BRACKNELL [*With a shiver, crossing to the sofa and sitting down*]. I do not know whether there is anything peculiarly exciting in the air of this part of Hertfordshire, but the number of engagements that go on seems to me considerably above the proper average that statistics have laid down for our guidance. I think some preliminary enquiries on my part would not be out of place. Mr. Worthing, is Miss Cardew at all connected with any of the larger railway stations in London? I merely desire information. Until yesterday I had no idea that there were any families or persons whose origin was a Terminus.

[JACK *looks perfectly furious, but restrains himself.*]

JACK [*In a clear, cold voice*]. Miss Cardew is the granddaughter of the late Mr. Thomas Cardew of 149, Belgrave Square, S.W.;[1] Gervase Park, Dorking, Surrey; and the Sporran, Fifeshire, N.B.[2]

LADY BRACKNELL. That sounds not unsatisfactory. Three addresses always inspire confidence, even in tradesmen. But what proof have I of their authenticity?

JACK. I have carefully preserved the Court Guides of the period. They are open to your inspection, Lady Bracknell.

LADY BRACKNELL [*Grimly*]. I have known strange errors in that publication.[3]

---

1   Another postal code, here indicating the southwestern postal region of London.

2   North Britain, or Scotland. As Robbins notes, a sporran "is an ornamental pouch of leather and fur, worn from the front of the kilt in traditional Highland dress" (34).

3   Here, as throughout *Earnest*, language is shown to be one means for conveying not only truth but, quite often, outright falsehood. Such a deconstruction of the Victorian investment in language and texts as sites

JACK. Miss Cardew's family solicitors are Messrs. Markby, Markby, and Markby.

LADY BRACKNELL. Markby, Markby, and Markby? A firm of the very highest position in their profession. Indeed I am told that one of the Mr. Markbys is occasionally to be seen at dinner parties. So far I am satisfied.

JACK [*Very irritably*]. How extremely kind of you, Lady Bracknell! I have also in my possession, you will be pleased to hear, certificates of Miss Cardew's birth, baptism, whooping cough, registration, vaccination, confirmation, and the measles; both the German and the English variety.

LADY BRACKNELL. Ah! A life crowded with incident, I see; though perhaps somewhat too exciting for a young girl. I am not myself in favour of premature experiences. [*Rises, looks at her watch*.] Gwendolen! the time approaches for our departure. We have not a moment to lose. As a matter of form, Mr. Worthing, I had better ask you if Miss Cardew has any little fortune?

JACK. Oh! about a hundred and thirty thousand pounds in the Funds.[1] That is all. Good-bye, Lady Bracknell! So pleased to have seen you.

LADY BRACKNELL [*Sitting down again*]. A moment, Mr. Worthing. A hundred and thirty thousand pounds! And in the Funds! Miss Cardew seems to me a most attractive young lady, now that I look at her. Few girls of the present day have any really solid qualities, any of the qualities that last, and improve with time. We live, I regret to say, in an age of surfaces.[2] [*To* CECILY.] Come over here, dear. [CECILY *goes across*.] Pretty

---

of truth lies at the heart of the humor of Wilde's play, since Jack and Algernon use language (false names, invented scenarios, and so on) to facilitate their Bunburying even as the play's embodiments of traditional morality (Lady Bracknell, Miss Prism, and Reverend Chasuble) hold fast to their shared faith in language as the register of truth.

1    Many well-to-do Victorians invested in "the funds," which guaranteed an annual return of three to five per cent. Such an investment would yield between £3900 and £6500 per year, somewhat less than Jack's income of £7000-£8000 per year but quite impressive nonetheless; for conversions to modern-day currency equivalents, see *E* 87n2.

2    Compare Lady Bracknell's pronouncement to Gwendolen's observation in act 1 that "we live ... in an age of ideals" (*E* 83), a contrast that reminds us of the various distinctions Wilde draws between the generations: in these examples, Gwendolen seems full of youthful optimism, whereas her mother seems the very voice of aged cynicism.

child! your dress is sadly simple, and your hair seems almost as Nature might have left it. But we can soon alter all that. A thoroughly experienced French maid produces a really marvellous result in a very brief space of time. I remember recommending one to young Lady Lancing,[1] and after three months her own husband did not know her.

JACK [*Aside*]. And after six months nobody knew her.

LADY BRACKNELL [*Glares at* JACK *for a few moments. Then bends, with a practised smile, to* CECILY]. Kindly turn round, sweet child. [CECILY *turns completely round.*] No, the side view is what I want. [CECILY *presents her profile.*] Yes, quite as I expected. There are distinct social possibilities in your profile.[2] The two weak points in our age are its want of principle and its want of profile. The chin a little higher, dear. Style largely depends on the way the chin is worn. They are worn very high, just at present. Algernon!

ALGERNON. Yes, Aunt Augusta!

LADY BRACKNELL. There are distinct social possibilities in Miss Cardew's profile.

ALGERNON. Cecily is the sweetest, dearest, prettiest girl in the whole world. And I don't care twopence about social possibilities.

LADY BRACKNELL. Never speak disrespectfully of Society, Algernon. Only people who can't get into it do that. [*To* CECILY.] Dear child, of course you know that Algernon has nothing but his debts to depend upon. But I do not approve of mercenary marriages. When I married Lord Bracknell I had no fortune of any kind. But I never dreamed for a moment of

---

1 A name retained from the title of Wilde's earlier four-act version, in which Lady Lancing serves as a version of Bunbury/Ernest in two ways: as an absent presence, invoked solely by the language of others, and as a figure of duplicity and change. In her transformation from one (kind of) woman to another, Lady Lancing becomes unrecognizable even to her husband, able to pass, so to speak, just as Jack and Algernon pass as or get by with the charade of being someone else in order to enjoy pleasures not allowed them in their respectable modes—that is, when they are "themselves."

2 Jackson references Wilde's comments on profile in his "Phrases and Philosophies for the Use of the Young": "If the poor only had profiles there would be no difficulty in solving the problem of poverty ... There is something tragic about the enormous number of young men there are in England at the present moment who start life with perfect profiles, and end by adopting some useful profession" (1244-45).

allowing that to stand in my way. Well, I suppose I must give my consent.

ALGERNON. Thank you, Aunt Augusta.

LADY BRACKNELL. Cecily, you may kiss me!

CECILY [*Kisses her*]. Thank you, Lady Bracknell.

LADY BRACKNELL. You may also address me as Aunt Augusta for the future.

CECILY. Thank you, Aunt Augusta.

LADY BRACKNELL. The marriage, I think, had better take place quite soon.

ALGERNON. Thank you, Aunt Augusta.

CECILY. Thank you, Aunt Augusta.

LADY BRACKNELL. To speak frankly, I am not in favour of long engagements. They give people the opportunity of finding out each other's character before marriage, which I think is never advisable.

JACK. I beg your pardon for interrupting you, Lady Bracknell, but this engagement is quite out of the question. I am Miss Cardew's guardian, and she cannot marry without my consent until she comes of age. That consent I absolutely decline to give.

LADY BRACKNELL. Upon what grounds may I ask? Algernon is an extremely, I may almost say an ostentatiously, eligible young man. He has nothing, but he looks everything. What more can one desire?

JACK. It pains me very much to have to speak frankly to you, Lady Bracknell, about your nephew, but the fact is that I do not approve at all of his moral character. I suspect him of being untruthful.

[ALGERNON *and* CECILY *look at him in indignant amazement.*]

LADY BRACKNELL. Untruthful! My nephew Algernon? Impossible! He is an Oxonian.[1]

---

1   Traditionally, alumni of Oxford University—"Oxonians"—were regarded as embodiments of culture and respectability; however, as Linda S. Dowling argues in *Hellenism and Homosexuality in Victorian Oxford*, by the late nineteenth century, the very public debates over Oxford's curriculum—specifically, whether classical studies glorified and encouraged same-sex "Platonic" relations between undergraduates—effectively unhinged Oxford from its position of respectability by re-defining the university as a dangerous, ambiguous site of learning and practice and thus characterizing its students as decadents and degenerates.

JACK. I fear there can be no possible doubt about the matter. This afternoon, during my temporary absence in London on an important question of romance, he obtained admission to my house by means of the false pretence of being my brother. Under an assumed name he drank, I've just been informed by my butler, an entire pint bottle of my Perrier-Jouet, Brut, '89; a wine I was specially reserving for myself.[1] Continuing his disgraceful deception, he succeeded in the course of the afternoon in alienating the affections of my only ward. He subsequently stayed to tea, and devoured every single muffin. And what makes his conduct all the more heartless is, that he was perfectly well aware from the first that I have no brother, that I never had a brother, and that I don't intend to have a brother, not even of any kind. I distinctly told him so myself yesterday afternoon.

LADY BRACKNELL. Ahem! Mr. Worthing, after careful consideration I have decided entirely to overlook my nephew's conduct to you.

JACK. That is very generous of you, Lady Bracknell. My own decision, however, is unalterable. I decline to give my consent.

LADY BRACKNELL [*To* CECILY]. Come here, sweet child. [CECILY *goes over.*] How old are you, dear?

CECILY. Well, I am really only eighteen, but I always admit to twenty when I go to evening parties.

LADY BRACKNELL. You are perfectly right in making some slight alteration. Indeed, no woman should ever be quite accurate about her age. It looks so calculating.... [*In a meditative manner.*] Eighteen, but admitting to twenty at evening parties. Well, it will not be very long before you are of age and free from the restraints of tutelage. So I don't think your guardian's consent is, after all, a matter of any importance.[2]

JACK. Pray excuse me, Lady Bracknell, for interrupting you again, but it is only fair to tell you that according to the terms

---

1   According to Raby, Perrier-Jouet was "a favorite drink of Wilde and Douglas" (*EOP* 367).

2   Uncharacteristically, Lady Bracknell implies that what is *not* important is authority and its embodiments, a notion suggested by Wilde's ironic titling of *The Importance of Being Earnest* as *A Trivial Comedy for Serious People.* Wilde lampooned earnestness in a similar way in *A Woman of No Importance,* as Donohue and Berggren observe (119n): Lord Illingworth opines that "One should never take sides in anything.... Taking sides is the beginning of sincerity, and earnestness follows shortly afterwards, and the human being becomes a bore" (471).

of her grandfather's will Miss Cardew does not come legally of age till she is thirty-five.

LADY BRACKNELL. That does not seem to me to be a grave objection. Thirty-five is a very attractive age. London society is full of women of the very highest birth who have, of their own free choice, remained thirty-five for years. Lady Dumbleton is an instance in point. To my own knowledge she has been thirty-five ever since she arrived at the age of forty, which was many years ago now. I see no reason why our dear Cecily should not be even still more attractive at the age you mention than she is at present. There will be a large accumulation of property.

CECILY. Algy, could you wait for me till I was thirty-five?

ALGERNON. Of course I could, Cecily. You know I could.

CECILY. Yes, I felt it instinctively, but I couldn't wait all that time. I hate waiting even five minutes for anybody. It always makes me rather cross. I am not punctual myself, I know, but I do like punctuality in others, and waiting, even to be married, is quite out of the question.

ALGERNON. Then what is to be done, Cecily?

CECILY. I don't know, Mr. Moncrieff.

LADY BRACKNELL. My dear Mr. Worthing, as Miss Cardew states positively that she cannot wait till she is thirty-five—a remark which I am bound to say seems to me to show a some-what impatient nature—I would beg of you to reconsider your decision.

JACK. But my dear Lady Bracknell, the matter is entirely in your own hands. The moment you consent to my marriage with Gwendolen, I will most gladly allow your nephew to form an alliance with my ward.[1]

LADY BRACKNELL [*Rising and drawing herself up*]. You must be quite aware that what you propose is out of the question.

JACK. Then a passionate celibacy is all that any of us can look forward to.

LADY BRACKNELL. That is not the destiny I propose for Gwendolen. Algernon, of course, can choose for himself. [*Pulls out her watch.*] Come, dear; [GWENDOLEN *rises*] we have

---

1 Another instance of the play's verbal echonomy: compare this to Lady Bracknell's language to Jack in act 1 refusing his request for Gwendolen's hand in marriage, in which she tells him that he cannot expect her or her husband to allow their daughter "to marry into a cloak-room, and form an alliance with a parcel" (*E* 90).

already missed five, if not six, trains. To miss any more might expose us to comment on the platform.

[*Enter* DR. CHASUBLE.]

CHASUBLE. Everything is quite ready for the christenings.

LADY BRACKNELL. The christenings, sir! Is not that somewhat premature?

CHASUBLE [*Looking rather puzzled, and pointing to* JACK *and* ALGERNON]. Both these gentlemen have expressed a desire for immediate baptism.

LADY BRACKNELL. At their age? The idea is grotesque and irreligious! Algernon, I forbid you to be baptised. I will not hear of such excesses.[1] Lord Bracknell would be highly displeased if he learned that that was the way in which you wasted your time and money.

CHASUBLE. Am I to understand then that there are to be no christenings at all this afternoon?

JACK. I don't think that, as things are now, it would be of much practical value to either of us, Dr. Chasuble.

CHASUBLE. I am grieved to hear such sentiments from you, Mr. Worthing. They savour of the heretical views of the Anabaptists,[2] views that I have completely refuted in four of my unpublished sermons. However, as your present mood seems to be one peculiarly secular, I will return to the church at once. Indeed, I have just been informed by the pew-opener that for the last hour and a half Miss Prism has been waiting for me in the vestry.

---

1   In this example of the play's verbal echonomy, Lady Bracknell's language echoes her insistence in act 1 that the circumstances of Jack's dubious upbringing "remind one of the worst excesses of the French Revolution" (*E* 89). By echoing only one key word, not an entire phrase, and a word of her own rather than one borrowed from a speech of another character, Lady Bracknell retains the authority she has claimed throughout the play. See the Introduction 38-42.

2   Anabaptists were a fundamentalist Protestant sect who practiced what was commonly called "believer's baptism," through which a young person or an adult offered a public demonstration of faith in Christian salvation. Chasuble's response to Jack's decision not to be baptized implies his condescension for those who regard baptism as primarily a public act, as something privileging "practical value" over spiritual meaningfulness.

LADY BRACKNELL [*Starting*]. Miss Prism! Did I hear you mention a Miss Prism?

CHASUBLE. Yes, Lady Bracknell. I am on my way to join her.

LADY BRACKNELL. Pray allow me to detain you for a moment. This matter may prove to be one of vital importance to Lord Bracknell and myself. Is this Miss Prism a female of repellent aspect, remotely connected with education?

CHASUBLE [*Somewhat indignantly*]. She is the most cultivated of ladies, and the very picture of respectability.

LADY BRACKNELL. It is obviously the same person. May I ask what position she holds in your household?

CHASUBLE [*Severely*]. I am a celibate, madam.

JACK [*Interposing*]. Miss Prism, Lady Bracknell, has been for the last three years Miss Cardew's esteemed governess and valued companion.

LADY BRACKNELL. In spite of what I hear of her, I must see her at once. Let her be sent for.

CHASUBLE [*Looking off*]. She approaches; she is nigh.

[*Enter* MISS PRISM *hurriedly.*]

MISS PRISM. I was told you expected me in the vestry, dear Canon. I have been waiting for you there for an hour and three quarters. [*Catches sight of* LADY BRACKNELL *who has fixed her with a stony glare.* MISS PRISM *grows pale and quails. She looks anxiously round as if desirous to escape.*]

LADY BRACKNELL [*In a severe, judicial voice*]. Prism! [MISS PRISM *bows her head in shame.*] Come here, Prism! [MISS PRISM *approaches in a humble manner.*] Prism! Where is that baby? [*General consternation.* THE CANON *starts back in horror.* ALGERNON *and* JACK *pretend to be anxious to shield* CECILY *and* GWENDOLEN *from hearing the details of a terrible public scandal.*] Twenty-eight years ago, Prism, you left Lord Bracknell's house, Number 104, Upper Grosvenor Street, in charge of a perambulator that contained a baby, of the male sex. You never returned. A few weeks later, through the elaborate investigations of the Metropolitan police, the perambulator was discovered at midnight, standing by itself in a remote corner of Bayswater.[1] It contained the manuscript of a three-volume novel of more than usually revolting sentimentality. [MISS PRISM *starts in involuntary indignation.*] But the baby was not

---

1 Leeming describes Bayswater as "an area of West London, not at all fashionable" at the time of Wilde's play (83).

there! [*Everyone looks at* MISS PRISM.] Prism! Where is that baby? [*A pause.*]

MISS PRISM. Lady Bracknell, I admit with shame that I do not know. I only wish I did. The plain facts of the case are these. On the morning of the day you mention, a day that is for ever branded on my memory, I prepared as usual to take the baby out in its perambulator. I had also with me a somewhat old, but capacious hand-bag in which I had intended to place the manuscript of a work of fiction that I had written during my few unoccupied hours. In a moment of mental abstraction, for which I never can forgive myself, I deposited the manuscript in the bassinette, and placed the baby in the hand-bag.

JACK [*Who has been listening attentively*]. But where did you deposit the hand-bag?

MISS PRISM. Do not ask me, Mr. Worthing.

JACK. Miss Prism, this is a matter of no small importance to me.[1] I insist on knowing where you deposited the hand-bag that contained that infant.

MISS PRISM. I left it in the cloak-room of one of the larger railway stations in London.

JACK. What railway station?

MISS PRISM [*Quite crushed*]. Victoria. The Brighton line. [*Sinks into a chair.*]

JACK. I must retire to my room for a moment. Gwendolen, wait here for me.

GWENDOLEN. If you are not too long, I will wait here for you all my life.

[*Exit* JACK *in great excitement.*]

CHASUBLE. What do you think this means, Lady Bracknell?

LADY BRACKNELL. I dare not even suspect, Dr. Chasuble. I need hardly tell you that in families of high position strange coincidences are not supposed to occur. They are hardly considered the thing.

[*Noises heard overhead as if someone was throwing trunks about. Everyone looks up.*]

---

1  Jack's phrase invokes the play's subtitle: what is important is not the known, the evident, but the unknown, the secret—a move that converts "Earnest"-ness from a visible quality (surface) to a hidden one (depth), from what may be seen to what has been, in effect, closeted (see the Introduction 21-23).

CECILY. Uncle Jack seems strangely agitated.

CHASUBLE. Your guardian has a very emotional nature.

LADY BRACKNELL. This noise is extremely unpleasant. It sounds as if he was having an argument. I dislike arguments of any kind. They are always vulgar, and often convincing.

CHASUBLE [*Looking up*]. It has stopped now. [*The noise is redoubled.*]

LADY BRACKNELL. I wish he would arrive at some conclusion.

GWENDOLEN. This suspense is terrible. I hope it will last.

[*Enter* JACK *with a hand-bag of black leather in his hand.*]

JACK [*Rushing over to* MISS PRISM]. Is this the hand-bag, Miss Prism? Examine it carefully before you speak. The happiness of more than one life depends on your answer.

MISS PRISM [*Calmly*]. It seems to be mine. Yes, here is the injury it received through the upsetting of a Gower Street omnibus in younger and happier days.[1] Here is the stain on the lining caused by the explosion of a temperance beverage, an incident that occurred at Leamington. And here, on the lock, are my initials. I had forgotten that in an extravagant mood I had had them placed there. The bag is undoubtedly mine. I am delighted to have it so unexpectedly restored to me. It has been a great inconvenience being without it all these years.

JACK [*In a pathetic voice*]. Miss Prism, more is restored to you than this hand-bag. I was the baby you placed in it.

MISS PRISM [*Amazed*]. You?

JACK [*Embracing her*]. Yes ... mother!

MISS PRISM [*Recoiling in indignant astonishment*]. Mr. Worthing! I am unmarried!

JACK. Unmarried! I do not deny that is a serious blow. But after all, who has the right to cast a stone against one who has suffered?[2] Cannot repentance wipe out an act of folly? Why

---

1  Raby observes that Gower Street is the location of both London University and the British Museum, which he characterizes as "suitable associations for Miss Prism" (*EOP* 368).

2  As Jackson notes, this phrase draws from a well-known Biblical maxim recording the teachings of Jesus Christ: "He that is without sin among you, let him first cast a stone [at the adulteress]" (John 8.7).

should there be one law for men, and another for women?[1] Mother, I forgive you. [*Tries to embrace her again.*]

MISS PRISM [*Still more indignant*]. Mr. Worthing, there is some error. [*Pointing to* LADY BRACKNELL.] There is the lady who can tell you who you really are.

JACK [*After a pause*]. Lady Bracknell, I hate to seem inquisitive, but would you kindly inform me who I am?

LADY BRACKNELL. I am afraid that the news I have to give you will not altogether please you. You are the son of my poor sister, Mrs. Moncrieff, and consequently Algernon's elder brother.[2]

JACK. Algy's elder brother! Then I have a brother after all. I knew I had a brother! I always said I had a brother! Cecily,—how could you have ever doubted that I had a brother. [*Seizes hold of* ALGERNON.] Dr. Chasuble, my unfortunate brother. Miss Prism, my unfortunate brother. Gwendolen, my unfortunate brother. Algy, you young scoundrel, you will have to treat me with more respect in the future. You have never behaved to me like a brother in all your life.

ALGERNON. Well, not till to-day, old boy, I admit. I did my best, however, though I was out of practice. [*Shakes hands.*]

GWENDOLEN [*To* JACK]. My own! But what own are you? What is your Christian name, now that you have become someone else?

JACK. Good heavens! ... I had quite forgotten that point. Your decision on the subject of my name is irrevocable, I suppose?

GWENDOLEN. I never change, except in my affections.

CECILY. What a noble nature you have, Gwendolen!

JACK. Then the question had better be cleared up at once. Aunt

---

1   Jackson reads this line alongside one of Hester's speeches in *A Woman of No Importance*: "Don't have one law for men and another for women" (483). Wilde offers an earlier version of this claim in *Lady Windermere's Fan* when Lord Darlington asks Lady Windermere, "Do you think that there should be the same laws for men as there are for women? ... I think life too complex a thing to be settled by these hard and fast rules" (423). The theme of sexual double-standards recurs throughout Wilde's work, forming pivotal moments in all four of his major comedies.

2   Lady Bracknell draws on language's performative power, speaking Jack into existence as Ernest—an existence Jack had already been enjoying for some time by way of his duplicitous use of the language of falsehood and secrecy, themselves the very opposite of Lady Bracknell's language of truth and revelation.

Augusta, a moment. At the time when Miss Prism left me in the hand-bag, had I been christened already?

LADY BRACKNELL. Every luxury that money could buy, including christening, had been lavished on you by your fond and doting parents.

JACK. Then I was christened! That is settled. Now, what name was I given? Let me know the worst.

LADY BRACKNELL. Being the eldest son you were naturally christened after your father.

JACK [*Irritably*]. Yes, but what was my father's Christian name?

LADY BRACKNELL [*Meditatively*]. I cannot at the present moment recall what the General's Christian name was. But I have no doubt he had one. He was eccentric, I admit. But only in later years. And that was the result of the Indian climate, and marriage, and indigestion, and other things of that kind.

JACK. Algy! Can't you recollect what our father's Christian name was?

ALGERNON. My dear boy, we were never even on speaking terms. He died before I was a year old.

JACK. His name would appear in the Army Lists[1] of the period, I suppose, Aunt Augusta?

LADY BRACKNELL. The General was essentially a man of peace, except in his domestic life. But I have no doubt his name would appear in any military directory.

JACK. The Army Lists of the last forty years are here. These delightful records should have been my constant study. [*Rushes to bookcase and tears the books out.*] M. Generals.... Mallam, Maxbohm,[2] Magley, what ghastly names they have—Markby, Migsby, Mobbs, Moncrieff! Lieutenant 1840, Captain, Lieutenant-Colonel, Colonel, General 1869, Christian names, Ernest John. [*Puts book very quietly down and speaks quite*

---

1 Quarterly government publications that recorded the names of officers, their regiments, and the dates of their commissions and retirements. In the four-act version, Jack distributes a comically eclectic set of books that includes one significant title, *The Green Carnation*—a real book, a venomous and thinly veiled attack on Wilde and his social-sexual circle, penned by Robert Hichens and published in 1894 (see *E* 69n1 and Appendix I1, 201n4).

2 Wilde's play contains a number of references to people who populated his life. Most agree that "Maxbohm" is a condensed version of Max Beerbohm, the theatre critic and caricaturist who sometimes portrayed Wilde to savage effect.

*calmly.*] I always told you, Gwendolen, my name was Ernest, didn't I? Well, it is Ernest after all. I mean it naturally is Ernest.

LADY BRACKNELL. Yes, I remember now that the General was called Ernest. I knew I had some particular reason for disliking the name.

GWENDOLEN. Ernest! My own Ernest! I felt from the first that you could have had no other name!

JACK. Gwendolen, it is a terrible thing for a man to find out suddenly that all his life he has been speaking nothing but the truth. Can you forgive me?

GWENDOLEN. I can. For I feel that you are sure to change.

JACK. My own one!

CHASUBLE [*To* MISS PRISM]. Lætitia! [*Embraces her.*]

MISS PRISM [*Enthusiastically*]. Frederick! At last!

ALGERNON. Cecily! [*Embraces her.*] At last!

JACK. Gwendolen! [*Embraces her.*] At last!

LADY BRACKNELL. My nephew, you seem to be displaying signs of triviality.

JACK. On the contrary, Aunt Augusta, I've now realised for the first time in my life the vital Importance of Being Earnest.[1]

TABLEAU.

CURTAIN.

---

1 Wilde punctuates Jack's final speech not only by closing with the play's title but also by celebrating its resolute absurdity with the intensifier "vital." As Christopher Craft argues, "the last words of the play swallow the first words of its title, [the play's] origin therefore dutifully assigned to a terminus" (34). The play's beginning, like the beginning of the married lives of its three couples, may thus be found only at the end of *Earnest*—and, significantly, at the end of earnestness itself.

# *Appendix A: Playbills for* The Importance of Being Earnest *(1895)*

[The playbills for *The Importance of Being Earnest* produced for the St. James's Theatre remind us of the enormous effect of Wilde's arrest on the playwright's reputation and legacy. The original playbill listed Wilde's name as playwright just below the play's title. Immediately following his arrest, however, Wilde's name was removed from all organs of publicity, as we see in the second playbill, produced during the final week of *Earnest*'s initial run. The second playbill almost exactly duplicates the original, with two exceptions: the play's production schedule has been updated, and—much more importantly—Wilde's name has been removed from the line beneath the play's title. Apparently, Victorians might still enjoy the author's work but felt a need to distance themselves from any appearance of support for its author and from any association with his tainted name.]

**1. The First, Uncensored Playbill. From Ellmann, *Oscar Wilde***

# ST. JAMES'S THEATRE.

SOLE LESSEE AND PROPRIETOR · · MR. GEORGE ALEXANDER.

PRODUCED THURSDAY, FEBRUARY 14th. 1895.

Every Evening at 9,

# The Importance of being Earnest,

A TRIVIAL COMEDY FOR SERIOUS PEOPLE,

## BY OSCAR WILDE.

| | | |
|---|---|---|
| John Worthing, J.P. | of the Manor House, Woolton, Hertfordshire | Mr. GEORGE ALEXANDER |
| Algernon Moncrieffe | (his Friend) | Mr. ALLAN AYNESWORTH |
| Rev. Canon Chasuble, D.D. | (Rector of Woolton) | Mr. H. H. VINCENT |
| Merriman | (Butler to Mr. Worthing) | Mr. FRANK DYALL |
| Lane | (Mr. Moncrieffe's Man-servant) | Mr. F. KINSEY PEILE |
| Lady Bracknell | | Miss ROSE LECLERCQ (By permission of Mr. J. COMYNS CARR.) |
| Hon. Gwendolen Fairfax | (her Daughter) | Miss IRENE VANBRUGH |
| Cecily Cardew | (John Worthing's Ward) | Miss VIOLET LYSTER |
| Miss Prism | (her Governess) | Mrs GEORGE CANNINGE |

**Time · · The Present.**

| | | |
|---|---|---|
| Act I. | Algernon Moncrieffe's Rooms in Piccadilly | (*H. P. Hall*) |
| Act II. | The Garden at the Manor House, Woolton | (*H. P. Hall*) |
| Act III. | Morning-Room at the Manor House, Woolton | (*Walter Hann*) |

Preceded, at 8.30, by a Play in One Act, by LANGDON E. MITCHELL, entitled

## IN THE SEASON.

| | |
|---|---|
| Sir Harry Collingwood | Mr. HERBERT WARING |
| Edward Fairburne | Mr. ARTHUR ROYSTON |
| Sybil March | Miss ELLIOTT PAGE |

Scene - A Room in Sir Harry Collingwood's House. Time - The Present.

**2. The Second, Censored Playbill. From** *Oscar Wilde: Trial and Punishment 1895-1897*

# ST. JAMES'S THEATRE.

SOLE LESSEE AND PROPRIETOR - - MR. GEORGE ALEXANDER.

PRODUCED THURSDAY, FEBRUARY 14th, 1895.

### Every Evening at 9 (Last Nights)

# The Importance of being Earnest,

A TRIVIAL COMEDY FOR SERIOUS PEOPLE.

| | | |
|---|---|---|
| John Worthing, J.P. { of the Manor House, Woolton, Hertfordshire } | | Mr. GEORGE ALEXANDER |
| Algernon Moncrieffe . (his Friend) . | | Mr. ALLAN AYNESWORTH |
| Rev. Canon Chasuble, D.D. . (Rector of Woolton) . | | Mr. H. H. VINCENT |
| Merriman . . (Butler to Mr. Worthing) . | | Mr. FRANK DYALL |
| Lane . . (Mr. Moncrieffe's Man-servant) . | | Mr. F. KINSEY PEILE |
| Lady Bracknell . . . . . . | | Mrs. EDWARD SAKER |
| Hon. Gwendolen Fairfax . (her Daughter) . | | Miss IRENE VANBRUGH |
| Cecily Cardew . (John Worthing's Ward) | | Miss ~~EVELYN MILLARD~~ *Violet Lyster* |
| Miss Prism . . (her Governess) . . | | Mrs GEORGE CANNINGE |

Time - - The Present.

Act I. - Algernon Moncrieffe's Rooms In Piccadilly (*H. P. Hall*)
Act II. - The Garden at the Manor House, Woolton (*H. P. Hall*)
Act III. - Morning-Room at the Manor House, Woolton (*Walter Hann*)

Preceded, at 8.30, by a Play in One Act, by LANGDON E. MITCHELL, entitled

## IN THE SEASON.

Sir Harry Collingwood . . . . Mr. HERBERT WARING
Edward Fairburne . . . . . Mr. ARTHUR ROYSTON
Sybil March . . . . . Miss ELLIOTT PAGE

Scene - A Room in Sir Harry Collingwood's House. Time - The Present.

# Appendix B: Reactions and Reviews

[Five reactions to and reviews of the London première of *Earnest* are excerpted below. Collectively, these provide a multi-faceted picture of the ways in which audiences received Wilde's play. These include glowing reviews from *The Daily Graphic* and *The World*; a mixed review from *The Observer*; a largely negative, dismissive review from *The Times*; and a quite caustic account of the play by Bernard Shaw. A final excerpt, from Max Beerbohm's recollection of the opening night of *Earnest*'s 1902 revival, provides a sense of the place Wilde had come to occupy in the cultural imagination just a short time after his imprisonment and death. Despite Shaw's somewhat hostile reaction to *Earnest*, he received a presentation copy of the first edition of Wilde's play (Dickson 1: xxiii). Beerbohm and William Archer, whose comments are among those excerpted below, also received presentation copies of the first edition of the play (Dickson 1: xxiii). Throughout the excerpts, original punctuation has been maintained.]

## 1. From *The Daily Graphic* (15 February 1895). Rpt. in Tydeman, 63-64

The empire of Mr Gilbert over Topseyturveydom is at last successfully challenged, and Mr Wilde may claim to reign

> Beyond dispute
> O'er all the realms of nonsense absolute.[1]

His three-act novelty at the St James's Theatre, announced as "a trivial comedy for serious people", is a veritable specimen of what, in a more propitious season, might be called midsummer madness. It has not a relish of reason or sparkle of sanity; it is absurd, preposterous, extravagant, idiotic, saucy, brilliantly clever, and unedifyingly diverting. The idea on which Voltaire constructed his *Ingénu*, that of an innocent and guileless savage speaking the truth in all presences and under all conditions—a notion subsequently elaborated upon by Mr Gilbert in the *Palace of Truth*—is once more employed. This time, however, everybody speaks truth through no magical influence of place, but through a hardened belief that what they think, do, and say is the same as is thought, done and said by the rest of the world.

---

1 William Tydeman notes that this line is taken from John Dryden's 1682 poem *Mac Flecknoe* (66n).

## 2. From William Archer, *The World* (20 February 1895). Rpt. in Tydeman, 66

It is delightful to see, it sends wave after wave of laughter curling and foaming round the theatre; but as a text for criticism it is barren and delusive. It is like a mirage-oasis in the desert, grateful and comforting to the weary eye—but when you come close up to it, behold! it is intangible, it eludes your grasp. What can a poor critic do with a play which raises no principle, whether of art or morals, creates its own canons and conventions, and is nothing but an absolutely wilful expression of an irrepressibly witty personality? Mr Pater, I think (or is it someone else?), has an essay on the tendency of all art to verge towards, and merge in, the absolute art—music. He might have found an example in *The Importance of Being Earnest*, which imitates nothing, represents nothing, means nothing, is nothing, except a sort of *rondo capriccioso*,[1] in which the artist's fingers run with crisp irresponsibility up and down the keyboard of life. Why attempt to analyse and class such a play? Its theme, in other hands, would have made a capital farce; but "farce" is too gross and commonplace a word to apply to such an iridescent filament of fantasy. Incidents of the same nature as Algy Moncrieff's "Bunburying" and John Worthing's invention and subsequent suppression of his scapegrace brother Ernest have done duty in many a French vaudeville and English adaptation; but Mr Wilde's humour transmutes them into something entirely new and individual. Amid so much that is negative, however, criticism may find one positive remark to make. Behind all Mr Wilde's whim and even perversity, there lurks a very genuine science, or perhaps I should say instinct, of the theatre. In all his plays, and certainly not least in this one, the story is excellently told and illustrated with abundance of scenic detail. Monsieur Sarcey[2] himself (if Mr Wilde will forgive my saying so) would "chortle in his joy"[3] over John Worthing's entrance in deep mourning (even down to his cane) to announce the death of his brother Ernest, when we know that Ernest in the flesh—a false but undeniable Ernest—is at that moment in the house making love to Cecily. The audience does not instantly awaken to the meaning of his

---

1   An instrumental selection with extensive repetitions ("rondo"), played in a lively and spontaneous ("capriccioso") style.

2   Tydeman describes Sarcey (1827-99) as "a highly exacting French dramatic critic" (66n).

3   A phrase taken from Lewis Carroll's famous mock-heroic ballad *Jabberwocky*, first published in *Through the Looking Glass and What Alice Found There* (1872).

inky suit, but even as he marches solemnly down the stage, and before a word is spoken, you can feel the idea kindling from row to row, until a "sudden glory" of laughter fills the theatre. It is only the born playwright who can imagine and work up to such an effect.

### 3. From *The Observer* (17 February 1895). Rpt. in Tydeman, 65

*The Importance of Being Earnest*, which is the awkward name of the new play by Mr Oscar Wilde, just produced with so much success by Mr George Alexander, is a title wherein lies concealed one of its author's characteristic jokes. Of course, Mr Wilde does not really mean that it is important to be earnest; he would be much more likely to urge the importance of being frivolous. He employs the adjective "earnest" by way of a pun upon the Christian name "Ernest", whereby a couple of eccentric, if attractive, girls are anxious to call their future husbands. It does not strike us as a particularly good joke, or one altogether worthy of the bright piece of nonsense to which it belongs. But at any rate it suggests clearly enough that in his latest work Mr Oscar Wilde has deliberately abandoned what he believes to be the methods of genuine comedy for those of avowed farce. He has provided a fresh, and to our way of thinking, a far more appropriate medium for the humour typified in the quasi-epigrams which he places in the mouths of all his *dramatis personae*, old men and maidens, lords and ladies, masters and servants indiscriminately. He has devised extravagant motives and extravagant proceedings to match their extravagant style of conversation and views of life. He has in fact accepted the situation, and since the public has shown itself most appreciative of his efforts as a drawing-room jester he has determined to jest without any laborious pretence of being serious. The plot on which Mr Wilde here hangs his airy witticisms and his favourite contradictions of accepted axioms is as slight as the web which may serve as setting for drops of dew. His epigrammatic heroes in the irreproachable frock-coats of contemporary civilisation are creations as fanciful as any clown who ever donned the motley. His ladylike heroines, with the diaries in which they take down their lovers' proposals from dictation, are as frankly creatures of burlesque as though they wore the garb of fairy queens and spoke in couplets of limping rhyme. The only two persons in the play who bear any relationship to comedy as distinguished from Gilbertian extravagance are the cynical dowager Lady Bracknell and the cynical manservant Lane ..., and even with these it is noticeable that their respective utterances of cynicism are in precisely the same key. But if the characters of Mr Wilde's "trivial comedy for serious people" all talk exactly alike it must be admitted that their talk is extremely entertaining, until through the monotony of its strain it becomes just a trifle wearisome.

## 4. From *The Times* (15 February 1895)

From serious comedy or frivolous drama Mr Oscar Wilde has passed to farce, a piece of this description being produced in his name last night at the St James's Theatre, under the title of *The Importance of Being Earnest....* It may only be the result of custom, but Mr Oscar Wilde's peculiar view of epigram does not accord too well with flippant action. Its proper setting is among serious people, in the drawing-room after dinner, or so at least we have been taught to think. In a farce it gives one the sensation of drinking wine out of the wrong sort of glass; it conveys to the palate a new sensation which in the end, however, is discovered to be not unpleasing. The public took very kindly last night to this further instalment of Mr Oscar Wilde's humour, and there is now little prospect of its true nature being discovered, until some one attempts to translate it into French. Whether in farce or drama, plot continues to be Mr Oscar Wilde's most vulnerable point. The story of this latest production is, indeed, almost too preposterous to go without music. Yet it sets a keynote of extravagance, which, being taken up by the actors, is speedily communicated to the house, and the result is an harmonious whole which is not unlikely to entertain the public of St James's for many months to come.

## 5. From Bernard Shaw, *Saturday Review* (1895). Rpt. in *Our Theatres in the Nineties*, 3 vols. (London: Constable and Company, 1932) 1: 41-44

I cannot say that I greatly cared for The Importance of Being Earnest. It amused me, of course; but unless comedy touches me as well as amuses me, it leaves me with a sense of having wasted my evening. I go to the theatre to be moved to laughter, not to be tickled or bustled into it; and that is why, though I laugh as much as anybody at a farcical comedy, I am out of spirits before the end of the second act, and out of temper before the end of the third, my miserable mechanical laughter intensifying these symptoms at every outburst. If the public ever becomes intelligent enough to know when it is really enjoying itself and when it is not, there will be an end of farcical comedy. Now in The Importance of Being Earnest there is plenty of this rib-tickling: for instance, the lies, the deceptions, the cross purposes, the sham mourning, the christening of the two grown-up men, the muffin eating, and so forth. These could only have been raised from the farcical plane by making them occur to characters who had, like Don Quixote, convinced us of their reality and obtained some hold on our sympathy. But that unfortunate moment of Gilbertism breaks our belief in the humanity of the play. Thus we are thrown back on the force and daintiness of its wit, brought home by an exquisitely grave, natural, and unconscious execution on the part of the actors. Alas! the latter is not forthcoming.... On the whole I must decline to accept The Importance of Being Earnest as a day less than ten years old; and I am altogether unable to perceive any uncommon excellence in its presentation.

### 6. From Max Beerbohm's Recollection of the Opening Night of the 1902 Revival of *The Importance of Being Earnest*, Collected in *Around Theatres*, 2 vols. (New York: Alfred A. Knopf, 1930). Rpt. in Popkin, 136–39

Last week, at the St. James', was revived "The Importance of Being Earnest," after an abeyance of exactly seven years—those seven years which, according to scientists, change every molecule in the human body, leaving nothing of what was there before. And yet to me the play came out fresh and exquisite as ever, and over the whole house almost every line was sending ripples of laughter—cumulative ripples that became waves, and receded only for fear of drowning the next line. In kind the play always was unlike any other, and in its kind it still seems perfect. I do not wonder that now the critics boldly call it a classic, and predict immortality. And (timorous though I am apt to be in prophecy) I join gladly in their chorus.... Mr. Wilde was a master in selection of words, and his words must not be amended.... Before we try to define how it should be acted, let us try to define its character. In scheme, of course, it is a hackneyed farce—the story of a young man coming up to London "on the spree," and of another young man going down conversely to the country, and of the complications that ensue. In treatment, also, it is farcical, in so far as some of the fun depends on absurd "situations," "stage-business," and so forth. Thus one might assume that the best way to act it would be to rattle through it. That were [*sic*] a gross error. For, despite the scheme of the play, the fun depends mainly on what the characters say, rather than on what they do.

# Appendix C: Ada Leverson's "The Advisability of Not Being Brought Up in a Handbag" (1895)

[One of Wilde's greatest and most constant friends and among the very few who stood by him following his release from prison, Ada Leverson was affectionately called "Sphinx" by Wilde, and it is she who, upon viewing with Wilde the extraordinary book of poems entitled *Silverpoints* by John Gray, famously suggested that Wilde write the perfect Aesthetic book, one of all margin. In the brief piece below, taken from the 2 March 1895 issue of *Punch; or, The London Charivari* and reproduced here in full, Leverson borrows from the plot and characters of Wilde's play, and she adds to the mix another of Wilde's personages, Dorian Gray, that notorious embodiment of the so-called Decadence and aberrant desires many readers associated with the book and its title character.

The inclusion of Dorian among Leverson's cast of characters heightens the homosexual subtext that lurks throughout *Earnest,* which is discussed at greater length in the Introduction (42-43 and 47-49). Dorian's assuming the role of the arranger of music for Aunt Augusta's party, a responsibility given to Algernon in act 1 of Wilde's play (*E* 81-82; see also *E* 82n1), underscores the coded nature of Aunt Augusta's references to German music. Algy's evasive—and thus not completely believable—remark to "Cicely," as it is spelled throughout, that he would rather spend time with her than dine at Willis's, also contributes to the homosocial context of Leverson's "Advisability," and although Wilde's play clearly serves as the major impetus for Leverson's spoof, one cannot but speculate that her knowledge of Wilde's private life also informs the erotic dynamics of this piece. Wilde's telegram, dated 15 February 1895, the day after *Earnest*'s première, indicates the delight he took in the title of his good friend's foray into *Earnest*'s playful, suggestive world. Original capitalization has been preserved throughout Leverson's short play.]

1. **Ada Leverson, "The Advisability of Not Being Brought Up in a Handbag,"** *Punch; or, The London Charivari* **(2 March 1895): 107**

THE ADVISABILITY OF NOT BEING BROUGHT UP IN A HANDBAG: A TRIVIAL TRAGEDY FOR WONDERFUL PEOPLE. (*Fragment found between the St. James's and Haymarket Theatres.*)

AUNT AUGUSTA (*an Aunt*).
COUSIN CICELY[1] (*a Ward*).
ALGY (*a Flutterpate*).
DORIAN (*a Button-hole*).
THE DUKE OF BERWICK.

TIME—*The other day. The* SCENE *is in a garden, and begins and ends with relations.*

*Algy* (*eating cucumber-sandwiches*). Do you know, Aunt AUGUSTA, I am afraid I shall not be able to come to your dinner tonight, after all. My friend BUNBURY has had a relapse, and my place is by his side.

*Aunt Augusta* (*drinking tea*). Really, ALGY! It will put my table out dreadfully. And who will arrange my music?

*Dorian. I* will arrange your music, Aunt AUGUSTA. I know all about music. I have an extraordinary collection of musical instruments. I give curious concerts every Wednesday in a long latticed room where wild gipsies tear mad music from little zithers, and I have brown Algerians who beat monotonously upon copper drums. Besides, I have set myself to music. And it has not marred me. I am still the same. More so, if anything.

*Cicely*. Shall you *like* dining at WILLIS'S with Mr. DORIAN to-night, Cousin ALGY?

*Algy* (*evasively*). It's much nicer being here with you, Cousin CICELY.

*Aunt Augusta*. Sweet child! I see distinct social probabilities in her profile. Mr. DORIAN has a beautiful nature. And it is *such* a blessing to think that he was not brought up in a handbag, like so many young men of the present day.

---

1  The misspelling of *Earnest*'s "Cecily" is perhaps Punch's error or perhaps Leverson's; at any rate; it appears as such throughout the original.

*Algy*. It is such a blessing, Aunt AUGUSTA, that a woman always grows exactly like her aunt. It is such a curse that a man never grows exactly like his uncle. It is the greatest tragedy of modern life.

*Dorian*. To be really modern one should have no soul. To be really mediæval one should have no cigarettes. To be really Greek——

[*The* Duke of BERWICK *rises in a marked manner, and leaves the garden.*]

*Cicely* (*writes in her diary, and then reads aloud dreamily*). "The Duke of BERWICK rose in a marked manner, and left the garden. The weather continues charming." ....[1]

## 2. Telegram from Oscar Wilde to Ada Leverson. From *The Complete Letters of Oscar Wilde*, 632

15 February 1895 Piccadilly

Title for *Punch* quite charming. Rely on you to misrepresent me. Your flowers are lovely. Will see you tonight.

OSCAR

---

1  The ellipsis appears in the original; this is the end of Leverson's piece.

# Appendix D: Three Works by Gilbert and Sullivan

[Wilde's association with W.S. Gilbert and Arthur Sullivan, and especially his complicated relationship to the comic opera *Patience; or, Bunthorne's Bride* (1881), remind us not only of the similar place occupied by these three celebrities in the late-Victorian cultural imagination but also of the ways in which all three addressed an overlapping set of issues, albeit from two distinct perspectives. Chiefly, these issues drew from codes, concerns, and anxieties about morals and manners, bodies and behaviors—tropes repeatedly and quite strikingly similarly lampooned throughout the works of all three men. Wilde's knowledge of *Patience*, the opera that skewered the Aesthetic movement, making him something of a laughing-stock in Britain and a celebrity in America, is reviewed in Appendices G4-G7, which feature excerpts and images that describe Wilde's American tour to promote Gilbert and Sullivan's opera.[1] The selections from *Patience* included below may have inspired Wilde as he composed *The Importance of Being Earnest*. Two other well-known works by Gilbert and Sullivan are also excerpted, since the plots of both *The Gondoliers* (1889) and *HMS Pinafore* (1878) offer moments that find echoes in Wilde's play.

Wilde attended the London première of *Patience*, the opera that mocked Aesthetic pretension, and he accompanied the touring company for the American production of Gilbert and Sullivan's piece as a living example of the Aesthetic type, most clearly represented in *Patience* by the poet Reginald Bunthorne (see the Introduction 26-27). *Patience* anticipates a central comic conceit in *The Importance of Being Earnest*, for everyone assumes poses to get what they want socially and romantically, yet they know these poses are mere ruses undertaken to give Society what it demands. *Patience* is unlike Wilde's play, however, in that at the end of the opera, the ultimate *poseur*, Bunthorne, is left alone and, in effect, mocked, signaling the failure of his pose to achieve its desired end. This proves a sharp contrast to the final moments of *Earnest* in which the pretences of the two male leads secure exactly what they desire and grant them the sanction of Society in general. Musically, *Patience* perhaps inspired Wilde's use of the strategies of pre-diction and echo (see the Introduction 38-42), as Grosvenor learns to mimic—to echo—the attitudes and platitudes Bunthorne has modeled shoring up his own power by securing the pleasures he desires.

---

1   See Appendix G4, 181n1.

*The Gondoliers* also anticipates aspects of *The Importance of Being Earnest*, particularly in regard to two characters: Inez, whose knowledge of the secret of the once-lost baby's identity pre-dicts Miss Prism's role in Wilde's play; and The Duke of Plaza Toro, whose snobbishness, whose jealous control of his daughter-to-be-wed, and whose attitude toward marriage as a means for maintaining financial and social stability all find echoes in Wilde's Lady Bracknell. Musically, *The Gondoliers* comments on the various types of masculinity the opera explores: when the gondoliers are portrayed as rather carefree youths, Gilbert and Sullivan rely on legato, free-flowing arias; but when the social stakes are raised and one or the other assumes he will be named King, the music shifts sharply. As the lyrics increasingly gesture toward concerns about gender, the male characters break into staccato marches, and the women maintain the legato arias associated with the carefree—that is, the irresponsible and, as Victorians would classify them, the *feminine*—gondoliers of the opera's earlier sections.[1]

*HMS Pinafore* explores two concepts Wilde draws on throughout *Earnest*. With the introduction of Dick Deadeye, Gilbert and Sullivan make light of the Victorian belief in somatic inscription, or the body's betrayal of the truths of the soul: to look at a person, Victorians imagined, is to know *who* the person is, to know *how* the person should be classified—a Victorian cultural obsession that went hand-in-hand with the contemporary mania for collecting and classifying all sorts of material objects. In a scene not reproduced here, the ridiculously lofty language Ralph employs to express his love for Josephine predicts the similarly high-flown language Algernon marshals as he makes love to Cecily, and Josephine's strategy of pretending to be angry at Ralph when in fact she is charmed by his efforts finds an echo in Cecily and Gwendolen's insistence on maintaining an increasingly false coldness to their suitors after they discover that neither is named "Ernest" after all.]

---

1   I am grateful to my assistant Nathan R. Wieting for his insight into the musicality of *The Gondoliers*, particularly how the opera addresses contemporary debates and anxieties about gender and power through shifts in musical style.

## 1. From W.S. Gilbert and Arthur Sullivan, *Patience; or, Bunthorne's Bride* (1881). Ed. Edmond W. Rickett (Milwaukee: Hal Leonard Publishing, 1982)

JANE (*L.C.,*[1] *suddenly*). Fools! (*They start, and turn to her.*)

ANGELA. I beg your pardon?

JANE. Fools and blind! The man loves—wildly loves!

ANGELA. But whom? None of us?

JANE. No, none of us. His weird fancy has lighted, for the nonce, on Patience, the village milkmaid!

SAPHIR. On Patience? Oh, it cannot be!

JANE. Bah! But yesterday I caught him in her dairy, eating fresh butter with a tablespoon. (16; act 1)

JANE (*coming L.C.*). There is a transcendentality of delirium—an acute accentuation of supremest ecstasy—which the earthy might easily mistake for indigestion. But it is *not* indigestion—it is aesthetic transfiguration! (22; act 1)[2]

DUKE. Oh ... I'm as cheerful as a poor devil can be expected to be who has the misfortune to be a Duke, with a thousand a day!

MAJOR. Humph! Most men would envy you!

DUKE. Envy *me*? Tell me, Major, are you fond of toffee?

MAJOR. Very!

COLONEL. We are all fond of toffee.

ALL. We are!

DUKE. Yes, and toffee in moderation is a capital thing. But to *live* on toffee—toffee for breakfast, toffee for dinner, toffee for tea—to have it supposed that you care for nothing *but* toffee, and that you would consider yourself insulted if anything but toffee were offered to you—how would you like *that*?

COLONEL. I can quite believe that, under those circumstances, even toffee would become monotonous.[3]

DUKE. For "toffee" read flattery, adulation, and abject deference, carried to such a pitch that I began, at last, to think that man was born bent at an angle of forty-five degrees! Great heavens, what is there to adulate in me? Am I particularly intelligent, or remarkably

---

1 The stage directions indicate that Jane speaks suddenly from a position left-center.

2 As in *Earnest*, here, excessive eating functions as a symptom of Aestheticism.

3 Wilde's play picks up on this argument, that the luxurious trappings of wealth and privilege prove so oppressive that one wishes for—and in the case of *Earnest*'s male leads, even invents—some means of escape.

studious, or excruciatingly witty, or unusually accomplished, or exceptionally virtuous?

COLONEL. You're about as commonplace a young man as ever I saw.

. . . .

DUKE. But who is the gentleman with the long hair?

. . . .

(*The Dragoons back to R., watching the entrance of the Ladies. Bunthorne enters, L.U.E.,*[1] *followed by the Ladies, two and two, playing on harps as before. He is composing a poem, and is quite absorbed. He sees no one, but walks across the stage, followed by the Ladies, who take no notice of the Dragoons—to the surprise and indignation of those officers.*) (33; act 1)

ANGELA. How purely fragrant!

SAPHIR. How earnestly precious!

PATIENCE. Well, it seems to me to be nonsense.

SAPHIR. Nonsense, yes, perhaps,—but oh, what precious nonsense!

COLONEL. This is all very well, but you seem to forget that you are engaged to us.

SAPHIR. It can never be. You are not Empyrean. You are not Della Cruscan. You are not even Early English. Oh, be Early English ere it is too late![2] (*Officers look at each other in astonishment.*)

JANE (*looking at uniform*). Red and yellow! Primary colors! Oh, South Kensington![3]

DUKE. We didn't design our uniforms, but we don't see how they could be improved!

JANE. No, you wouldn't. Still, there *is* a cobwebby gray velvet, with a tender bloom like cold gravy, which, made Florentine fourteenth century, trimmed with Venetian leather and Spanish altar lace, and surmounted with something Japanese—it matters not what—would at least be Early English! Come, maidens. (47; act 1)

---

1   Left upper entrance.

2   As in *Earnest*, here we see the comic idea that love is predicated upon identity, anticipating the links Wilde will expose throughout his play between what is assumed to be deep and true (love) and what is wholly superficial (names, labels). Gilbert and Sullivan's language also underscores the notion that identity is a changeable type, that by taking on a different label or name, one becomes a different thing altogether—and thus becomes, consequently, more or less desirable.

3   South Kensington was associated with Aestheticism and all of its excesses, such as the unusual pairing of strong colors.

BUNTHORNE.[1] Am I alone,
    And unobserved? I am!
Then let me own,
    I'm an aesthetic sham!
This air severe
    Is but a mere
        Veneer!
This cynic smile
    Is but a wile
        Of guile!
This costume chaste
    Is but good taste
        Misplaced!
    Let me confess!
A languid love for lilies does *not* blight me!
Lank limbs and haggard cheeks do *not* delight me!
I do *not* care for dirty greens
    By any means.
I do *not* long for all one sees
    That's Japanese.
I am *not* fond of uttering platitudes
    In stained-glass attitudes.
In short, my mediaevalism's affectation,
Born of a morbid love of admiration![2] (52-54; act 1)

(*As the Dragoons and Girls are embracing, enter Grosvenor, R.U.E.,[3] reading. He takes no notice of them, but comes slowly down, still reading. The Girls are strangely fascinated by him. The Chorus divides, L. and R., and the Girls are held back by the Dragoons, as they attempt to throw themselves at Grosvenor. Fury of Bunthorne, who recognizes a rival.*)

---

1  Bunthorne's recitative, commonly titled "If You're Anxious for to Shine in the High Aesthetic Line," lampoons the Aesthetic personality: an obsession with matters of dress and style; physical weakness; cynicism; a fondness for lilies, drab colors ("dirty greens"), Japanese designs, and all things medieval; a propensity for epigrams; and an affiliation with the Pre-Raphaelite movement, to which the song alludes by way of the phrase "stained-glass attitudes." The song exposes each of these as merely a pose adopted to attract women, just as in Wilde's play Jack and Algernon assume the pose of earnestness to attract Gwendolen and Cecily.

2  Bunthorne's song concludes with his admission that his supposed identity is false and that he has assumed such a pose only in order to secure the things he desires—attention and love—just as Wilde's male leads will do when they present themselves to Gwendolen and Cecily as "Ernest."

3  Right upper entrance.

. . . .

GROSVENOR. I am a broken-hearted troubadour,
  Whose mind's aesthetic and whose tastes are pure!
ANGELA. Aesthetic! He is aesthetic!
GROSVENOR. Yes, Yes—I am aesthetic and poetic!
MAIDENS. Then, we love you![1] (109-12; act 1)

PATIENCE (*very tenderly*). But you *do* love me, don't you?
GROSVENOR. Madly, hopelessly, despairingly![2] (144; act 2)

COLONEL (*attitude*[3]). Yes, it's quite clear that our only chance of making a lasting impression on these young ladies is to become as aesthetic as they are.
MAJOR (*attitude*). No doubt. The only question is how far we've succeeded in doing so. I don't know why, but I've an idea that this is not quite right.
DUKE (*attitude*). *I* don't like it. I never did. I don't see what it means. I do it, but I don't like it.
COLONEL. My good friend, the question is not whether we like it, but whether they do. They understand these things—we don't. Now I shouldn't be surprised if this is effective enough—at a distance.
MAJOR. I can't help thinking we're a little stiff at it. It would be extremely awkward if we were to be "struck"[4] so!
COLONEL. I don't think we shall be struck so. Perhaps we're a little awkward at first—but everything must have a beginning. Oh here they come! 'Tention! (163; act 2)

---

1 The Maidens' line is key to the link between *Patience* and an aspect central to the success of Wilde's play: the reduction of love to conditions of attitude, to posings. Just as Gwendolen and Cecily love their suitors *because* they believe the men are named Ernest, so too do the Maidens love Grosvenor because they believe he is an Aesthete, as their telling use of the word "Then" indicates. In short, the Maidens' love for Grosvenor is prompted by his claiming of an "aesthetic and poetic" sensibility, which is as much a pose, a fiction, as are Jack's and Algernon's claims to be Ernest.

2 Grosvenor's catalogue of adverbs finds an echo in Algernon's announcement to Cecily that "I have dared to love you wildly, passionately, devotedly, hopelessly" (*E* 112).

3 An "attitude" is an intentionally affected pose, which underscores how conscious the Colonel, the Major, and the Duke remain that they are presenting themselves to the world by way of playing specific roles, much as in Wilde's play Jack and Algernon present themselves to the world, when they so choose, as Ernest.

4 To be bewitched or rendered motionless. The *Oxford English Dictionary* cites this use in *Patience* as exemplary of its definition 46e for "strike."

PATIENCE. Oh, Reginald, I'm so happy! Oh, dear, dear Reginald, I cannot express the joy I feel at this change. It will no longer be a duty to love you, but a pleasure—a rapture—an ecstasy!

BUNTHORNE. My darling! (*embracing her*)

PATIENCE. But—oh, horror! (*recoiling from him*)

BUNTHORNE. What's the matter?

PATIENCE. It is quite certain that you have absolutely reformed—that you are henceforth a perfect being—utterly free from defect of any kind?

BUNTHORNE. It is quite certain. I have sworn it.

PATIENCE. Then I never can be yours! (*crossing to R.C.*)

BUNTHORNE. Why not?

PATIENCE. Love, to be pure, must be absolutely unselfish, and there can be nothing unselfish in loving so perfect a being as you have now become!

BUNTHORNE. But stop a bit! I don't want to change—I'll relapse—I'll be as I was—interrupted![1] (184; act 2)

## 2. From W.S. Gilbert and Arthur Sullivan, *The Gondoliers; or, The King of Barataria* (1889). In Bradley, ed., 859-967

DON ALHAMBRA. I stole the Prince, and I brought him here,
    And left him gaily prattling
With a highly respectable gondolier,
Who promised the Royal babe to rear,
And teach him the trade of a timoneer
    With his own beloved bratling.

    Both of the babes were strong and stout,
        And, considering all things, clever.
    Of that there is no manner of doubt—
    No probable, possible shadow of doubt—
        No possible doubt whatever.

    No possible doubt whatever.

---

1  Both Patience and Bunthorne understand that "being" is a matter of choosing, that one can become this person or that merely by claiming such an identity and acting accordingly. Such a notion anticipates Wilde's longstanding belief that identity is fluid, that there is nothing natural or constant about it, which is reflected throughout *Earnest* in the shifting attitudes and mercurial poses of the young lovers as well as in the proto-social-constructionist stance of Miss Prism (see Appendix I2, 205n1).

But owing, I'm much disposed to fear,
　　To his terrible taste for tippling,
That highly respectable gondolier
Could never declare with a mind sincere
Which of the two was his offspring dear,
　　And which the Royal stripling!

　　　Which was which he could never make out
　　　　Despite his best endeavour.
　Of *that* there is no manner of doubt—
　　　No probable, possible shadow of doubt—
　　　　No possible doubt whatever. (891; act 1)

CASILDA. Then do you mean to say that I am married to one of two
gondoliers, but it is impossible to say which?
DON ALHAMBRA. Without any doubt of any kind whatever. But be
reassured: the nurse to whom your husband was entrusted is the
mother of the musical young man who is such a past-master of that
delicately modulated instrument (*indicating the drum*). She can, no
doubt, establish the King's identity beyond all question.[1] (893; act
1)

DUKE. I am a courtier grave and serious
　　　Who is about to kiss your hand:
　　Try to combine a pose imperious
　　　With a demeanour nobly bland.
MARCO *and* GUISEPPE. Let us combine a pose imperious
　　　　With a demeanour nobly bland.[2] (959; act 2)

DON ALHAMBRA. Now let the loyal lieges gather round—
The Prince's foster-mother has been found!

---

1　Inez functions as a precursor for *Earnest*'s Miss Prism, for her recollection of
the suspicious circumstances surrounding a young child proves key to the revelation of that child's true identity and, consequently, to the success of a
hoped-for romance. Similarly, another character from *The Gondoliers*, the
Duke of Plaza-Toro, anticipates *Earnest*'s Lady Bracknell in his position as a
presumed figure of respectability, tradition, and propriety and as one whose
pronouncements, like hers, unmask his utterly ridiculous aspects.
2　As in *Patience*, here male characters understand that to assume an identity is
simply to pose as it. In addition, this combination of haughtiness and modesty
anticipates the extremes in demeanour the double-lives Jack and Algernon
exemplify throughout *Earnest*.

She will declare, to silver clarion's sound,
The rightful King—let him forthwith be crowned!

. . . .

| | |
|---|---|
| TESSA. | Speak, woman, speak— |
| DUKE. | We're all attention! |
| GIANETTA. | The news we seek— |
| DUCHESS. | This moment mention. |
| CASILDA. | To us they bring— |
| DON ALHAMBRA. | His foster-mother. |
| MARCO. | Is he the King? |
| GUISEPPE. | Or this my brother? |
| ALL. | Speak, woman, speak, etc. |

INEZ. The Royal Prince was by the King entrusted
   To my fond care, ere I grew old and crusted;
   When traitors came to steal his son reputed,
   My own small boy I deftly substituted!
   The villains fell into the trap completely—
   I hid the Prince away—still sleeping sweetly:
   I called him "son" with pardonable slyness—
   His name, Luiz! Behold his Royal Highness!

(*Sensation.* LUIZ *ascends the throne, crowned and robed as King.*)

. . . .

ALL. Then hail, O King of a Golden Land,
   And the high-born bride who claims his hand!
   The past is dead, and you gain your own,
   A royal crown and a golden throne! (963, 965, 967; act 2)

## 3. From W.S. Gilbert and Arthur Sullivan, *HMS Pinafore; or, The Lass That Loved a Sailor* (1878). In Bradley, ed., 113-85

BOATSWAIN. Aye, Little Buttercup—and well called—for you're the rosiest, the roundest, and the reddest beauty in all Spithead.[1]

BUTTERCUP. Red, am I? and round—and rosy! May be, for I have dissembled well! But hark ye, my merry friend—hast ever thought that beneath a gay and frivolous exterior there may lurk a canker-worm which is slowly but surely eating its way into one's very heart?

---

1 The Boatswain's speech sets the tone for this entire passage, which plays on the Victorian belief in physiognomy, or the correspondence between looks and character, a sentiment echoed several times throughout *Earnest*, most notably when Algernon insists Jack must be Ernest because he is "the most earnest looking person I ever saw in my life" (*E* 75; see also *E* 75n2) and when Lady Bracknell says of her nephew Algernon that "[h]e is an extremely, I may almost say an ostentatiously, eligible young man. He has nothing, but he looks everything. What more can one desire?" (*E* 135).

BOATSWAIN. No, my lass, I can't say I ever thought that.

(*Enter* DICK DEADEYE. *He pushes through sailors, and comes down.*)

DICK. *I* have thought it often. (*All recoil from him.*)

BUTTERCUP. Yes, you look like it! What's the matter with the man? Isn't he well?

BOATSWAIN. Don't take no heed of *him*; that's only poor Dick Deadeye.

DICK. I say—it's a beast of a name, ain't it—Dick Deadeye?

BUTTERCUP. It's not a nice name.

DICK. I'm ugly too, ain't I?

BUTTERCUP. You are certainly plain.

DICK. And I'm three-cornered too, ain't I?

BUTTERCUP. You are rather triangular.

DICK. Ha! ha! That's it. I'm ugly, and they hate me for it; for you all hate me, don't you?

ALL. We do!

DICK. There!

BOATSWAIN. Well, Dick, we wouldn't go for to hurt any fellow-creature's feelings, but you can't expect a chap with such a name as Dick Deadeye to be a popular character—now can you?

DICK. No.

BOATSWAIN. It's asking too much, ain't it?

DICK. It is. From such a face and form as mine the noblest sentiments sound like the black utterances of a depraved imagination. It is human nature—I am resigned. (121, 123; act 1)[1]

SAILORS. His nose should pant and his lips should curl,
　　His cheeks should flame and his brow should furl,
　　His bosom should heave and his heart should glow,
　　And his fist be ever ready for a knock-down blow.

ENSEMBLE. His foot should stamp and his throat should growl,
　　His hair should twirl and his face should scowl,
　　His eyes should flash and his breast protrude,
　　And this should be his customary attitude—(*pose*).[2] (153; act 1)

---

1　As in *Earnest*, here image is everything, for in the culture of *H.M.S. Pinafore*, as in Wilde's own day, surface and depth, superficiality and truth, are assumed to be one and the same. See also the Introduction 21-23.

2　Like the posings in attitude seen in the excerpt from *Patience*, here the descriptions and poses of the sailors and the ensemble remind us that ideal men are created by the act of pretending to be what is already perceived as ideal, just as throughout Wilde's play readers realize that earnestness is a pose, a sham, and thus it is the very antithesis of what it purports to be.

BUTTERCUP.[1] Things are seldom what they seem,
   Skim milk masquerades as cream;
   Highlows[2] pass as patent leathers;
   Jackdaws strut in peacock's feathers.[3]
CAPTAIN (*puzzled*). Very true,
   So they do.
BUTTERCUP. Black sheep dwell in every fold;
   All that glitters is not gold;
   Storks turn out to be but logs;
   Bulls are but inflated frogs.
CAPTAIN (*puzzled*). So they be,
   Frequentlee.[4]
BUTTERCUP. Drops the wind and stops the mill;
   Turbot is ambitious brill;[5]
   Gild the farthing[6] if you will,
   Yet it is a farthing still.
CAPTAIN (*puzzled*). Yes, I know,
   That is so. (157; act 2)


BUTTERCUP.[7] A many years ago,
  When I was young and charming,
    As some of you may know,
  I practised baby-farming.

---

1  The exchange between Buttercup and the Captain offers a meditation on the dilemma introduced by Buttercup's first line, that "things are seldom what they seem," just as in Wilde's play Jack and Algernon present themselves to Gwendolen and Cecily as something each is not (although of course in the end each finds that he is).

2  Laced boots worn by many Victorian women as everyday wear, vastly different from the more expensive and formal patent leather shoes.

3  In *The Complete and Annotated Gilbert and Sullivan*, Ian Bradley glosses this line as an allusion to one of Æsop's fables, in which a jackdaw tries to impress the other birds by wearing peacock's feathers, only for his masquerade finally to fall apart and for him to be unmasked as a fool (156).

4  As spelled by Gilbert and Sullivan, indicating how the final vowel sound should be drawn out.

5  Bradley notes that turbot and brill are fish of similar same size and shape, but turbot "is regarded as a considerable delicacy, while [brill] is not" (156).

6  A coin of very small value.

7  Buttercup's confession anticipates a similar moment at the end of *The Gondoliers* when Inez reveals her mix-up of the infants (albeit intentional, in her case). Thus, both operas pre-dict the final act of *Earnest*, when all eyes and ears turn to Miss Prism as she reveals, finally, the truth about her mislaying of Jack and Jack's real identity as Ernest.

ALL. Now this is most alarming!
　　When she was young and charming,
　　She practiced baby-farming,
　　　　A many years ago.
BUTTERCUP. Two tender babes I nussed:[1]
　　One was of low condition,
　　The other, upper crust,
　　　　A regular patrician.
ALL (*explaining to each other*). Now, this is the position:
　　One was of low condition,
　　The other a patrician,
　　　　A many years ago.
BUTTERCUP. Oh, bitter is my cup!
　　　　However could I do it?
　　I mixed those children up,
　　And not a creature knew it!
ALL. However could you do it?
　　Some day, no doubt, you'll rue it,
　　Although no creature knew it,
　　　　So many years ago.
BUTTERCUP. In time each little waif
　　　　Forsook his foster-mother
　　The well-born babe was Ralph—
　　　　Your captain was the other!!! (179; act 2)

RALPH *and* JOSEPHINE. Oh bliss, oh rapture!
CAPTAIN *and* BUTTERCUP. Oh rapture, oh bliss!
SIR JOSEPH. Sad my lot and sorry,
　　What shall I do? I cannot live alone!
HEBE. Fear nothing—while I live I'll not desert you.
　　I'll soothe and comfort you in your declining days.
SIR JOSEPH. No, don't do that.
HEBE. Yes, but indeed I'd rather—
SIR JOSEPH (*resigned*). Oh, very well then.
　　To-morrow morn our vows shall all be plighted
　　Three loving pairs on the same day united![2] (181; act 2)

---

1　Nursed; a cue for pronunciation, as with "frequentlee" above.
2　This series of exchanges anticipates the conclusion of *Earnest*: the nearly
　　perfect echoes uttered by the pairs of lovers in the first two lines of this
　　excerpt find form in the closing lines of Wilde's play as the trio of lovers look
　　forward to their lives together.

# Appendix E: From J.G.F. Nicholson, Love in Earnest (London: Elliot Stock, 1892)

[Appearing just two years after the scandalous American publication of "The Picture of Dorian Gray" in *Lippincott's Monthly Magazine* and just a year after *Dorian Gray*'s slightly less risqué book-length British debut in its censored form, J.G.F. Nicholson's *Love in Earnest* celebrated the joys of same-sex love openly and without apology. Although Wilde's knowledge of this volume cannot be conclusively established, he was certainly familiar with Nicholson's work, since both were contributors to the single issue of the Oxford magazine *The Chameleon* (Smith xix; see the Introduction 32-33 and *E* 75n3). Indeed, the poems below suggest the presence in London literary circles of what today might be considered a homosexual subculture, a readership whose sexual sophistication would have equipped them to pick up on the several suggestions throughout *Earnest* that what appears on stage as heterosexual horseplay may gesture to same-sex knowledge, activity, and pleasures, an alternative reading of the play that has risen to prominence in recent years (see the Introduction 42-43 and 47-49). Of particular interest to readers of Wilde's play is Nicholson's ballad "Of Boys' Names," which celebrates the delights of a whole range of male characters and which proclaims "Ernest" as the name that "sets [the poet's] heart a-flame" in a refrain at the end of each of the four stanzas. Not only does Nicholson's poem anticipate Gwendolen's admission that the name Ernest "produces vibrations" (*E* 84), but more generally, and more importantly, Nicholson's line establishes that name, for some readers, as a recognizable "gay" code.]

OF BOYS' NAMES
To W.E.M.
"*Sets my heart a-flame, O!*"—Princess Ida.[1]

Old memories of the Table Round
    In Percival and Lancelot dwell,
Clement and Bernard bring the sound
    Of anthems in the cloister-cell,
    And Leonard vies with Lionel

---

1  Title character of another comic opera by Gilbert and Sullivan.

In stately step and kingly frame,
  And Kenneth speaks of field and fell,
And Ernest sets my heart a-flame.

One name can make my pulses bound,
  No peer it owns, nor parallel,
By it is Vivian's sweetness drowned,
  And Roland, full as organ-swell;
  Though Frank may ring like silver bell,
And Cecil softer music claim,
  They cannot work the miracle,—
'Tis Ernest sets my heart a-flame.

Cyril is lordly, Stephen crowned
  With deathless wreaths of asphodel,
Oliver whispers peace profound,
  Herbert takes arms his foes to quell,
  Eustace with sheaves is laden well,
Christopher has a nobler fame,
  And Michael storms the gates of Hell,
But Ernest sets my heart a-flame.

  ENVOY[1]
 My little Prince, Love's mystic spell
Lights all the letters of your name,
  And you, if no one else, can tell
Why Ernest sets my heart a-flame.


## THE BOY IN THE BOAT
(FOR A PAINTING BY W.H. BARTLETT.)

Where sapphire waters in their summer splendour
  Reflect the clouds that idly float,
Stripped for the plunge, the boy of figure slender
  Stands in the open boat.

Vaguely I see his comrades round him swimming,—
  To him is given my gaze alone
As he leans o'er them, innocently dimming
  Their beauty by his own.

---

1   An envoy (sometimes spelled as the French *envoi*) is a brief closing stanza that
  dedicates the poem to a patron or some other addressee; an envoy may also
  summarize the poem's main claims.

His silent sunburnt face is downward drooping,
    He rests his hands upon his knees:
The careless posture of that lithe form stooping
    Is full of grace and ease.

The sunny afternoon so gaily beaming
    Across the opalescent sea,
The distant ship, the far-off headland gleaming,
    Are not so fair as he.

O, what a charm is thine, sweet youthful swimmer,
    Thy praise I sing with feeble note,
As thou art standing in the sunlight's shimmer,
    O, bright boy in the boat!

# Appendix F: Conduct Manuals

[Published just two years after *Earnest*'s première, Mrs. Humphrey's *Manners for Men* exemplifies contemporary conduct books designed for aspiring gentlemen. Set alongside Wilde's play, *Manners for Men* demonstrates the prevalence of the values, ideas, and behaviors Wilde's play lampoons: the excerpts below describe the "ideal man" and emphasize the gentleman's duties at tea, his behavior at proposing marriage, and his response to overly eager advances from women—all situations central to *Earnest*'s plot. Mrs. Julia McNair Wright's *Practical Life; or, Ways and Means for Developing Character and Relations* provides insight regarding what American readers were encouraged to believe about phenomena central to Wilde's play, including the dandy and the dangers of his extravagance, the French Revolution and its effect on marriage, and the importance of earnestness to a successful and respectable adulthood.]

## 1. From Mrs. Humphrey, *Manners for Men* (London: James Bowden, 1897)

Like every other woman, I have my ideal of manhood. The difficulty is to describe it. First of all, he must be a gentleman; but that means so much that it, in its turn, requires explanation. Gentleness and moral strength combined must be the salient characteristics of the "gentleman," together with that polish that is never acquired but in one way: constant association with those so happily placed that they have enjoyed the influences of education and refinement all through their lives. He must be thoughtful for others, kind to women and children and all helpless things, tenderhearted to the old and the poor and the unhappy, but never foolishly weak in giving where gifts do harm instead of good—his brain must be as fine as his heart, in fact. There are few such men; but they do exist. I know one or two. (1-2; ch. 1)

Gentlemen are in great request at five o'clock tea. Their duties are rather onerous if there are but one or two men and the usual crowd of ladies. They have to carry teacups about, hand sugar, cream, and cakes or muffins, and keep up all the time a stream of small talk, as amusing as they can make it. They must rise every time a lady enters or leaves the room, opening the door for her exit if no one else is nearer to it, and, if his hostess requests him, he must see the lady downstairs to her carriage or cab.

With regard to the viands,[1] a man helps himself, but not till he has seen that all the ladies in his vicinity have everything they can possibly want. His hostess, or some lady deputed by her to preside at the tea-table, gives him tea or coffee, and he adds sugar and cream. (94; ch. 15)

The old-fashioned rule that a man must approach the father of a girl before offering himself in marriage to her has now, to some extent, died out. At the same time it is considered dishonourable for any one to propose to a girl in the face of the decided disapprobation of her family. Clandestine courtship is also regarded as dishonourable, except in circumstances where the girl is unhappy or oppressed and needs a champion. (108; ch. 18)

Worldly girls have often sufficient wisdom of the serpent to bring a reluctant wooer to the point and, by immediately announcing the engagement to their friends, to make it extremely difficult for him to retreat.

Sometimes a girl falls so wildly in love with a man that she creates a kind of corresponding, though passing, fervour in him, and while it lasts he believes himself in love, though his emotions are only a mixture of gratified vanity and that physical attraction which needs true love to redeem it from the fleshly sort. Should marriage follow upon such courtships as these, where the girl takes ever the initiative, the union is very seldom a happy one. The wife never feels sure that her husband really loves her or would have chosen her. She knows that he was her choice, rather than she his, and a racking jealousy seizes her and makes her not only miserable herself, but a very uncomfortable companion for him. He, too, often finds when it is too late that she fulfils none of his ideals, and is in many ways a contrast to the girl he would have chosen if she had not whirled him into the vortex of her own strong feeling. And he occasionally wonders if she may not some day experience a similar strength of attraction for some other man and let herself be carried away by it as she had been by her feeling for him. "Hot fires soon burn out," he thinks, and remembers the warning given to Othello: "She hath deceived her father, and may thee." (110-11; ch. 18)

---

1 Articles of food.

## 2. From Julia McNair Wright, *Practical Life; or, Ways and Means for Developing Character and Resources* (Philadelphia: J.C. McCurdy, 1881)

"Which is the worst extreme," asked Robert —"a sloven or a dandy?"

"One is about as bad as the other. The sloven is usually a boor in his manners, ill furnished in mind, and negligent in business, because he carries his untidy dispositions into all that he does. The dandy is usually too self-conceited to care to learn, too fond of his appearance to be willing to work, and so mad after dress that he does not consider what he can afford, and *extravagance is twin-brother to dishonesty*."

"You speak as if dress and actions had close relationship."

"And indeed they do. Extremes, either in negligence or show, arise out of a coarse or frivolous mind. They indicate what is in the disposition, and serve to intensify it. You will have observed that people are more mannerly and at ease when they are well dressed. Ill-fitting, ill-made, ill-looking garments help to destroy one's self-respect. I wish all parents would remember this: if they wish their sons to be mannerly, obliging, cheerful, quick, easy in society or business, they must not burden them with a sense of negligence and inferiority by means of outgrown, patched, miserable garments. It is true that poverty often obliges parents to dress their children less neatly than they would wish. But in any case they can make them scrupulously tidy, and patches can be neatly put on, matching in color and in thread, and well sewed. Many parents allow their children to be carelessly dressed from mere greed or negligence. They do not realize that they are thus doing much to destroy the future of their children. When a boy's clothes are whole and well-fitted, and the *barber has cut his hair*, and he has a nail-brush, clothes-brush, tooth-brush, shoe-brush, he is much more likely to be self-respecting, honorable, and diligent than if he owns none of these things. Good manners are of themselves a large business capital."

"Some people," said John Frederick, "make *muffs*[1] of their boys, by keeping them too long in childish clothes. I remember a long-legged youngster of eleven, whose mother kept him in pumps, knee-breeches, fancy striped stockings, ruffled shirts, lace collars, and long yellow curls. He went to dancing school, and out on parade along the avenues. He was a cry-baby, a tell-tale, a dreadful little liar; and had various other interesting ugly ways; all because he was never taught anything reasonable and manly."

---

1 Generally, a fool; more specifically, given this context, a boy who remains a child too long, a feminine boy who will face a difficult transition into manhood.

"O, John Frederick! and you lay *all that* to his dress!" cried Dora.

"Well, a deal of it," said John Frederick; "a mother who had so little sense as to bring up a *boy* in that style was not likely to have sense enough to give him instructions that would make him manly and honorable. He and his clothes were all of a piece."[1]

"A boy," said the Stranger, "should certainly be taken out of the long-hair-and-fancy-clothes age as early as is prudent, and made active, muscular, fearless. He should be taught frankness, industry, honorable ideas, to help other people, aid and defend the weak, and aim to be thoroughly manly." (315-16)

"Are there any statistics that show that divorce is on the increase?" asked Catherine.

"Let me tell you that at present in New England alone two thousand divorces occur annually. These directly concern four thousand individuals; but indirectly, considering children, parents, near friends, and parties that marry with these who are divorced, the number must reach some ten thousand, annually interfered with in their domestic relations. In one hundred years, ending 1785, New England divorces were 4.3 annually. In 1800 about one divorce for every one hundred marriages; but by 1864 the ratio was one divorce to every ten marriages. The ratio of divorce now in New England is greater than in France at the lawless period of the Revolution. In the West, though that portion of territory is connected with very loose ideas as regards divorce, the ratio is one divorce to twelve marriages. A newspaper correspondent, in one of the finest Western cities, says: 'Divorce has become a deadly epidemic which no one can explain.'"

"Pause one moment just there," interrupted the doctor; "I wish to bring before your minds a tremendous moral fact: *the contagion of crime; vice as an epidemic.* We doctors have learned but little about contagious and epidemic diseases—we are learning how to handle them—but our *moral physicians,* our social scientists, know less and interfere less concerning the *contagion of crime.* A mania for divorce, did one say? So there starts up a mania for arson, for forgery, for suicide. Cases of these crimes do not stand alone: one more, always. I tell you young

---

1  Wright expresses a common Victorian belief, pervasive in both Britain and America, that "manliness" is not a natural condition but instead is purely a social construction (see Appendix I2, 205n1). In other words, little boys do not "naturally" grow up to be "manly" men: they must be taught how to become so—and, thus, how to avoid the alternative, the supposedly "unnatural" feminine man. In this way, Wright unintentionally exposes all modes of gendered embodiment as equally unnatural, an argument Wilde makes throughout his career.

people you need not at all dread physical sickness and death in comparison with the way in which you should dread *sin*: SIN, my children, is the very quintessence of death. Beware then of lightly regarding *evil*, for, bad in itself, it is worse as the root of further evil. Never be restive against the legitimate restraints of crime: it is as necessary as the restraint of smallpox or the plague. Crime is the most fatal of epidemics!"[1]

"What do you suppose," asked Laura, "was the reason of the sudden increase of the divorce ratio from 1780 to 1820?"

"No doubt the corrupting influence of French infidelity and the lawlessness of the French Revolution. France was at that time a horrible moral sore on the face of the earth, corrupting every nation that had any dealings there."

"And yet France has been purified and bettered in every way, by that awful outbreak," said Robert.

"Thus poor France sloughed off the garnered corruption and iniquity of centuries of the most demoralizing and fatal rule and instruction," said the doctor, "and some of the poison thrown off by France then interfered with the moral health of every civilized community." (456-57)

These are words of warning needed by the young in their zeal for success. But let calm assurance prohibit alike thirsty ambition and anxious care. Self-denial, industry, uprightness,[2] will secure for every one both honor and competence. (600)

---

1 Throughout this paragraph, attributed, importantly, to "the doctor," crime is connected to illness, to disease, a pathology that intuits Degeneration theory as articulated by Cesare Lombroso and, later, Max Nordau (see the Introduction 34).

2 Taken together, self-denial, industry, and uprightness form the core of what the Victorians thought of as "earnestness," and thus Mrs. Wright's conduct manual closes by advocating the very quality Wilde's play would expose a decade and a half later as a sham, as the very opposite of the pose itself.

# Appendix G: On Dandyism and on Wilde as a Dandy

[Wilde's place in late-Victorian culture as the presumed leader of the Aesthetic movement incited countless detractors. For many, the so-called decadence embodied and celebrated in the writer and his work contained the seeds of Victorian Britain's undoing and, more largely, of the complete collapse of Western civilization. Chief among these was Max Nordau, whose book-length study of *Degeneration* devoted an entire section to Wilde, whom Nordau considered emblematic of the pernicious influence of *fin-de-siècle* arts and culture (see the Introduction 34). Yet Wilde's cultural presence loomed large in a much more positive register, exemplified by the influence his works, personal habits, and modes of self-representation exacted upon many aspects of British style, from patterns of speech to tastes in interior decoration to men's and women's fashions. Wilde's double-position in his culture offers a real-life model for the kinds of double-lives celebrated throughout *Earnest*, and the material in this Appendix focuses on the ways in which Wilde was represented—and thus perceived—both at home and abroad, in England and in America, where Wilde's curtain speeches preceding the 1882 performances of Gilbert and Sullivan's *Patience; or, Bunthorne's Bride* established the writer as the fashionable, witty gentleman-about-town, a truly cosmopolitan creature of the very sort *Patience* mocks (see Appendix D1).

The three caricatures of Wilde included here remark on the writer's larger-than-life presence as well as on the other side of his fame, the opportunities his eccentricities provided for those who would mock the writer's devotion to beauty, his cultivation of an "artistic" persona, and his vexed relationship to prevailing modes of masculinity (see the Introduction 25-35 and Appendix D1). These include a title-page image from a preposterous, imagined biography of Wilde, privately printed by the writer and illustrator Charles Kendrick; an image by George Frederick Keller from San Francisco's *Wasp* magazine, which depicts Wilde as "The Modern Messiah" posed amidst a tableau of figures who had gained widespread notoriety by the time Wilde's American tour reached the West coast; and an image by Linley Sambourne of Wilde as a sunflower surrounded by the trappings of his trade—papers and cigarettes—as well as a waste receptacle, one of many savage send-ups of Wilde that appeared in *Punch; or, The London Charivari*. Like Sambourne's caricature, Keller's image from *Wasp* depends on the cultural associations of Wilde with the sunflower, which, like the lily, had become a widely recognized symbol for the

Aestheticism Wilde promoted. Both of these cartoonists use the sunflower to mock Wilde, Keller by crowning "The Modern Messiah" with a sunflower-like halo and placing an American dollar sign in the head of the flower Wilde holds, and Sambourne by reducing Wilde to the sunflower itself, thereby limiting and constraining the artist to (only) the superficial beauty Aestheticism celebrated, or so its critics claimed, a gesture repeated in the lines below Sambourne's image. (For another caricature of Wilde that introduces the sunflower as a symbol for Aestheticism, see "Strike Me With a Sunflower" from the Introduction [28].)

The selection excerpted from Lloyd Lewis and Henry Justin Smith's *Oscar Wilde Discovers America*, a record of Wilde's speaking tour undertaken in 1882 to publicize the American stagings of Gilbert and Sullivan's *Patience* and to educate Americans about the so-called Aesthetic Movement, describes the writer's departure from America on 27 December 1882. In so doing, the closing gesture of *Oscar Wilde Discovers America* demonstrates the problematic double-place Wilde had come to occupy in the American cultural imagination by the end of his American tour ("Good-by, Oscar; we shan't miss you," one paper was reported to have printed). Such a double-place proves quite like the one that finds form in the three opening caricatures, which suggests the divided response of the general public to Wilde and to the many contradictions he is imagined to represent—genius and fool, prophet and charlatan.

Finally, two images from the American publications *Harper's Weekly* and *The Washington Post* compare Wilde and his Aestheticism to animalistic desire, aligning Aestheticism with Degeneration, and an image from *The Daily Graphic* reminds readers that for many New Yorkers, during the time of his American tour Wilde became a figure easily mocked, particularly for the profits his dedication to Aestheticism had secured.]

1. From Charles Kendrick, [Title-page drawing of Oscar Wilde], *Ye Soul Agonies in Ye Life of Oscar Wilde* (New York, 1882)

2. George Frederick Keller, "The Modern Messiah," *Wasp* (31 March 1882)

### 3. Linley Sambourne, "O.W. [Punch's Fancy Portraits 37]," *Punch; or, The London Charivari* (25 June 1881)

PUNCH'S FANCY PORTRAITS.—No. 37.

"O. W."

"O, I eel just as happy as a bright Sunflower
*Lays of Christy Minstrelsy*

Æsthete of Æsthetes!
What's in a name?
The poet is WILDE,
But his poetry's tame.

## 4. From Lloyd Lewis and Henry Justin Smith, "No Wave of His Chiseled Hand," *Oscar Wilde Discovers America* (New York: Harcourt, Brace, and Company, 1936), 444-45

Whatever of a showman's trappings Oscar Wilde might be prepared to drop overboard on the voyage was not visible to a reporter who, on the morning of December 27th, saw the poet tell America farewell.

The steamer *Bothnia* stood at the Cunard dock quivering from the strokes of her impatient engines, and to it, a little before ten o'clock, came a carriage driven by a coachman in dark green livery with silver buttons. Out stepped Oscar Wilde and two well-dressed friends—one of them the owner of the carriage, said the reporter, though he didn't bother to inquire.

Although his wide Western hat was pulled well down, Oscar's face was still noted by the onlookers as "clean-shaven, with remarkably long eyelashes, which appeared as though they had been freshly penciled." He "mounted the gangplank with the languid grace of a Bunthorne."[1]

The longshoremen stared at him, but he paid no heed. He went straight to his cabin, which held flowers, "conspicuous among them a large sunflower." A Japanese umbrella or two had been hung on the walls.

He returned to the deck and, as the ship moved off with her tugs, he waved farewell to his two loyal friends.

Back on the mainland, squibs of printer's ink, "comic, without being amusing," fired a parting salute:

"Good-by[e], Oscar; we shan't miss you."

"We know a charlatan when we see one."

"Oscar Wilde has abandoned us without a line of farewell, slipped away without giving us a last goodly glance, left without a wave of his chiseled hand or a friendly nod of his classic head."

"This is the end of the aesthetic movement."

---

1  This reference reinforces the link in the American imagination between Wilde and the character Bunthorne from Gilbert and Sullivan's opera *Patience*; see Appendix D1.

5. "Aestheticism as Oscar Understands It" (1882). Rpt. in
   Lewis and Smith, 53

6. "Mr. Wild [*sic*] of Borneo" (1882). Rpt. in Lewis and Smith, 101

HOW FAR IS IT FROM

THIS

TO

THIS?

7. W.H. Beard, "The Aesthetic Monkey" (1882). Rpt. in Lewis and Smith, 82

# Appendix H: Other Works by Wilde

[These selections offer a sense of the place of *Earnest* in Wilde's larger *oeuvre*, commenting directly and otherwise on the importance of the play to Wilde's reputation as well as on the prevalence of the play's style and themes to other works in the Wilde canon. In general, all of these selections in some way prefigure, emphasize, or further develop concepts central to the play.

Selections from three of Wilde's more provocative sets of epigrams—"A Few Maxims for the Instruction of the Over-Educated" from the *Saturday Review* (November 1894), "Phrases and Philosophies for the Use of the Young" from *The Chameleon* (December 1894), and the Preface to the book version of *The Picture of Dorian Gray* (1891)—stress the writer's preference for pretence over reality, for art over nature, and they address the importance to late-Victorian culture of education, manners, and other socially constructed behavioral codes. "The Decay of Lying" (1889) laments the decline of untruthfulness in Victorian life and conversation, along the way elevating lying to an art akin to poetry and celebrating neither truth nor transparency but rather the mask as the ultimate ideal. *De Profundis* (January-March 1897), a long letter written to Lord Alfred Douglas during Wilde's imprisonment but not published in full until many years after Wilde's death (1962), addresses the writer's awareness of his status as a figure symbolic of the excesses and failures of his own age; the originally untitled letter also considers the failure of the selfishly invested philosophy of the ego celebrated in so many of Wilde's works, *The Importance of Being Earnest* and *The Picture of Dorian Gray* chief among them.

Selections from more of Wilde's letters close Appendix H so that the author may speak on his own terms about *Earnest*, sometimes directly and sometimes by way of addressing the styles and concerns the play engages as well as the cultural critique in which it participates. These include a letter to Philip Houghton remarking on the need for masks; three letters to George Alexander, Wilde's producer, on the original idea for *Earnest*, on Wilde's interest in launching an American production of the play, and on the first copy of the play Wilde sent to Alexander under the title *Lady Lancing*; letters to an unidentified correspondent and to Lord Alfred Douglas on Douglas's father's plan to interrupt *Earnest*'s opening night and to call attention to Wilde's relationship with his son, a scheme whose foiling Wilde gleefully recounts; and a letter to R.V. Shone canceling Lord Alfred Douglas's father's reserved seat for that première.]

## 1. From "A Few Maxims for the Instruction of the Over-Educated" (1894), *The Complete Works of Oscar Wilde*. Ed. Merlin Holland and Rupert Hart-Davis (Glasgow: Harper Collins, 1996), 1242–43

The English are always degrading truths into facts. When a truth becomes a fact it loses all its intellectual value.

The only thing that can console one for being rich is economy.

One should never listen. To listen is a sign of indifference to one's hearers.

## 2. From "Phrases and Philosophies for the Use of the Young" (1894), *The Complete Works of Oscar Wilde*. Ed. Merlin Holland and Rupert Hart-Davis (Glasgow: Harper Collins, 1996), 1244–45

The first duty in life is to be as artificial as possible. What the second duty is no one has yet discovered.

Wickedness is a myth invented by good people to account for the curious attractiveness of others.

A really well-made buttonhole is the only link between Art and Nature.[1]

The well-bred contradict other people. The wise contradict themselves.

Nothing that actually occurs is of the smallest importance.

If one tells the truth, one is sure, sooner or later, to be found out.

It is only by not paying one's bills that one can hope to live in the memory of the commercial classes.

Only the shallow know themselves.

Any preoccupation with ideas of what is right or wrong in conduct shows an arrested intellectual development.

---

1   See the play's reference to a buttonhole at *E* 103 and in the related n2.

It is only the superficial qualities that last.

The condition of perfection is idleness.

### 3. From "Preface," *The Picture of Dorian Gray* (1891). Ed. Donald L. Lawler (New York: Norton, 1988), 3-4

No artist has ethical sympathies. An ethical sympathy in an artist is an unpardonable mannerism of style.

Vice and virtue are to the artist materials for an art.

All art is at once surface and symbol. Those who go beneath the surface do so at their peril.

It is the spectator, and not life, that art really mirrors.

### 4. From "The Decay of Lying" (1889), *The Complete Works of Oscar Wilde*. Ed. Merlin Holland and Rupert Hart-Davis (Glasgow: Harper Collins, 1996), 1071-92

After all, what is a fine lie? Simply that which is its own evidence.

Lying and poetry are arts—arts, as Plato saw, not unconnected with each other—and they require the most careful study, the most disinterested devotion.

The only real people are the people who never existed.... In point of fact what is interesting about people in good society ... is the mask that each one of them wears, not the reality that lies behind the mask.

Fact, occupied as Fact usually is, with trying to reproduce Fiction....

The only form of lying that is absolutely beyond reproach is lying for its own sake, and the highest development of this is, as we have already pointed out, Lying in Art.

## 5. From *De Profundis* (January-March 1897) [Posthumously Published Version (1962) of a Letter to Lord Alfred Douglas],[1] *The Complete Letters of Oscar Wilde*. Ed. Merlin Holland and Rupert Hart-Davis (New York: Henry Holt, 2000), 683-780

The supreme vice is shallowness. (685)

The trivial in thought and action is charming. I had made it the key-stone of a very brilliant philosophy expressed in plays and paradoxes. (692)

And I remember that afternoon, as I was in the railway-carriage whirling up to Paris, thinking what an impossible, terrible, utterly wrong state my life had got into, when I, a man of world-wide reputation, was actually forced to run away from England, in order to try and get rid of a friendship that was entirely destructive of everything fine in me either from the intellectual or ethical point of view: the person from whom I was flying being no terrible creature sprung from sewer or mire into modern life with whom I had entangled my days, but you yourself, a young man of my own social rank and position, who had been at my own college at Oxford, and was an incessant guest at my house. (693)

I don't regret for a single moment having lived for pleasure. I did it to the full, as one should do everything that one does to the full. There was no pleasure I did not experience. I threw the pearl of my soul into a cup of wine. I went down the primrose path to the sound of flutes. I lived on honeycomb. But to have continued the same life would have been wrong because it would have been limiting. I had to pass on. The other half of the garden had its secrets for me also. (739-40)

In their heavy inaccessibility to ideas, their dull respectability, their tedious orthodoxy, their worship of vulgar success, their entire preoc-

---

1 While incarcerated at Reading Gaol, Wilde composed a lengthy letter to Lord Alfred Douglas, which he entrusted to Robbie Ross upon his release. In an effort to protect those named in the letter as well as to secure Wilde's literary estate against lawsuits, Ross, as executor, published carefully selected excerpts of the letter, to which he gave the name *De Profundis* ("from the depths"). Ross entrusted the complete manuscript of the letter to the British Museum in 1909 under the condition that it remain sealed for fifty years. In 1949, the suppressed portions of *De Profundis* were published by Wilde's son, Vyvyan Holland, and the complete, unexpurgated text was published in 1962 in Vyvyan Holland and Rupert-Hart Davis's *Letters of Oscar Wilde*.

cupation with the gross materialistic side of life, and their ridiculous estimate of themselves and their importance, the Jew of Jerusalem in Christ's day was the exact counterpart of the British Philistine of our own. (751)

### 6. "[Letter to Philip Houghton]" (February 1894), *The Complete Letters of Oscar Wilde*. Ed. Merlin Holland and Rupert Hart-Davis (New York: Henry Holt and Company, 2000), 586

[? Late February 1894]                                   16 Tite Street

Dear Sir, I will send you a manuscript copy of my play, a little incomplete, but still enough to give you an idea of its ethical scheme. Your letter has deeply moved me. To the world I seem, by intention on my part, a dilettante and dandy merely—it is not wise to show one's heart to the world—and as seriousness of manner is the disguise of the fool, folly in its exquisite modes of triviality and indifference and lack of care is the robe of the wise man. In so vulgar an age as this we all need masks.

I, at any rate, am your friend                 OSCAR WILDE

### 7. "[Letter to George Alexander]" (July 1894), *The Complete Letters of Oscar Wilde*. Ed. Merlin Holland and Rupert Hart-Davis (New York: Henry Holt and Company, 2000), 595-97

[? July 1894]                                            16 Tite Street

My dear Aleck, Thanks for your letter. There really is nothing more to tell you about the comedy beyond what I said already. I mean that the real charm of the play, if it is to have charm, must be in the dialogue. The plot is slight, but, I think, adequate.

Act I. Evening party. 10 p.m.

Lord Alfred Rufford's rooms in Mayfair. Arrives from country Bertram Ashton his friend: a man of 25 or 30 years of age: his great friend. Rufford asks him about his life. He tells him that he has a ward, etc. very young and pretty. That in the country he has to be serious, etc. that he comes to town to enjoy himself, and has invented a fictitious younger brother of the name of George—to whom all his misdeeds are put down. Rufford is deeply interested about the ward.

Guests arrive: the Duchess of Selby and her daughter, Lady Maud Rufford, with whom the guardian is in love—Fin-de-Siècle talk, a lot of guests—the guardian proposes to Lady Maud on his knees—enter Duchess—Lady Maud: "Mamma, this is no place for you."

Scene: Duchess enquires for *her son Lord Alfred Rufford*:[1] servant comes in with note to say that Lord Alfred has been suddenly called away to the country. Lady Maud vows eternal fidelity to the guardian whom she only knows under the name of *George* Ashton.

(PS The disclosure of the guardian of his double life is occasioned by Lord Alfred saying to him "You left your handkerchief here the last time you were up" (or cigarette case). The guardian takes it—the Lord A. says "but why, dear George, is it marked Bertram—who *is* Bertram Ashton?" Guardian discloses plot.)

### Act II. The guardian's home—pretty cottage.

Mabel Harford, his ward, and her governess, Miss Prism. Governess of course dragon of propriety. Talk about the profligate George: maid comes in to say "Mr George Ashton". Governess protests against his admission. Mabel insists. Enter Lord Alfred. Falls in love with ward at once. He is reproached with his bad life, etc. Expresses great repentance. They go to garden.

Enter guardian: Mabel comes in: "I have a great surprise for you—your brother is here." Guardian of course denies having a brother. Mabel says "You cannot disown your own brother, whatever he has done"—and brings in Lord Alfred. Scene: also scene between two men alone. Finally Lord Alfred arrested for debts contracted by guardian: guardian delighted: Mabel, however, makes him forgive his brother and pay up. Guardian looks over bills and scolds Lord Alfred for profligacy.

Miss Prism backs the guardian up. Guardian then orders his brother out of the house. Mabel intercedes, and brother remains. Miss Prism has designs on the guardian—matrimonial—she is 40 at least—she believes he is proposing to her and accepts him—his consternation.

### Act III. Mabel and the false brother.

He proposes and is accepted. When Mabel is alone, Lady Maud, who only knows the guardian under the name of George, arrives alone. She tells Mabel she is engaged "to George"—scene naturally. Mabel

---

1    The italics indicate Wilde's underlining in the hand-written letter.

retires: enter George, he kisses his sister naturally. Enter Mabel and sees them. Explanations, of course. Mabel breaks off the match on the ground that there is nothing to reform in George: she only consented to marry him because she thought he was bad and wanted guidance. He promises to be a bad husband—so as to give her an opportunity of making him a better man; she is a little mollified.

Enter guardian: he is reproached also by Lady Maud for his respectable life in the country: a JP: a country-councillor: a church-warden: a philanthropist: a good example. He appeals to his life in London: she is mollified, on condition that he never lives in the country: the country is demoralising: it makes you respectable. "The simple fare at the Savoy: the quiet life in Piccadilly: the solitude of Mayfair is what you need etc."

Enter Duchess in pursuit of her daughter—objects to both matches. Miss Prism, who had in early days been governess to the Duchess, sets it all right, without intending to do so—everything ends happily.

Result
Curtain
Author called
Cigarette called
Manager called

Royalties for a year for author.

Manager credited with writing the play. He consoles himself for the slander with bags of red gold.
Fireworks

Of course this scenario is open to alterations: the third act, after entrance of Duchess, will have to be elaborated: also, the local doctor, or clergyman, must be brought in, in the play for Prism.

Well, I think an amusing thing with lots of fun and wit might be made. If you think so, too, and care to have the refusal of it—do let me know—and send me £150. If when the play is finished, you think it too slight—not serious enough—of course you can have the £150 back—I want to go away and write it—and it could be ready in October—as I have nothing else to do—and Palmer is anxious to have a play from me for the States "with no real serious interest"—just a comedy.

Kind regards to Mrs Aleck. Yours ever        OSCAR

## 8. "[Letter to George Alexander]" (September 1894), *The Complete Letters of Oscar Wilde*. Ed. Merlin Holland and Rupert Hart-Davis (New York: Henry Holt and Company, 2000), 610

[? September 1894]                                    5 Esplanade, Worthing

My dear Aleck, I can't make out what could have become of your letter. I thought from your silence that you thought the play too farcical in incident for a comedy theatre like your own, or that you didn't like my asking you to give me some money. I thought of telegraphing to you, but then changed my mind.

As regards the American rights: when you go to the States, it won't be to produce a farcical comedy. You will go as a romantic actor of modern and costume pieces. My play, though the dialogue is sheer comedy, and the best I have ever written, is of course in idea farcical: it could not be made part of a repertoire of serious or classical pieces, except for fun—once—as Irving[1] plays Jeremy Diddler[2] to show the Bostonians how versatile he is, and how a man who can realise Hamlet for us, can yet hold his own with the best of fantastic farce-players.

I would be charmed to write a modern comedy-drama for you, and to give you rights on both sides of the disappointing Atlantic Ocean, but you, of all our young actors, should not go to America to play farcical comedy. You might just as well star at Philadelphia in *Dr. Bill*.[3] Besides, I hope to make at least £3000 in the States with this play, so what sum could I ask you for, with reference to double rights? Something that you, as a sensible manager, would not dream of paying. No: I want to come back to you. I would like to have my play done by you (I must tell you candidly that the two young men's parts are equally good), but it would be neither for your artistic reputation as a star in the States, nor for my pecuniary advantage, for you to produce it for a couple of nights in each big American town. It would be throwing the thing away.

---

1   Henry Irving (1838-1905), the pre-eminent actor-manager of the late Victorian era and the first actor ever to be knighted (1895). Irving was managed by Bram Stoker, whose novel *Dracula* has been read as a veiled attack on Wilde; see Gladden's "*Dracula*'s Earnestness: Stoker's Debt to Wilde."

2   A ne'er-do-well from the 1803 farce *Raising the Wind*, by James Kenney. Holland and Hart-Davis (610n2) mention that Irving chose to play this character for a comic relief from the tragic parts that he played so frequently and so famously.

3   Evidently an obscure American adaptation of a French farce, *Le Docteur Jo-Jo* (1888), according to an 1890 review in the *New York Times*.

I may mention that the play is an admirable play. I can't come up to town, I have no money. (Why doesn't Hardacre[1] give us something more?) Write me your views—about this whole business. Ever yours

OSCAR

## 9. "[Letter to George Alexander]" (October 1894), *The Complete Letters of Oscar Wilde*. Ed. Merlin Holland and Rupert Hart-Davis (New York: Henry Holt and Company, 2000), 620

[Circa 25 October 1894]                                            16 Tite Street

My dear Aleck, I have been ill in bed for a long time, with a sort of malarial fever, and have not been able to answer your kind letter of invitation. I am quite well now, and, as you wished to see my somewhat farcical comedy, I send you the first copy of it. It is called *Lady Lancing* on the cover: but the real title is *The Importance of Being Earnest*. When you read the play, you will see the punning title's meaning. Of course, the play is not suitable to you at all: you are a romantic actor: the people it wants are actors like Wyndham and Hawtrey.[2] Also, I would be sorry if you altered the definite artistic line of progress you have always followed at the St James's. But, of course, read it, and let me know what you think about it. I have very good offers from America for it.

I read charming accounts of your banquet at Birmingham, and your praise of the English dramatist. I know and admire Pinero's work, but *who is Jones*?[3] Perhaps the name as reported in the London papers was a misprint for something else. I have never heard of Jones. Have you?

Give my kind regards to Mrs Aleck, and believe me, sincerely yours

OSCAR WILDE

---

1  J. Pitt Hardacre managed touring productions of plays, including an 1892 tour of *Lady Windermere's Fan*.
2  Charles Wyndham (1837-1919) was an actor and the manager of the Criterion Theatre, and Charles Hawtrey (1858-1923; knighted 1922) was an actor-manager who created the role of the dandy Lord Goring in Wilde's *An Ideal Husband*. Both were among the leading comic actors of the time.
3  Arthur Wing Pinero (1855-1934) and Henry Arthur Jones (1851-1929) were among the celebrated playwrights of Wilde's day, best known for their "well-made plays"; see the Introduction 12-16. Wilde is surely being playful in suggesting he has never heard of Jones.

10. "[Letter to an Unidentified Correspondent]" (February 1895), *The Complete Letters of Oscar Wilde*. Ed. Merlin Holland and Rupert Hart-Davis (New York: Henry Holt and Company, 2000), 632

[14 February 1895]

Bosie's father is going to make a scene tonight. I am going to stop him.

11. "[Letter to Lord Alfred Douglas]" (February 1895), *The Complete Letters of Oscar Wilde*. Ed. Merlin Holland and Rupert Hart-Davis (New York: Henry Holt and Company, 2000), 632-33

[Circa 17 February 1895]     Tho[ma]s Cook & Son, 33 Piccadilly

Dearest Boy, Yes: the Scarlet Marquis made a plot to address the audience on the first night of my play! Algy Bourke revealed it, and he was not allowed to enter.

He left a grotesque bouquet of vegetables for me! This of course makes his conduct idiotic, robs it of dignity.

He arrived with a prize-fighter!! I had all Scotland Yard—twenty police—to guard the theatre. He prowled about for three hours, then left chattering like a monstrous ape. Percy is on our side.

I feel now that, without your name being mentioned, all will go well.

I had not wished you to know. Percy wired without telling me. I am greatly touched by your rushing over Europe. For my own part I had determined you should know nothing. ·

I will wire to Calais and Dover, and you will of course stay with me till Saturday. I then return to Tite Street, I think.

Ever, with love, all love in the world, devotedly your

OSCAR

12. "[Letter to R.V. Shone]" (February 1895), *The Complete Letters of Oscar Wilde*. Ed. Merlin Holland and Rupert Hart-Davis (New York: Henry Holt and Company, 2000), 631-32

[13 February 1895]

Dear Mr Shone, Lord Queensberry is at Carter's Hotel, Albemarle Street. Write to him from Mr Alexander that you regret to find that the seat given to him was already sold, and return him his money.

This will prevent trouble, I hope. Truly yours     OSCAR WILDE

# Appendix I: From the Original Four-Act Version

[The passages that follow are taken from the manuscript and typescript pages for the original, four-act version of Wilde's play, which was titled *Lady Lancing: A Serious Comedy for Trivial People*. (See the Introduction and the Note on the Text for a more detailed history of the development of the play that would become *The Importance of Being Earnest: A Trivial Comedy for Serious People*.) The passages below illustrate aspects of Wilde's play that did not survive his editing of the original work as required by his producer, George Alexander. Nonetheless, these exchanges provide fascinating insights into a key subplot omitted from the three-act version of the play as well as into more complex aspects of the characters Miss Prism and Lady Bracknell, or Lady "Brancaster," as she was originally named. Collectively, this excised material contributes to one of *Earnest*'s overriding interests: the hypocrisy of a culture that insists on a singular and stable identity, that resists the kind of pleasure and play celebrated throughout *Earnest* by the act of Bunburying and authorized by the sometimes surprisingly progressive, playful attitudes of even the play's most staunchly "Victorian" characters, its embodiments of tradition and cultural morality (see the Introduction 11-12).

Except where noted, all passages below are taken from Oscar Wilde, *Lady Lancing: A Serious Comedy for Trivial People, In Four Acts as Originally Written [The Importance of Being Earnest]*, 1894. Ed. Sarah Augusta Dickson. 2 vols. Arents Tobacco Collection 6 (New York: New York Public Library, 1956).]

## 1. Passages Regarding Algernon's and Ernest's Past-due Accounts

*From Act 1*

ALGERNON. ... Ah! ... Just let me look at those cucumber sandwiches again. [Lane *hands the sandwiches*.] Any brute try to see me this morning?

LANE. The wine merchant waited in the hall, sir, from ten to a quarter to one.[1]

---

1 This is the four-act play's first allusion to the debts that result from a life of excess, a theme that will become increasingly prevalent as *Lady Lancing* moves to the arrival in act 2 of the solicitor Gribsby at Jack's country house to arrest Ernest for unpaid bills at the Savoy Hotel. This sub-plot does not survive in the three-act version of Wilde's play.

ALGERNON. I hope you gave him an uncomfortable chair....Wish to goodness some ass would leave me a large fortune. Can't go on as I am going on now. It is ridiculous. (Wilde, ed. Dickson 1: 4)

JACK. Well, I can't dine at the Savoy. I owe them about £700. They are always getting judgments and things against me. They bother my life out.

ALGERNON. Why on earth don't you pay them? You have got heaps of money.

JACK. Yes, but Ernest hasn't, and I must keep up Ernest's reputation. Ernest is one of those chaps who never pay a bill. He gets writted[1] about once a week. He is always being writted.

ALGERNON. Well, let us dine at Willis's. (Wilde, ed. Berggren 75-76)

*From Act 2*

MERRIMAN [*To* Ernest]. I beg your pardon, sir, there is an elderly gentleman wishes to see you. He has just come in a cab from the station. [*Hands card on salver.*]

ALGERNON. To see me?

MERRIMAN. Yes, sir.[2]

ALGERNON [*Reads card*]. "Parker and Gribsby, Solicitors." I don't know anything about them. Who are they?

JACK [*Takes card*]. Parker and Gribsby. I wonder who they can be. I expect, Ernest, they have come about some business for your friend Bunbury. Perhaps Bunbury wants to make his will, and wishes you to be executor. [*To* Merriman.] Show Messrs. Parker and Gribsby in at once.

MERRIMAN. There is only one gentleman in the hall, sir.

JACK. Show either Mr. Parker or Mr. Gribsby in.

MERRIMAN. Yes, sir.

[*Exit.*]

---

1  Legally cited for unpaid debts. The implication here is that Ernest refuses to pay for his extravagances, and so his creditors are forever pressing him for payment.

2  Merriman's exchanges with Algernon pre-dict his exchange with Cecily at the beginning of *Lady Lancing*'s act 3 upon the arrival and introduction of Gwendolen. Such pre-diction positions the one who is thus introduced here, Gribsby, as a character parallel to the one who will be introduced in act 3, Gwendolen, underscoring what Wilde implies throughout the whole of the Gribsby episode: the supposed guardians of law, order, and morality are in fact just as equally invested in pleasure and play, a doubleness embodied first in Jack and Algy and now in Gribsby and Gwendolen. See Appendix I1, 200n3.

JACK. I hope, Ernest, that I may rely on the statement you made to me last week when I finally settled all your bills for you. I hope you have no outstanding accounts of any kind.

ALGERNON. I haven't any debts at all, dear Jack. Thanks to your generosity I don't owe a penny, except for a few neckties I believe.

JACK. I am sincerely glad to hear it.

MERRIMAN. Mr. Gribsby.

[*Enter* Gribsby.]

GRIBSBY [*To* Canon Chasuble]. Mr. Ernest Worthing?

MISS PRISM. This is Mr. Ernest Worthing.

GRIBSBY. Mr. Ernest Worthing?

ALGERNON. Yes.

GRIBSBY. Of B.4, The Albany—?[1]

ALGERNON. Yes, that is my address.

GRIBSBY. I am very sorry, Mr. Worthing, but we have a writ of attachment[2] for 20 days against you at the suit of the Savoy Hotel Co. Limited for £762.14.2.

ALGERNON. What perfect nonsense! I never dine at the Savoy at my own expense. I always dine at Willis's. It is far more expensive. I don't owe a penny to the Savoy.

GRIBSBY. The writ is marked as having been on you personally at The Albany on May the 27th. Judgement was given in default against you on the fifth of June. Since then we have written to you no less than thirteen times, without receiving any reply. In the interest of our clients we had no option but to obtain an order for committal of your person. But, no doubt, Mr. Worthing, you will be able to settle the account without any further unpleasantness. Seven and

---

1  For the significance of the play's references to The Albany, see *E* 75n3.

2  An arrest warrant. In other words, Gribsby has obtained written orders to take Ernest into custody and transfer him to prison—or to provide him the opportunity to settle his debt instead. In his edition of *Earnest*, Kenneth Krauss notes that "British currency at this time consisted of pounds (£), shillings (s.), and pence (d.); there were 12 pennies to a shilling and 20 shillings to the pound. The sum Jack owes the Savoy roughly translates into $3,800 [in 1890s dollars], an enormous amount" (46n). In 1895, a British pound (£) would be the equivalent of about £480 in 2009, making the debt "Ernest" owes the Savoy approximately £365,760 or roughly $678,338 in American dollars—amounts surely indicative of the stunningly lavish life Ernest has led, as in fact did Wilde, whose own weekly debts during his courtship of Lord Alfred Douglas regularly amounted to around £100, or the 2009 equivalent of £48,091 (McKenna 275; www.measuringworth.com).

six[1] should be added to the bill of costs for expense of the cab which was hired for your convenience in case of any necessity of removal, but that, I am sure, is a contingency that is not likely to occur.

ALGERNON. Removal! What on earth do you mean by removal? I haven't the smallest intention of going away. I am staying here for a week. I am staying with my brother. [*Points to* Jack.]

GRIBSBY [*To* Jack]. Pleased to meet you, sir.

ALGERNON [*To* Gribsby]. If you imagine I am going up to town the moment I arrive you are extremely mistaken.

GRIBSBY. I am merely a solicitor myself. I do not employ personal violence of any kind. The officer of the court whose function it is to seize the person of the debtor is waiting in the fly[2] outside. He has considerable experience in these matters. In the point of fact he has arrested in the course of his duties nearly all the younger sons[3] of the aristocracy, as well as several eldest sons, besides of course a good many members of the House of Lords. His style and manner are considered extremely good. Indeed, he looks more like a betting man than a court-official. That is why we always employ him. But no doubt you will prefer to pay the bill.

ALGERNON. Pay it? How on earth am I going to do that? You don't suppose I have got any money? How perfectly silly you are. No gentleman ever has any money.[4]

GRIBSBY. My experience is that it is usually relatives who pay.

JACK. Kindly allow me to see this bill, Mr. Gribsby ... [*Turns over immense folio.*] ... £762.14.2 since last October.... I am bound to say I never saw such reckless extravagance in all my life.[5] [*Hands it to Dr. Chasuble.*]

---

1   That is, seven shillings and six pence (7s.6d.), or just over a third of a pound.

2   A public carriage drawn by a single horse; also called a hansom.

3   In the British tradition of primogeniture, estates generally passed to the eldest son rather than being divided among heirs. Therefore younger sons of the aristocracy were generally raised with expensive tastes but little means to support them, and daughters were encouraged to marry "well."

4   Algernon's speech reminds readers that gentlemanliness and respectability proceed from pure pose, not substance—the appearance of wealth, but no guarantee of money. The phrase "no gentleman ever" will be echoed by Jack in *Lady Lancing*'s act 4, underscoring the men's function as doubles throughout the play.

5   Wilde peppers his play with the adjective "reckless," perhaps most powerfully here and in a speech by the solicitor Gribsby shortly to follow. Jack's language and his attitude follow from the judgmental position Lady Bracknell adopts in act 1 when she speaks of "the worst excesses of the French Revolution" (*E* 89), there fearing, as Jack fears here, the complete breakdown of all order. These speeches thus connect two quite different characters—the youthful/pro-

MISS PRISM. 762 pounds for eating! How grossly materialistic! There can be little good in any young man who eats so much, and so often.

CHASUBLE. It certainly is a painful proof of the disgraceful luxury of the age. We are far away from Wordsworth's plain living and high thinking.[1]

JACK. Now, Dr. Chasuble, do you consider that I am in any way called upon to pay this monstrous account for my brother?

CHASUBLE. I am bound to say that I do not think so. It would be encouraging his profligacy.[2]

MISS PRISM. As a man sows, so let him reap.[3] This proposed incarceration might be most salutary. It is to be regretted that [it] is only for 20 days.[4]

JACK. I am quite of your opinion.

ALGERNON. My dear fellow, how ridiculous you are! You know perfectly well that the bill is really yours.

JACK. Mine?

ALGERNON. Yes, you know it is.

---

gressive/duplicitous Jack and the older/traditional/judgmental Bracknell—and therefore remind us that what seem to be distinctions between characters are often composite aspects of single individuals, an argument that throws completely into question the notion of what Wilde's culture might have considered a "stable" identity.

1  William Wordsworth (1770-1850), the English poet and pillar of the Romantic movement, was known for his reverence for nature and for the common people. These comments from Miss Prism and Reverend Chasuble emphasize the play's links between extremes in appetites of all sorts—for food and for love, the gustatorial and the erotic—and the subversion of traditional society, chiefly by those who reject social codes of behavior in favor of selfish pleasures. Further, Wilde clearly casts the decadent, dandiacal lives of Jack and Algernon in sharp contrast to Wordsworthian Romanticism, implying the obvious distinction between an artistic movement that turns to nature as a source and site of truth (Romanticism) and one that follows the Symboliste doctrine of "*l'art pour l'art*" ("art for art's sake," or what is generally known as Aestheticism).

2  See *E* 91n2 for Cohen's interpretation of the various resonances of the term "profligacy": here, as before, what seems a measure of personal morality and the management of desire may also embed a reference to transgressive sexuality.

3  This is the second time Miss Prism has invoked this proverb. That Miss Prism's language exactly echoes her earlier words implies her equation of the fates of Bunbury and Ernest—a quite precise understanding of the play's alignment of those twin embodiments of irresponsibility.

4  The word "it" has been inserted for clarity, thereby correcting an omission in the manuscript and typescript of *Lady Lancing*.

CHASUBLE. Mr. Worthing, if this is a jest, it is out of place.

MISS PRISM. It is gross effrontery.[1] Just what I expected from him.

CECILY. It is ingratitude. I didn't expect that.

JACK. Never mind what he says. This is the way he always goes on. You mean now to say that you are not Ernest Worthing, residing at B.4, The Albany? I wonder, as you are at it, that you don't deny being my brother at all. Why don't you?

ALGERNON. Oh! I am not going to do that, my dear fellow; it would be absurd. Of course, I'm your brother. And that is why you should pay this bill for me. What is the use of having a brother, if he doesn't pay one's bills for one?[2]

JACK. Personally, if you ask me, I don't see any use in having a brother. As for paying your bill, I have not the smallest intention of doing anything of the kind. Dr. Chasuble, the worthy Rector of this parish, and Miss Prism, in whose admirable and sound judgment I place great reliance, are both of opinion that incarceration would do you a great deal of good. And I think so, too.

GRIBSBY [Pulls out watch]. I am sorry to disturb this pleasant family meeting, but time presses. We have to be at Holloway not later than four o'clock; otherwise it is difficult to obtain admission. The rules are very strict.[3]

ALGERNON. Holloway![4]

GRIBSBY. It is at Holloway that detentions of this character take place always.

---

1  Miss Prism's phrase pre-dicts Gwendolen's language upon her discovery that the men are eating muffins (E 127). Both speeches eschew excess in the consumption of food, whether in inappropriate amounts (here) or at inappropriate times (there). Throughout the play, food operates as a metaphor for desire (see the Introduction 43-46), and eating functions as a displacement for erotic engagement; Algernon's excessive consumption may thus be likened to licentiousness, to wantonness or promiscuity, again linking the Bunburyist to one who leads a "profligate" life of selfish, excessive, erotic gratification.

2  Algernon's language pre-dicts the speeches in the play's final act following Jack's discovery that Algernon is his younger brother, where Algernon's sentiment gets reversed—echoed—for comic effect, when Jack introduces Algernon as his brother to those assembled in the room.

3  Gribsby's concerns about time and transportation pre-dict similar anxieties voiced by Lady Brancaster in her final speech in the play, reminding readers again of the connections between these minor and major characters and, thus, that just as Gribsby is both an embodiment of law and order and a figure of pleasure and play, so, too, may be Lady Brancaster, even though all we see of her throughout the play is her (supposed) earnestness.

4  A prison located just outside London—and the very one in which Wilde would be held from 5 April to 7 May 1895 as he awaited trial.

ALGERNON. Well, I really am not going to be imprisoned in the suburbs for having dined in the West End.[1] It is perfectly ridiculous.[2]

GRIBSBY. The bill is for suppers, not for dinners.[3]

ALGERNON. I really don't care. All I say is that I am not going to be imprisoned in the suburbs.

GRIBSBY. The surroundings, I admit, are middle class; but the gaol itself is fashionable and well-aired, and there are ample opportunities of taking exercise at certain stated hours of the day. In the case of a medical certificate, which is always easy to obtain, the hours can be extended.

ALGERNON. Exercise! Good God! No gentleman ever takes exercise. You don't seem to understand what a gentleman is.

GRIBSBY. I have met so many of them, sir, that I am afraid I don't. There are the most curious varieties of them. The result of cultivation, no doubt.[4] Will you kindly come now, sir, if it will not be inconvenient to you.

ALGERNON [*Appealingly*]. Jack!

MISS PRISM. Pray be firm, Mr. Worthing.

CHASUBLE. This is an occasion on which any weakness would be out of place. It would be a form of self-deception.

---

1   London's theatre district, where the Savoy Hotel is located. The hotel is attached to the Savoy Theatre, where many of the most famous works of Gilbert and Sullivan were first produced. Wilde kept a suite of rooms and slept with Lord Alfred Douglas in the Savoy, one of the most respectable and expensive of the city's luxury hotels, and members of the Savoy staff were called to testify during Wilde's trials about the comings and goings of Wilde and his all-male entourage.

2   Algernon's complaint is that a person of privilege should be treated as anything else when incarcerated: in Wilde's day, the West End was London's site of wealth and affluence; the suburbs, of economy.

3   In Wilde's culture, "suppers" denoted evening meals, and "dinners" denoted those taken at mid-day.

4   Wilde aligns the sort of gentleman Algernon invokes with the "curious" and with "cultivation." In Wilde's day, the word "curious" functioned as a code for what we would now call homosexuality; in the present speech, all of these qualities are posed in opposition to lawfulness and to the lawfully minded, whom Gribsby represents—in sharp contrast to dandies like Algernon, who love nonsense and ridiculousness—unless and until such attitudes affect them negatively. Subsequent drafts of the play contain a speech by Lady Brancaster near the end of the fourth act making reference to a novel called *The Green Carnation*, which describes, as she says, "the cultivation of exotics"; for more on Hichens's *The Green Carnation*, see *E* 69n1 and *E* 143n1, as well as the Introduction 33.

JACK. I am quite firm; and I don't know what weakness or deception of any kind is.[1]

CECILY. Uncle Jack! I think you have a little money of mine haven't you? Let me pay this bill. I wouldn't like your own brother to be in prison.

JACK. Oh, you can't pay it, Cecily, that is nonsense.

CECILY. Then you will, won't you? I think you would be sorry if you thought your own brother was shut up. Of course, I am quite disappointed with him.

JACK. You won't speak to him again, Cecily, will you?

CECILY. Certainly not, unless, of course, he speaks to me first; it would be very rude not to answer him.

JACK. Well, I'll take care he doesn't speak to you. I'll take care he doesn't speak to anybody in this house. The man should be cut, Mr. Gribsby—

GRIBSBY. Yes, sir.

JACK. I'll pay this bill for my brother. It is the last bill I shall ever pay for him, too. How much is it?

GRIBSBY. £762.14.2. May I ask your full name, sir?

JACK. Mr. John Worthing, J.P., The Manor House, Woolton. Does that satisfy you?

GRIBSBY. Oh, certainly, sir, certainly! It was a mere formality. [*To Miss Prism.*] Handsome place. Ah! the cab will be 5/9 extra—hired for the convenience of the client.

JACK. All right.

MISS PRISM. I must say that I think such generosity quite foolish. Especially paying the cab.

CHASUBLE [*With a wave of the hand*]. The heart has its wisdom as well as the head, Miss Prism.

JACK. Payable to Gribsby and Parker, I suppose.

GRIBSBY. Yes, sir. Kindly don't cross the cheque.[2] Thank you.

JACK. You are Gribsby, aren't you? What is Parker like?

GRIBSBY. I am both, sir. Gribsby when I am on unpleasant business, Parker on occasions of a less serious kind.[3]

---

1 Pre-dicts Lady Bracknell's language in act 3: "On this point, as indeed on all points, I am firm" (*E* 131).

2 To "cross the cheque" means to make it non-transferable: perhaps Gribsby will use this money to pay someone else.

3 Gribsby's speech shows that even representatives of the law may lead double-lives, that the kind of life such figures enjoy does not necessarily exclude other kinds of life altogether. Charles Parker is the name of one of the individuals with whom Wilde was reported to have committed acts of gross indecency in the spring of 1893, well before he began writing *Earnest*. "Parker" perhaps

JACK. The next time I see you I hope you will be Parker.

GRIBSBY. I hope so, sir. [*To* Dr. Chasuble.] Good day. [Dr. Chasuble *bows coldly*.] Good day. [Miss Prism *bows coldly*.] Hope I shall have the pleasure of meeting you again. [*To* Algernon.]

ALGERNON. I sincerely hope not. What ideas you have of the sort of society a gentleman wants to mix in. No gentleman ever wants to know a solicitor who wants to imprison one in the suburbs.

GRIBSBY. Quite so, quite so.

ALGERNON. By the way, Gribsby. Gribsby, you are not to go back to the station in that cab. That is my cab. It was taken for my convenience. You and the gentleman who looks like the betting-man have got to walk to the station. And a very good thing, too. Solicitors don't walk nearly enough. They bolt. But they don't walk. I don't know any solicitor who takes sufficient exercise. As a rule they sit in stuffy offices all day long neglecting their business.

JACK. You can take the cab, Mr. Gribsby.

GRIBSBY. Thank you, sir.

[*Exit.*] (Wilde, ed. Dickson 1: 74-82)

## 2. Passages Illuminating the Characters and Roles of Miss Prism and Canon Chasuble

*From Act 2*

MISS PRISM. Cecily, that sounds like Socialism. And I suppose you know where Socialism leads to?[1] (Wilde, ed. Dickson 1: 57)

---

functions, like "Bunbury," as a signifier not only of an individual but of the type of person whom society would perceive as living purely for pleasure. As such, the name may also embed one of the play's several noddings to Wilde's private life.

1   Another moment of verbal echonomy (see the Introduction 38-42): Miss Prism directly echoes Lady Brancaster's rejection of the French Revolution in the speech that includes the rhetorical question, "And I presume you know what that unfortunate movement led to?" (*E* 89). Such an echo suggests the similarity between Miss Prism and Lady Brancaster, for although at times they are pitted against each other, especially in the three-act version of *Earnest*, these women stand as embodiments of morality in Wilde's play, unwittingly adding to the play's comic effects when they say, do, and think things that register on transgressive levels in ways apparently unknown to them. Ignorance of such double meanings may thus function as simple naïveté or as a cloak for hypocrisy, showing Wilde's audience, to its delight, that even the most uptight among late-Victorian society remained blind to social transgressions, all the while (unknowingly) endorsing them.

CHASUBLE. Fruits grown in the pleasant garden of memory, I doubt not. [*Aside.*] An admirable woman, though somewhat slow of wit.

MISS PRISM. A sluggish intellect, though a good man. More violent measures are necessary.[1] Dr. Chasuble, we have had quite a long walk. May I offer you a glass of sherry? (Wilde, ed. Dickson 1: 66)

CHASUBLE. ... I do not know, however, if you would care to join them at the Font. Personally I do not approve myself of the obliteration of class-distinctions. I think they were ordered for our profit and instruction.[2] (Wilde, ed. Dickson 1: 70)

MISS PRISM. To partake of two luncheons in one day would not be liberty. It would be licence.[3]

CHASUBLE. Even the pagan philosophers condemned excess in eating. Aristotle speaks of it with severity. He uses the [same] terms about it as he does about usury.

ALGERNON. But I have an extremely good appetite. Country air gives me almost as good an appetite as town air does. I've not been so hungry since yesterday.

MISS PRISM. The appetites were given us to be checked, not to be gratified.[4] Cecily, luncheon is waiting. Let us set an example of punctuality. (Wilde, ed. Dickson 1: 84)

---

1   Although not so marked by stage directions, the first two sentences of Miss Prism's speech are meant as an aside, as are Dr. Chasuble's previous lines. Miss Prism's critique of Reverend Chasuble, as well as his remarks about her immediately above, were both removed from later drafts of *Earnest*, which construct these characters as much more simple beings, uncomplicated by the kind of critical, metacognitive tendencies Wilde suggests here.

2   Wilde's lines remind us of the connection between Chasuble and other characters in the play who embody pretentiousness and traditional morality, such as Lady Brancaster and Miss Prism. These lines thus suggest that Chasuble should be grouped with them as one kind of character in the play, while the younger couples, the doubles Jack/Algy and Gwendolen/Cecily, embody what is essentially an alternative, progressive perspective.

3   Compare Lady Brancaster's response in the four-act play to Jack's status as having lost both parents ("To lose one parent may be regarded as a misfortune. To lose both seems like carelessness" [Wilde, ed. Dickson 1: 29]), an echo that aligns Miss Prism with Lady Brancaster.

4   Miss Prism's speech underscores her role as an embodiment of traditional morality, since above all else she encourages keeping the appetite(s) in check.

*From Act 3*

MISS PRISM. Profligacy is apt to dull the senses, Mr. Worthing.[1]
(Wilde, ed. Dickson 1: 98)

MISS PRISM. My sweet child! Good-bye, Mr. Worthing. Ah! If you
had only remembered that as a man sows so shall he reap[2] you
would not find yourself now in such a painful and humiliating position. [*To* Cecily.] You really think the strings are better tied at the
side?[3] (Wilde, ed. Dickson 1: 99)

*From Act 4*

MISS PRISM [*Who has shuddered visibly at the expression: the naked
truth*]. I have to thank you for so flattering a testimonial, Mr. Montford.[4] Should you find time to commit it to writing the document
will remain the sole consolation of a life that I fear will be extremely
solitary. For it is my duty to leave. It had never occurred to me before
that as a woman sows, so shall she reap. I had thought that that apho-
rism only applied to the male sex. I was in error. And besides I have
really nothing more to teach dear Cecily. In the very difficult accom-
plishment of getting married, I fear my sweet and clever pupil has far
outstripped her teacher. (Wilde, ed. Dickson 1: 174)

---

1 While her proto-social-constructionist perspective may make Miss Prism seem
 rather progressive, here Wilde exposes her more traditional, conservative side:
 the belief that "profligacy is apt to dull the senses" parallels contemporary
 Degeneration theory, most fully articulated in Max Nordau's *Degeneration* (on
 profligacy, see *E* 91n2). An entire section of Nordau's book focuses on the
 Aesthetes and targets Wilde as one of many cultural threats gaining visibility
 and influence throughout Europe.
2 Miss Prism's third invocation of this proverb emphasizes her role as an
 embodiment of traditional and unforgiving morality. The final line of *this*
 speech, however, shifts abruptly from the serious to the superficial, from substance to style, thus aligning Miss Prism with Cecily and, through her, with
 Wilde and the Aesthetic philosophy articulated in his "Phrases and Philosophies for the Use of the Young" (see Appendix H2).
3 In asking Cecily about the best way to tie her bonnet, Miss Prism's shift from
 serious concerns to the apparently trivial reminds readers of Wilde's strategy
 of shifting from seriousness to triviality—so much so that, by the play's end,
 we appreciate how and to what effect Wilde collapses the distinctions between
 them.
4 "Montford," Algy's last name in earlier hand-written drafts of the play, was
 entered here inadvertently.

CHASUBLE. Lætitia, when I entered this room a short time ago I found it a scene of painful discord. It is to you, and to you alone, that the present harmony is due. It is to you also that our esteemed and honoured host owes the fact that we can still look up to him as a man of the very strictest veracity even in details about his family life, a point in which most men as a rule go sadly astray.... I have also come to the conclusion that the Primitive Church was in error on certain points. Corrupt readings seem to have crept into the text.... Lætitia, I beg to solicit the honour of your hand.

MISS PRISM. Frederick, at the present moment words fail me to express my feelings. But I will forward you this evening the three last volumes of my diary; in these you will be able to peruse a full account of the sentiments that I have entertained towards you for the last eighteen months.[1] (Wilde, ed. Dickson 1: 175)

## 3. Additional Passages

*From Act 1*

LADY BRANCASTER. I cannot say that I approve of so strange an inversion[2] of the more customary procedure in such matters. But, as I am told, you are fond of useful information, Gwendolen,—a taste of which I cannot say that I approve in one of your years—you will be interested to learn that you are not engaged at all. (Wilde, ed. Dickson 1: 25)

---

1 Here, Miss Prism, that figure of rationality and order who eschews Cecily's flights of fancy and encourages her to focus instead on a rather dry sort of education, gets unmasked as an older version of her pupil, for just as the pupil has preceded her teacher into marriage, so too has the pupil modeled a behavior her teacher publicly discouraged yet privately, secretly, indulged—diary-keeping and, as Wilde's audience learned from the initial meeting of Cecily and Algernon, the conversion-via-writing of imagination into reality, of fiction into fact.

2 In addition to suggesting a reversal, the term "inversion" was also used by the German sexologists Karl Westphal and Karl Ulrichs to describe what is now understood as male homosexuality. This particular meaning entered late-Victorian culture as the sexologists' work became more widely known; many men who experienced same-sex desire were called, and sometimes even called themselves, "inverts." Inversion is a key aspect examined in Max Nordau's tome *Degeneration*, and it also forms the core of Havelock Ellis's book-length study *Sexual Inversion*, which was published in 1897, the same year Wilde was released from Reading Gaol. For other instances of inversion in the play, see *E* 124n1.

ALGERNON. Oh, no good chap makes a good husband. If a chap makes a good husband there must have been something rather peculiar about him when he was a bachelor. To be a good husband requires considerable practice.[1] (Wilde, ed. Dickson 1: 33)

JACK. ... And after all what does it matter whether a man has ever had a father and mother or not? Mothers, of course, are all right. They pay a chap's bills and don't bother him. But fathers bother a chap and never pay his bills. I don't know a single chap at the club who speaks to his father.

ALGERNON. Yes. Fathers are certainly not popular just at present.[2]

JACK. Popular! I bet you anything you like that there is not a single chap, of all the chaps that you and I know, who would be seen walking down St. James's Street with his own father. [*Throws cigarette away.*] (Wilde, ed. Dickson 1: 35-36)

JACK. ... [*Throws cigarette away.*] Don't think much of these cigarettes of yours, Algy.

ALGERNON. Yes, I see you throw them away almost as soon as you have lit them.

JACK. I am tired of gold-tipped cigarettes. You can get them quite cheap now. No particular advantage in smoking them any longer.

ALGERNON. Ah! those cigarettes are rather smart. They have got my monogram on each of them.

JACK [*Sneeringly*]. I don't quite see how that can make the tobacco any better.

---

1  Like identity throughout *Earnest*, Algernon's speech proves curiously double: it implies that good husbands result from bachelors who have a lot of practice, presumably at romancing, yet its use of the words "peculiar" and "bachelor" introduce an entirely different element of erotic experience, since by the time of Wilde's writing of the play, both were circulating as code words for what we would now refer to as "homosexual." Whichever reading of these terms one follows, homosexual or heterosexual, something decidedly sexual lurks throughout in Algernon's speech, reminding readers of the erotic undercurrent that percolates throughout Wilde's comedy of manners, just as within the play, dubious secret lives and moments of disrespectability go hand-in-hand with honesty and respectability—and, indeed, these together compose the complex quality that is earnestness.

2  Many critics see this as Wilde's dig at The Marquis of Queensberry, the father of Wilde's lover Lord Alfred Douglas, who had been following Wilde and "Bosie," as Lord Alfred was known, from place to place, loudly and often publicly accusing them of improprieties. His accusations eventually led to Wilde's three trials and his conviction and incarceration for such acts. See the Introduction 32-34 and the Chronology for the year 1895.

ALGERNON. It does, to me.[1] (Wilde, ed. Dickson 1: 37-38)

JACK. What are you doing to-morrow?

ALGERNON [*Pleasantly and buoyantly*]. To-morrow, my dear fellow? To-morrow I go to the country, Bunburying.

JACK. Nonsense.

ALGERNON. I do really. I start in the morning. It will probably be a capital day for Bunburying.

JACK. Where are you going to Bunbury at?

ALGERNON. I'll tell you when I come back. Come and sup at the Club to-morrow night at twelve, and I'll possibly let you know whether I have had a successful Bunbury or not.

JACK. Oh, I don't want to know anything about it. All I say is that you'll get yourself into a serious scrape some day.

ALGERNON. I like scrapes. They are the only things that are never serious.

JACK. I have made up my mind to kill that brother of mine.

ALGERNON. It is rather heartless of you. He has been a very good brother to you, and very useful.

JACK. My dear fellow, you have never had a brother. I have had a brother for the last eight months. Quite long enough for anyone to have a brother, I should fancy.

ALGERNON. Well, Bunbury is no relation of mine, but I wouldn't kill him for anything. I couldn't live without Bunbury.

JACK. Ah! I am engaged you see, and I think it is high time to give up all that sort of nonsense. (Wilde, ed. Dickson 1: 39-40)

*From Act 2*

MISS PRISM. Cecily, this will never do. Pray open your Schiller at once.

CECILY. But I don't like German.

MISS PRISM. You should not talk flippantly of a language whose

---

1 Late-Victorian dandies flaunted many modes of affectation, such as mono-grammed cigarettes. Following the première of *Lady Windermere's Fan*, Wilde shocked audiences by offering a curtain speech while smoking a cigarette, a defiant gesture that helped solidify his reputation as a dandy and a hedonist, as one who refused to conform to social convention. Wilde's own cigarettes, usually bought on account from Robert Lewis's shop at 19 St. James's Street in London, were gold-tipped and monogrammed with his initials, suggesting a close identification of the playwright with his creation. See also *E* 73n2.

grammar displays such interesting varieties of syntax, gender, and expression.[1]

CECILY. Yes ... but it isn't at all a becoming language, at any rate for a young girl. I know perfectly well that I always look quite plain after my German lesson, if I have given it any attention at all. But I don't often do that, do I?[2] (Wilde, ed. Dickson, 1: 51-52)

CECILY. Uncle Jack, whose health has been sadly undermined by the late hours you keep in town, has been ordered by his London doctor to have *pâté-de-foie-gras* sandwiches and 1874 champagne at 12. I don't know if such invalid's fare would suit you.[3] (Wilde, ed. Dickson 1: 63)

ALGERNON. It is all very well, but one can't Bunbury when one is hungry....[4] (Wilde, ed. Dickson 1: 86)

---

1  Those among Wilde's audience familiar with the (homo)erotic resonances of the metaphor of Germanness would certainly find humor in this line, which acknowledges that language's "interesting varieties of [...] gender." See *E* 82n1, *E* 97n1, and *E* 129n1; see also Appendix I3, 209n2.

2  Like the references to German music in act 1, this reference to German lessons also provides a homoerotic subtext. Cecily realizes that her association with Germanness renders her completely unattractive, as indeed any woman would be to the eye of a man inclined to "Germanness," or same-sex desire. See *E* 82n1, *E* 97n1, and *E* 129n1; and Appendix I3, 209n1.

3  Compare this to the exchange that opens act 1 in which Algernon and Lane attribute the excessive consumption of champagne to bachelors and lament the lack of good champagne in married households (*E* 69-70). Given that context, here Wilde comically suggests that the bachelor's repast is essentially the same as the invalid's, thereby introducing two complicated yet apt equations for the bachelor, first with illness and weakness—and, by cultural logic, with femininity; and second with the play's actual invalid, Bunbury. Bunbury thus stands in for the bachelor and vice versa, and it is Bunbury himself and Bunburying itself that guarantee otherwise respectable, "healthy" men the "invalid"—indeed, the in-valid—pleasures of bachelorhood, the flight from adult masculine responsibility.

4  Algernon's comment proves telling for readers of the play who understand "Bunburying" as a code for illicit behavior, particularly of a homosexual sort: since food functions throughout the play as a metaphor for desire (see the Introduction 43-46), Algernon's observation that "one can't Bunbury when one is hungry" juxtaposes hunger (or desire) with Bunburying, suggesting that Bunburying is hunger's opposite—satisfaction, satiation, and so on. To hunger is to desire; to Bunbury is to be, or to become, satisfied.

*From Act 3*

CECILY. Ah! Believe me, dear Miss Prism, it is only the superficial
qualities that last. Man's deeper nature is soon found out.[1] (Wilde,
ed. Dickson 1: 96)

CECILY. Ah! that, dear Ernest, is clearly a metaphysical speculation,
and like most metaphysical speculations quite profitless as far as
any actual relation to practical life is concerned.[2] (Wilde, ed.
Dickson 1: 110)

CECILY. Dear sweet boy he is![3] (Wilde, ed. Dickson 1: 114)

*From Act 4*

LADY BRANCASTER. ... During the whole course of my married
life I have never undeceived Lord Brancaster about anything. As a
natural consequence, he has the most perfect trust in whatever I tell
him. (Wilde, ed. Dickson 1: 145)

ALGERNON [*Behind screen to* Cecily *who is whispering and laughing*].
Hush!
LADY BRANCASTER. Mr. Worthing, is it you who keeps on saying
"Hush" whenever I am talking?

---

1   Cecily's speech echoes two aphorisms from Wilde's "Phrases and Philosophies
    for the Use of the Young": "In all unimportant matters, style, not sincerity, is
    the essential. In all important matters, style, not sincerity, is the essential" and
    "If one tells the truth, one is sure, sooner or later, to be found out" (1244). Of
    course, Gwendolen repeats the first of these—thus demonstrating that she is
    of the same type as her "frenemy" Cecily—at the beginning of act 3 of
    *Earnest*: "In matters of grave importance, style, not sincerity is the vital thing"
    (*E* 128).
2   Cecily's line almost exactly repeats Gwendolen's response in act 1 to Jack's
    query about whether she could love him if his name were not Ernest—exactly
    the conundrum Algernon tries to work out with Cecily here. Such an echo
    reminds readers that Gwendolen and Cecily are less individuals than types,
    just as might be said of Jack and Algernon as well as of both romantic rela-
    tionships developed between the play's younger characters.
3   Here, Cecily seems to take Algernon/Ernest at his word and to believe him,
    therefore, to be sincere. In the three-act version, however, Wilde altered
    Cecily's speech to characterize Algernon/Ernest not as "sweet" but as
    "impetuous" (*E* 114), therefore marking what she loves about him not as his
    sincerity or depth but as his shallowness, his superficiality and, as "impetu-
    ous" connotes, his inconsistency and irresponsibility.

JACK. No, Lady Brancaster. I have been listening with the deepest interest to everything you say.

LADY BRANCASTER. It is clear then that there is someone who says "Hush" concealed in this apartment. The ejaculation has reached my ears more than once. It is not at any time a very refined expression, and its use, when I am talking, is extremely vulgar, and indeed insolent. I suspect it to have proceeded from the lips of someone who is of more than usually low origin.

JACK. I really think you must be mistaken about it, Lady Brancaster. There is a sort of echo I believe in this room. I have no doubt it is that.

LADY BRANCASTER [*With a bitter smile*]. In the course of my travels I have visited many of the localities most remarkable for their echoes, both at home and abroad. I am ready to admit that the accuracy of their powers of repetition has been grossly overestimated, no doubt for the sake of gain, but in no instance have I ever found an echo to say "Hush" in answer to an observation. Such an occurrence would be most improper. It would be a kind of miracle. It would tend to superstition. My hearing, I may mention, is unusually acute, as indeed are all my senses: my sight, my touch, my capacity for discerning odours. [*Looks about the room carefully with her lorgnette. Finally, catching sight of a glance between* Jack *and* Gwendolen, *she turns her attention to the screen. She glares at it for a short time.*] Mr. Worthing, might I ask you to be kind enough to move aside that screen?

JACK [*Cheerily*]. What screen, Lady Brancaster?

LADY BRANCASTER [*Stonily*]. That screen, if you please. I see no other in the room. [Jack *is obliged to move back the screen.* Algernon *and* Cecily *are discovered; they are holding each other's hands.*] Algernon! You here? (Wilde, ed. Dickson 1: 146–47)

LADY BRANCASTER. Child! never fall into the habit, so unfortunately common now-a-days, of talking trivially about serious things.[1] (Wilde, ed. Dickson 1: 153)

---

1 Lady Brancaster's admonishment alludes to the play's original subtitle, "A Serious Comedy for Trivial People," which Wilde modified for the three-act version of the play. In its rejection of triviality, Lady Brancaster's comment re-emphasizes her function throughout the production as an embodiment of tradition, of morality, as are the Reverend Chasuble and Miss Prism. In Wilde's four-act version, Miss Prism virtually overtakes the lead as such a person from Lady Brancaster, but in the three-act, the re-named Lady Bracknell clearly lords her moral superiority over all others.

ALGERNON [*Coming over and taking* Cecily *by the two hands*]. Cecily is the prettiest girl in the whole world.

GWENDOLEN [*In indignant surprise*]. Algy!

ALGERNON. The prettiest girl in the whole world, for me.[1] (Wilde, ed. Dickson 1: 154)

JACK. ... Nothing could induce me to give my consent. In this matter I am firm, as indeed in all matters I am firm.[2] I do not allow Miss Cardew to become engaged to your nephew. I forbid it absolutely. (Wilde, ed. Dickson 1: 156)

JACK. ... No gentleman ever corroborates a thing that he knows to be untrue.[3] (Wilde, ed. Dickson 1: 158)

---

1  This marks the third and final time in *Lady Lancing* that Algernon refers to Cecily as "the prettiest girl in the whole world," making Algernon the only character other than Miss Prism to speak a phrase of his/her own more than twice. In so doing, both characters attempt to establish authority, but where in Miss Prism's case such relentless insistence ironically undercuts her, in Algernon's, such repetition seems merely another of his excesses, like eating, and thus a mark of his dandiacal charm.

2  Jack echoes Lady Brancaster's earlier pronouncement that "On this point, as indeed on all points, I am firm" (*E* 131). In so doing, Jack effectively claims power from Lady Brancaster, undercutting her prior pronouncement of certainty through this taunting, mocking gesture (see the Introduction 38-42).

3  Jack's line begins with an echo of a linguistic formation that marks one of Algernon's speeches in act 2, the haughty "no gentleman ever ...", thereby underscoring the men's function as doubles throughout Wilde's play. See also Appendix I1, 201 and 198n4.

# Bibliography

## Works Cited and Consulted

Adams, James Eli. Afterword. *Dandies and Desert Saints: Styles of Victorian Manhood*. Ithaca: Cornell UP, 1995. 229-31.

"Aestheticism as Oscar Understands It." *The Daily Graphic* 11 January 1882: n. pag. Rpt. in Lewis and Smith, *Oscar Wilde Discovers America* 53.

Applebaum, Stanley, ed. *The Importance of Being Earnest: A Trivial Comedy for Serious People*. By Oscar Wilde. New York: Dover Publications, 1990. Dover Thrift Editions.

Archer, William. "[Review of *The Importance of Being Earnest*]." *The World* 20 February 1895. Rpt. in Tydeman 66.

Arnold, Matthew. *Culture and Anarchy: An Essay in Political and Social Criticism*. 1869. Ed. Samuel Lipman. New Haven: Yale UP, 1994.

Auden, W.H. "An Improbable Life." 1963. Ellmann, ed., 116-37.

Beard, W.H. "The Aesthetic Monkey." *Harper's Weekly* 28 January 1882. Rpt. in Lewis and Smith, *Oscar Wilde Discovers America* 82.

Beckson, Karl. Chronology. *The Oscar Wilde Encyclopedia*. New York: AMS P 1998. xv-xviii.

——, "Love in Earnest: The Importance of Being Uranian." *London in the 1890s: A Cultural History*. New York: W.W. Norton, 1992. 186-212.

——, ed. *Aesthetes and Decadents of the 1890s: An Anthology of British Poetry and Prose*. 1981. Chicago: Academy Chicago Publishers, 1993.

——, ed. *Oscar Wilde: The Critical Heritage*. London: Routledge and Kegan Paul, 1971. The Critical Heritage Series.

Beerbohm, Max. "In Defence of Cosmetics." 1894. Beckson, ed., *Aesthetes and Decadents of the 1890s* 47-63.

——. ["A Letter to the Editor."] 1894. Beckson, ed., *Aesthetes and Decadents of the 1890s* 63-66.

——. ["Recollection of the opening night of *The Importance of Being Earnest* by Max Beerbohm, originally written in 1902."] *Around Theatres*. 2 vols. New York: Alfred A. Knopf, 1930. 1: 240-43. Rpt. in Popkin, ed., 136-39.

Belford, Barbara. *Oscar Wilde: A Certain Genius*. New York: Random House, 2000.

Bentley, Eric. "*The Importance of Being Earnest*." Ellmann, ed., 111-15.

Biggs, John. *Ernest Worthing: A Musical Play in Three Acts.* Ventura: Consort P, 1997.

Blanchard, Mary Warner. *Oscar Wilde's America: Counterculture in the Gilded Age.* New Haven: Yale UP, 1998.

Bradley, Ian, ed. *The Complete and Annotated Gilbert and Sullivan.* New York: Oxford UP, 1996.

Bristow, Joseph. *Effeminate England: Homoerotic Writing after 1885.* New York: Columbia UP, 1995.

———. Introduction. The Importance of Being Earnest *and Related Writings.* By Oscar Wilde. Ed. Bristow. New York: Routledge, 1992. 1-26. Routledge English Texts.

Brown, Julia Prewitt. *Cosmopolitan Criticism: Oscar Wilde's Philosophy of Art.* Charlottesville: UP of Virginia, 1997.

Cave, Richard Allen, ed. The Importance of Being Earnest *and Other Plays.* By Oscar Wilde. New York: Penguin Books, 2000. Penguin Classics.

Cohen, Ed. *Talk on the Wilde Side: Toward a Genealogy of a Discourse on Male Sexualities.* New York: Routledge, 1993.

Craft, Christopher. "Alias Bunbury: Desire and Termination in *The Importance of Being Earnest." Representations* 31 (Summer 1990): 19-46.

Daniel, Anne Margaret. "Wilde the Writer." Roden, ed., 36-71.

Darwin, Charles. *The Origin of Species* [*On the Origin of Species by Means of Natural Selection, or The Preservation of Favoured Races in the Struggle for Life*]. 1859. New York: Oxford UP, 1998. Oxford World's Classics.

Dellamora, Richard. *Masculine Desire: The Sexual Politics of Victorian Aestheticism.* Chapel Hill: U of North Carolina P, 1990.

Denisoff, Dennis. "Oscar Wilde, Commodity, Culture." Roden, ed., 119-42.

Dickson, Sarah Augusta. "Notes [to the Arents Edition]." Wilde, *Lady Lancing, passim.*

Dollimore, Jonathan. *Sexual Dissidence: Augustine to Wilde, Freud to Foucault.* Oxford: Clarendon, 1991.

Donohue, Joseph, and Ruth Berggren, eds. *Oscar Wilde's* The Importance of Being Earnest: *A Reconstructive Edition of the First Production. St. James's Theatre, London, 1895. Annotated and Illustrated from Contemporary Sources and Edited with Introductory Essays on the Play and its Text.* Gerrards Cross: Colin Smythe, 1995.

Doody, Noreen. "Oscar Wilde: Nation and Empire." Roden, ed., 246-66.

Dowling, Linda S. *Hellenism and Homosexuality in Victorian Oxford.* Ithaca: Cornell UP, 1994.

Ellmann, Richard. "The Critic as Artist as Wilde." 1973. Rpt. in Lawler, ed., 414-22.

——. *Oscar Wilde*. New York: Knopf, 1988.

——, ed. *Oscar Wilde: A Collection of Critical Essays*. Englewood Cliffs: Prentice-Hall, 1969.

Fineman, Joel. "The Significance of Literature: *The Importance of Being Earnest*." *Critical Essays on Oscar Wilde*. Gagnier, ed., 1991. 108-18.

Foldy, Michael S. *The Trials of Oscar Wilde: Deviance, Morality, and Late-Victorian Society*. New Haven: Yale UP, 1997.

Forster, E.M. *Maurice: A Novel*. 1971. New York: Norton, 1987.

Freedman, Jonathan, ed. *Oscar Wilde: A Collection of Critical Essays*. Upper Saddle River: Prentice-Hall, 1996.

Gagnier, Regenia, ed. *Critical Essays on Oscar Wilde*. New York: G.K. Hall and Company, 1991.

Gilbert, W.S., and Arthur Sullivan. *The Gondoliers; or, The King of Barataria*. 1889. Bradley, ed., 859-967.

——. *HMS Pinafore; or, The Lass That Loved a Sailor*. 1878. Bradley, ed., 113-85.

——. *Patience; or, Bunthorne's Bride*. 1881. Ed. Edmond W. Rickett. Milwaukee: Hal Leonard Publishing, 1982.

Gladden, Samuel Lyndon. "*Dracula*'s Earnestness: Stoker's Debt to Wilde." *ELN* [*English Language Notes*] 43.1 (June 2005): 62-75.

——. "Passages: The Long and Difficult Death of the Victorian Era, 1893-1945." *Ghosts of the Victorian*. Ed. David Latané and Elisabeth Rose Gruner. Spec. issue *Victorians Institute Journal* 31 (2003): 41-56.

Glavin, John. "Deadly Earnest and Earnest Revised: Wilde's Four-Act Play." *Nineteenth-Century Studies* 1 (1987): 13-24.

Goodman, Jonathan, comp. *The Oscar Wilde File*. London: Allison and Busby, 1988.

Guy, Josephine, and Ian Small. *Oscar Wilde's Profession: Writing and the Culture Industry in the Late Nineteenth Century*. New York: Oxford UP, 2000.

Hall, N. John. *Max Beerbohm: Caricatures*. New Haven: Yale UP, 1997.

Hawthorne, Melanie C. "'Comment Peut-on Être Homosexuel?': Multinational (In)Corporation and the Frenchness of *Salomé*." *Perennial Decay: On the Aesthetics and Politics of Decadence*. Ed. Liz Constable, Dennis Denisoff, and Matthew Potolsky. Philadelphia: U of Pennsylvania P, 1999. 159-82.

Hern, Patricia. "Oscar Wilde: 1854-1900." Hern and Lemming, eds., v-xi.

——, and Glenda Lemming, eds. *Oscar Wilde:* The Importance of Being Earnest: *A Trivial Play for Serious People.* 1981. London: Methuen Drama, 1988. Methuen Student Edition 10.

Hichens, Robert. *The Green Carnation.* 1894. New York: D. Appleton and Co., 1895.

Holland, Merlin. *Irish Peacock and Scarlet Marquess: The Real Trial of Oscar Wilde.* London: Fourth Estate, 2003.

——, and Rupert Hart-Davis. "Chronological Table." Holland and Hart-Davis, eds., vii-xi.

——, and Rupert Hart-Davis, eds. *The Complete Letters of Oscar Wilde.* New York: Henry Holt and Company, 2000.

Hyde, H. Montgomery. "Leading Dates Relating to the Wilde Trials." Hyde, ed., *The Trials of Oscar Wilde*, 102-04.

——, ed. *The Annotated Oscar Wilde: Poems, Fiction, Plays, Lectures, Essays, and Letters.* New York: Clarkson N. Potter, 1982.

——, ed. *The Trials of Oscar Wilde: Regina (Wilde) v. Queensberry, Regina v. Wilde and Taylor.* London: William Hodge and Company, 1948. Notable British Trials 70.

*The Importance of Being Earnest.* Dir. Anthony Asquith. Perf. Michael Redgrave, Michael Denison, and Edith Evans. Janus Films, 1952.

*The Importance of Being Earnest.* Dir. Oliver Parker. Perf. Rupert Everett, Colin Firth, Reese Witherspoon, Judi Dench. Miramax Films and Ealing Studios, 2002.

Irigaray, Luce. *Elemental Passions.* 1982. Trans. Joanne Collie and Judith Still. New York: Routledge, 1992.

Jackson, Russell, ed. *The Importance of Being Earnest: A Trivial Comedy for Serious People.* By Oscar Wilde. 1980. New York: W.W. Norton, 2001. New Mermaids.

Kaufman, Moises. *Gross Indecency: The Three Trials of Oscar Wilde.* New York: Vintage, 1998.

Kaye, Richard A. "Gay Studies/Queer Theory and Oscar Wilde." Roden, ed., 189-223.

Keller, George Frederick. "The Modern Messiah." *Wasp* 31 March 1882: n. pag.

Kendrick, Charles. *Ye Soul Agonies in Ye Life of Oscar Wilde.* New York, 1882.

Kopelson, Kevin. "Wilde, Barthes, and the Orgasmics of Truth." *Genders* 7 (March 1990): 22-31.

Krauss, Kenneth. "The World of Oscar Wilde." Krauss, ed., ix-xii.

——, ed. The Importance of Being Earnest *and Four Other Plays.* By Oscar Wilde. New York: Barnes and Noble, 2003. Barnes and Noble Classics.

Lalonde, Jeremy. "A 'Revolutionary Outrage': *The Importance of*

*Being Earnest* as Social Criticism." *Modern Drama* 48.4 (Winter 2005): 659-76.

Lawler, Donald L. "Oscar Wilde: A Chronology." Lawler, ed., 458-60.

——, ed. *The Picture of Dorian Gray*. By Oscar Wilde. 1890 and 1891. New York: W.W. Norton, 1988. 171-281; 7-170. Norton Critical Editions.

Le Gallienne, Richard. *The Romantic '90s*. 1926. London: Robin Clark Ltd., 1993.

Leeming, Glenda. "[Notes.]" Hern and Lemming, eds., 74-83.

Leverson, Ada. "The Advisability of Not Being Brought Up in a Handbag." *Punch; or, The London Charivari* 2 March 1895: 107.

Lewis, Lloyd, and Henry Justin Smith. "No Wave of His Chiseled Hand." Lewis and Smith, *Oscar Wilde Discovers America* 444-45.

——. *Oscar Wilde Discovers America*. 1882. New York: Harcourt, Brace, and Company, 1936.

Litvak, Joseph. *Strange Gourmets: Sophistication, Theory, and the Novel*. Durham: Duke UP, 1997.

McKenna, Neil. *The Secret Life of Oscar Wilde: An Intimate Biography*. 2003. New York: Basic Books, 2005.

Moers, Ellen. *The Dandy: Brummell to Beerbohm*. 1960. Lincoln: U of Nebraska P, 1978.

"Mr. Wild [*sic*] of Borneo." *The Washington Post* 22 January 1882: n. pag. Rpt. in Lewis and Smith, *Oscar Wilde Discovers America* 101.

Mrs. Humphrey. *Manners for Men*. London: James Bowden, 1897. Kent: Pryor Publications, n.d.

Nicholson, J.G.F. *Love in Earnest*. London: Elliot Stock, 1892.

Nordau, Max. *Degeneration*. 1892; trans. 1895. Lincoln: University of Nebraska P, 1993.

O'Mahoney, John Sean. *The Musical Importance of Being Earnest: A Musical, Based on* The Importance of Being Earnest *by Oscar Wilde*. New York: Samuel French, 1988.

Osborne, Charles. *The Importance of Being Earnest: A Trivial Novel for Serious People. Adapted from the Play by Oscar Wilde*. New York: St. Martin's, 1999.

*Oscar Wilde: Trial and Punishment 1895-1897*. London: The National Portrait Gallery, 1998.

Paglia, Camille. "The English Epicene: Wilde's *The Importance of Being Earnest*." *Sexual Personæ: Art and Decadence from Nefertiti to Emily Dickinson*. New Haven: Yale UP, 1990. 531-71.

Pockriss, Lee, and Anne Croswell. *Ernest in Love. A New Musical Based on Oscar Wilde's* The Importance of Being Earnest. Columbia, 1960. LP. Columbia Masterworks.

Popkin, Henry, ed. The Importance of Being Earnest: *An Authoritative Text Edition*. New York: Avon Books, 1965.

Powell, Kerry. "Algernon's Other Brothers." Gagnier, ed., 138-54.

——. "The Importance of Being at Terry's." *Oscar Wilde and the Theatre of the 1890s.* 108-23.

——. *Oscar Wilde and the Theatre of the 1890s.* Cambridge: Cambridge UP, 1990.

Raby, Peter. "Chronology." Raby, The Importance of Being Earnest: *A Reader's Companion,* ix-xii.

——. "Chronology." Raby, ed., *The Cambridge Companion,* xix-xxii.

——. The Importance of Being Earnest: *A Reader's Companion.* New York: Twayne Publishers, 1995. Twayne's Masterwork Studies.

——. "Wilde's Comedies of Society." Raby, ed., *The Cambridge Companion to Oscar Wilde,* 143-60.

——, ed. *The Cambridge Companion to Oscar Wilde.* New York: Cambridge UP, 1997.

——, ed. The Importance of Being Earnest *and Other Plays.* New York: Oxford UP, 1995. Oxford World's Classics/Oxford English Drama.

Rev. of *The Importance of Being Earnest,* by Oscar Wilde. *The Daily Graphic* 15 February 1895: n. pag. Rpt. in Tydeman, ed., 63-64.

Rev. of *The Importance of Being Earnest,* by Oscar Wilde. *The Observer* 17 February 1895: n. pag. Rpt. in Tydeman, ed., 65.

Rev. of *The Importance of Being Earnest,* by Oscar Wilde. *The Times* 15 February 1895: n. pag. Rpt. in Tydeman, ed., 62.

Robbins, Ruth. *The Importance of Being Earnest.* London: York P, 1999. York Notes Advanced.

Roden, Frederick S., ed. *Palgrave Advances in Oscar Wilde Studies.* New York: Palgrave Macmillan, 2004. Palgrave Advances.

Rose, David. "Chronology." Roden, ed., xiv-xxxix.

Sambourne, Linley. "O.W. [Punch's Fancy Portraits 37]." *Punch; or, The London Charivari* 25 June 1881: n. pag.

Sammells, Neil. *Wilde Style: The Plays and Prose of Oscar Wilde.* New York: Longman, 2000.

Schmidgall, Gary. *The Stranger Wilde: Interpreting Oscar.* New York: Dutton, 1994.

Sedgwick, Eve Kosofsky. "Tales of the Avunculate: *The Importance of Being Earnest." Tendencies.* Durham: Duke UP, 1993. 52-72. Series Q.

Shaw, Bernard. Rev. of *The Importance of Being Earnest,* by Oscar Wilde. 1895. *Our Theatres in the Nineties.* 3 vols. London: Constable and Company, 1932. 1: 41-44.

Showalter, Elaine. *Sexual Anarchy: Gender and Culture at the Fin de Siècle.* New York: Viking, 1990.

Siebold, Thomas, ed. *Readings on* The Importance of Being Earnest.

San Diego: Greenhaven, 2000. Greenhaven Press Literary Companions to British Literature.

Sinfield, Alan. *The Wilde Century: Effeminacy, Oscar Wilde, and the Queer Moment*. London: Cassell, 1994. Cassell Lesbian and Gay Studies.

Sloan, John. *Authors in Context: Oscar Wilde*. New York: Oxford UP, 2003. Oxford World's Classics.

Smith, Timothy D'Arch. Introduction. *Love in Earnest: Some Notes on the Lives and Writings of English "Uranian" Poets from 1889 to 1930*. London: Routledge and Kegan Paul, 1970. xvii-xxiii.

Stevenson, Robert Louis. *Strange Case of Dr. Jekyll and Mr. Hyde*. 1886. Ed. Martin Danahay. 2nd ed. Peterborough, ON: Broadview, 2005. Broadview Literary Texts.

Tennyson, Lord Alfred. "The Lady of Shallot." 1832, 1842. *The Longman Anthology of British Literature*. Gen. ed. David Damrosch. 2nd ed. 2 vols. New York: Longman, 2003. 2: 1141-46.

*The Trials of Oscar Wilde*. Dir. Ken Hughes. Perf. Peter Finch. Warwick Productions, 1960.

Tydeman, William, ed. *Comedies: A Casebook:* Lady Windermere's Fan, A Woman of No Importance, An Ideal Husband, The Importance of Being Earnest. New York: Macmillan P, 1982.

Waldrep, Shelton. *The Aesthetics of Self-Invention: Oscar Wilde to David Bowie*. Minneapolis: U of Minnesota P, 2004.

Ware, James M. "Algernon's Appetite: Oscar Wilde's Hero as Restoration Dandy." *English Literature in Transition (1880-1920)* 13.1 (1970): 17-26.

*Wilde*. Dir. Brian Gilbert. Perf. Stephen Fry and Jude Law. Sony Pictures Classics and Samuelson Entertainment, 1997.

Wilde, Oscar. "The Canterville Ghost." 1887. Wilde, *Complete Works*, 184-95.

——. *Complete Works of Oscar Wilde*. 1948. Ed. Merlin Holland and Rupert Hart-Davis. Glasgow: HarperCollins, 1996. Collins Classics.

——. "The Critic as Artist." 1890. Wilde, *Complete Works*, 1108-55.

——. *De Profundis*. 1962. Holland and Hart-Davis, eds., 683-780.

——. "The Decay of Lying." 1889. Wilde, *Complete Works*, 1071-92.

——. *The Definitive Four-Act Version of* The Importance of Being Earnest: A Trivial Comedy for Serious People, *by Oscar Wilde*. Ed. Ruth Berggren. New York: Vanguard P, 1987.

——. "A Few Maxims for the Instruction of the Over-Educated." 1894. Wilde, *Complete Works*, 1242-43.

——. "A Handbook to Marriage [Review of Reverend Hardy's *How to be Happy Though Married*]." 1885. *Oscar Wilde: Selected Journalism*. Ed. Anya Clayworth. New York: Oxford UP, 2004. 10-11. Oxford World's Classics.

———. *An Ideal Husband.* 1899. Wilde, *Complete Works*, 515-82.

———. *Lady Lancing: A Serious Comedy for Trivial People, In Four Acts as Originally Written* [*The Importance of Being Earnest*]. 1894. Ed. Sarah Augusta Dickson. 2 vols. New York: New York Public Library, 1956. Arents Tobacco Collection 6.

———. *Lady Windermere's Fan.* 1893. Wilde, *Complete Works*, 420-64.

———. "[Letter to George Alexander.]" July 1894. Holland and Hart-Davis, eds., 595-97.

———. "[Letter to George Alexander.]" September 1894. Holland and Hart-Davis, eds., 610.

———. "[Letter to George Alexander.]" c. October 1894. Holland and Hart-Davis, eds., 620.

———. "[Letter to the Home Secretary.]" July 1896. Holland and Hart-Davis, eds., 656-60.

———. "[Letter to Lord Alfred Douglas.]" c. February 1895. Holland and Hart-Davis, eds., 632-33.

———. "[Letter to Philip Houghton.]" February 1894. Holland and Hart-Davis, eds., 586.

———. "[Letter to R.V. Shone.]" February 1895. Holland and Hart-Davis, eds., 631-32.

———. "[Letter to an unidentified correspondent.]" February 1895. Holland and Hart-Davis, eds., 632.

———. "Pen, Pencil, and Poison." 1889. Wilde, *Complete Works*, 1093-1107.

———. "Phrases and Philosophies for the Use of the Young." 1894. Wilde, *Complete Works*, 1244-45.

———. *The Picture of Dorian Gray.* 1890, 1891. Lawler, ed., 171-281; 3-170.

———. "The Portrait of Mr. W.H." 1889. Wilde, *Complete Works*, 302-50.

———. "The Remarkable Rocket." 1888. Wilde, *Complete Works*, 294-301.

———. *Salomé: A Tragedy in One Act.* 1894. Trans. Lord Alfred Douglas. Illus. Aubrey Beardsley. New York: Dover, 1967.

———. ["Telegram to Ada Leverson."] 15 February 1895. Holland and Hart-Davis, eds., 632.

———. *A Woman of No Importance.* 1894. Wilde, *Complete Works*, 465-514.

Wren, Gayden. *"Patience." A Most Ingenious Paradox: The Art of Gilbert and Sullivan.* New York: Oxford UP, 2001. 93-120.

Wright, Mrs. Julia McNair. *Practical Life; or, Ways and Means for Developing Character and Resources.* Philadelphia: J.C. McCurdy, 1881.

## Recommended Reading and Viewing

The selections below include a list of sources relevant to *The Importance of Being Earnest* in terms of the cultural, contextual, and theoretical issues raised throughout this Broadview edition. These references are subdivided into categories to make for easier use by readers.

*Biographical Studies of Wilde and His Circle*

Amor, Anne Clark. *Mrs. Oscar Wilde: A Woman of Some Importance.* London: Sidgwick and Jackson, 1983.

Bentley, Joyce. *The Importance of Being Constance.* New York: Beaufort Books, 1983.

Croft-Cooke, Rupert. *The Unrecorded Life of Oscar Wilde.* London: W.H. Allen, 1972.

Douglas, Lord Alfred. *Oscar Wilde and Myself.* London: J. Long, 1914.

———. *A Summing Up.* London: Duckworth, 1940.

———. *Without Apology.* London: Richards, 1938.

Holland, Merlin. *The Wilde Album.* 1996. New York: Holt, 1997.

Holland, Vyvyan. *Son of Oscar Wilde.* Oxford: Oxford UP, 1954.

Murray, Douglas. *Bosie.* New York: Hyperion, 2000.

*General Criticism of Wilde's Works*

Beckson, Karl. *The Oscar Wilde Encyclopedia.* New York: AMS P, 1998.

Behrendt, Patricia Flanagan. *Oscar Wilde: Eros and Aesthetics.* New York: St. Martin's, 1991.

Bloom, Harold, ed. *Oscar Wilde.* New York: Chelsea House, 1985.

Brown, Julia Prewitt. *Cosmopolitan Criticism: Oscar Wilde's Philosophy of Art.* Charlottesville: U of Virginia P, 1997.

Clayworth, Anya. "*The Woman's World*: Oscar Wilde as Editor." *Victorian Periodicals Review* 30.2 (Summer 1997): 84-101.

Eltis, Sos. *Revising Wilde: Society and Subversion in the Plays of Oscar Wilde.* Oxford: Clarendon P, 1996.

Gagnier, Regenia. *Idylls of the Marketplace: Oscar Wilde and the Victorian Public.* Stanford: Stanford UP, 1986.

———. "Stages of Desire: Oscar Wilde's Comedies and the Consumer." *Genre* 15 (1982): 315-36.

Gillespie, Michael Patrick. *Oscar Wilde and the Poetics of Ambiguity.* Gainesville: UP of Florida, 1996. Syracuse: Syracuse UP, 2002.

Gladden, Samuel Lyndon. "'Sebastian Melmoth': Wilde's Parisian Exile as the Spectacle of Sexual, Textual Revolution." *Victorians Institute Journal* 28 (2000): 39-63.

Kaplan, Joel H., and Sheila Stowell. "The Dandy and the Dowager: Oscar Wilde and Audience Resistance." *New Theatre Quarterly* 15.4 (1999): 319-31.

Keane, Robert N., ed. *Oscar Wilde: The Man, His Writings, and His World*. New York: AMS P, 2003. AMS Studies in the Nineteenth Century 32.

Knox, Melissa. *Oscar Wilde: A Long and Lovely Suicide*. New Haven: Yale UP, 1994.

Kohl, Norbert. *Oscar Wilde: The Works of a Conformist Rebel*. Cambridge: Cambridge UP, 1989.

McCormack, Jerusha, ed. *Wilde the Irishman*. New Haven: Yale UP, 1998.

Nunokawa, Jeff. *Tame Passions of Wilde: The Styles of Manageable Desire*. Princeton: Princeton UP, 2003.

Raby, Peter. *Oscar Wilde*. Cambridge: Cambridge UP, 1988.

Smith, Philip E., II, ed. *Approaches to Teaching the Works of Oscar Wilde*. New York: Modern Language Association, 2009. Approaches to Teaching World Literature.

Stetz, Margaret Diane. "The Bi-Social Oscar Wilde and 'Modern' Women." *Nineteenth-Century Literature* 55.4 (March 2001): 515-37.

Stokes, John. *Oscar Wilde: Myths, Miracles and Imitations*. Cambridge: Cambridge UP, 1996.

——. "Wilde Interpretations." *Modern Drama* 37.1 (Spring 1994): 156-74.

Tanitch, Robert. *Oscar Wilde on Stage and Screen*. London: Methuen, 1999.

Tydeman, William, ed. *Wilde, Comedies: A Selection of Critical Essays*. London: Macmillan, 1982.

Criticism of The Importance of Being Earnest

Beckson, Karl. "Oscar Wilde and the Importance of Not Being Earnest." *Oscar Wilde: The Man, His Writings, and His World*. Ed. Robert N. Keane. New York: AMS P, 2003. 1-14. AMS Studies in the Nineteenth Century 32.

Brown, Keith. "Art for Ernest's Sake." *English: The Journal of the English Association* 33 (Autumn 1994): 235-46.

Cohen, Ed. "Laughing in Earnest: The Trying Context of Wilde's

'Trivial' Comedy." *LIT: Literature Interpretation Theory* 3.1 (1991): 57-64.

Gillespie, Michael Patrick. "From Beau Brummell to Lady Bracknell: Reviewing the Dandy in *The Importance of Being Earnest.*" *Victorians Institute Journal* 21 (1993): 119-42.

Gurfinkel, Helena. "'Yet Each Man Kills the Thing He Loves': Murder and Sexual Transgression in *The Importance of Being Earnest,* 'Lord Arthur Saville's Crime,' and *Salomé.*" *Oscar Wilde: The Man, His Writings, and His World.* Ed. Robert N. Keane. New York: AMS P, 2003. 163-74. AMS Studies in the Nineteenth Century 32.

Harrison, S.J. "Prunes and Prism: Wilde and Dickens." *Notes and Queries* 44.3 (September 1997): 350-52.

Kaplan, Joel H. "Ernest Worthing's London Address: A Reconsideration." *Canadian Journal of Irish Studies* 11.1 (1985): 53-54.

Mackie, W. Craven. "Bunbury Pure and Simple." *Modern Drama* 41.2 (Summer 1998): 327-30.

Poague, L.A. "*The Importance of Being Earnest*: The Texture of Wilde's Irony." *Modern Drama* 16 (1973): 251-57.

Poznar, Walter. "Life and Play in Wilde's *The Importance of Being Earnest.*" *Midwest Quarterly: A Journal of Contemporary Thought* 30.4 (Summer 1989): 515-28.

Raby, Peter. "The Origins of *The Importance of Being Earnest.*" *Modern Drama* 37.1 (Spring 1994): 139-47.

——. "'The Persons of the Play': Some Reflections on Wilde's Choice of Names in *The Importance of Being Earnest.*" *Nineteenth-Century Theatre* 23.1-2 (Summer-Winter 1995): 67-75.

Stone, Geoffrey. "Serious Bunburyism: The Logic of *The Importance of Being Earnest.*" *Essays in Criticism* 26 (1976): 28-41.

Thienpont, Eva. "From Faltering Arrow to Pistol Shot: *The Importance of Being Earnest.*" *Cambridge Quarterly* 33.3 (2004): 245-55.

Toliver, Harold E. "Wilde and the Importance of 'Sincere and Studied Triviality'." *Modern Drama* 5 (1963): 389-99.

Walkowitz, Rebecca L. "Ethical Criticism: *The Importance of Being Earnest.*" *Contemporary Literature* 43.1 (Spring 2002): 187-93.

Ware, J.A. "Algernon's Appetite: Oscar Wilde's Hero as Restoration Dandy." *English Literature in Transition* 13 (1970): 17-26.

*Cultural and Literary Contexts*

Beckson, Karl. *London in the 1890s: A Cultural History.* New York: W.W. Norton, 1993.

Gladden, Samuel Lyndon. "Conclusion: Re-Tracing Seduction: The Influence of Shelley on Nineteenth-Century British Culture." *Shelley's Textual Seductions: Plotting Utopia in the Erotic and Political Works*. New York: Routledge, 2002. 285-318. Major Literary Authors 8.

Green, Stephanie. "Oscar Wilde's *The Woman's World*." *Victorian Periodicals Review* 30.2 (1997): 102-20.

Hoare, Philip. *Oscar Wilde's Last Stand: Decadence, Conspiracy, and the Most Outrageous Trial of the Century*. New York: Arcade, 1997.

Ledger, Sally, and Scott McCracken, eds. *Cultural Politics at the Fin de Siècle*. Cambridge: Cambridge UP, 1995.

Stokes, John, ed. *Fin de Siècle/Fin du Globe: Fears and Fantasies of the Late Nineteenth Century*. New York: St. Martin's, 1992.

Swisher, Clarice, ed. *Victorian England*. San Diego: Greenhaven, 2000. Turning Points in World History.

Winwar, Frances. *Oscar Wilde and the Yellow 'Nineties*. New York: Harper, 1940.